GLOBAL DEMOCRACY

'This is a most timely publication as the world experiences a huge reverse in democracy and fragmentation. Instead it offers a pragmatic vision of a unified world based on global democracy and equal global citizenship. The book illuminates how political institutions function in the modern world and how this is inadequate. In particular, it provides us with stories of people who followed their vision and fought for a fair and democratic world. Motivating and inspiring!'

—**Gulnara Shahinian**, founder of Democracy Today and former UN Special Rapporteur on Contemporary Forms of Slavery

'This publication is a thought-provoking and timely contribution on why a democratic layer of government is needed at the global scale. There is no doubt that the current international system needs urgent reform to meet the ever growing threat to peace, security and social development.'

—**Livingstone Sewanyana**, UN Independent Rapporteur on the Promotion of an Equitable and Democratic International Order

'Gilad and Freeman have produced forthright advocacy for democratic world federation in the 21st century. For major global problems beyond the capacity of national states to solve alone, democratic world federation is presented as the necessary and possible solution. They foresee pathways analogous to the historical origins of national democracies. A stirring book that is complemented by a series of YouTube videos for young audiences. The old ideal of a union of peoples to create a world of peace and justice still lives!'

—**Joseph Baratta**, Emeritus Professor of History and Political Science at Worcester State University, and author of *The Politics of World Federation* (2004)

'An enlightening and timely book given the global nature of today's challenges. One of the first books about world federalism to bring a feminist and post-colonial lens to global structures and processes. A great contribution to world federalist thought and action.'

—**Amy Oloo**, Executive Director, World Federalist Movement

'This book is one of the most complete attempts at making the case for federalism and democracy at the global scale. From an appropriate diagnosis of current crises, the authors conclude that the global order needs drastic changes. Deep crisis used to provoke radical institutional innovations in the past, as the creation of the UN and the European Union have shown. Let's hope that this extraordinary book will provide good guidance in the coming years and for the long-term future of humanity.'

—**Fernando Iglesias**, Co-President of the World Federalist Movement and Member of the Chamber of Deputies of Argentina

'I want my children to receive a world passport as global citizens. This book convincingly shows how that can become a reality.'

—**Tadashi Inuzuka**, Co-President of the World Federalist Movement and former Senator in the House of Councilors of the Japanese Parliament

'This is an exciting book! It argues for nothing short of full democratic world federalism, and does so in a way that is nuanced and clear-eyed about the obstacles ahead and how they might be overcome. It is thorough and carefully argued, while also crisply written and accessible, excellent for classroom or reading group use. Best of all, it gives detailed biographical narratives on some of the crucial but understudied figures in the world government traditions, including Rosika Schwimmer, Jawaharlal Nehru, and Hideki Yukawa. Highly recommended.'

—**Luis Cabrera**, Associate Professor of Political Science, Griffith University, Australia, Co-Convenor of the World Government Research Network, and author of *The Practice of Global Citizenship* (2010)

'Passionate advocacy to move us from an international to a truly global commons. A needed jolt of aspirational idealism, with faith in democratic governance at its heart.'

—**Manu Bhagavan**, Professor of History, Human Rights, and Public Policy at Hunter College and the Graduate Center-CUNY, and author of *The Peacemakers: India and the Quest for One World* (2012)

ABOUT THIS PUBLICATION

This book is based on the text of lectures that were first written for a series of videos produced by One World: Movement for Global Democracy and released in 2022. The authors would like to thank Workable World Trust for the generous grant which made the production of the video lectures possible.

The videos are available online at www.oneworld.network/lectures and at the *Global Democracy and Justice Lecture Series* YouTube channel.

ABOUT THE AUTHORS

ODED GILAD is the Director of One World: Movement for Global Democracy. From 2014-2020 he was a member of the Council of the World Federalist Movement. He is a regular international speaker and has published several articles on global democracy and world federalism in the Federalist Debate, Eén Wereld, Fédéchoses, and on Open Democracy.

DENA FREEMAN is the Deputy Director of One World: Movement for Global Democracy and a member of the International Advisory Board of Democracy Without Borders. She has published widely on the topics on globalisation, development and democracy and is the author of several books, including most recently *Can Globalization Succeed?* (2020).

ABOUT THE PUBLISHER

DEMOCRACY WITHOUT BORDERS is an international civil society organization with chapters around the world that promotes democracy from the local to the global level, global citizenship and world federalism.

GLOBAL DEMOCRACY

The Key to Global Justice

Oded Gilad
Dena Freeman

Published by
Democracy Without Borders
Berlin, 2022

Paperback ISBN 978-3-942282-22-2
Ebook ISBN 978-3-942282-23-9

Visit our website at
www.democracywithoutborders.org

Contents

Preface

This book advocates a fundamental change to the world system: the expansion of democracy beyond the borders of individual countries to the entire planet. While references to 'global democracy' are often used to describe the proliferation of democracy across the world's nation-states, Oded Gilad and Dena Freeman use the term to refer to a truly 'global' democracy, a unified democratic polity in which everyone on the planet would be equal citizens. As the latest wave of national democratization that gathered momentum after the end of the Cold War is now receding, if not reversing into a trend of autocratisation, the authors boldly argue that the solution is to push democracy up to the global level.

The key argument of the book revolves around the ongoing dramatic mismatch between the level of government and the level at which major issues play out. The former continues to reside in separate nation-states but the latter often is planetary, the management of global commons such as the atmosphere or the COVID pandemic being key examples. As they show with great clarity, this mismatch is undermining fair development, human rights, democracy, climate action and the fight against inequality, to name but a few fields. In particular, national democracy will remain under constant pressure in an undemocratic global framework that is not fit for purpose.

The solution that they offer is straightforward: a federal democratic layer of government needs to be added on top of existing nation-states. Or in other words, the solution is to create a democratic world federation. This new layer would make every human being a world citizen in the literal legal sense of global citizenship and terminate their arbitrary confinement in nation-states that is primarily determined by the accident of birth. Humanity as a collective of global citizens would be represented in a democratically elected global parliament.

This book builds on decades of thinking and activism around this idea. It is being published 75 years after the adoption of the Montreux Declaration on World Federal Government, which was adopted in Switzerland in 1947 and was a milestone in forming the global movement advocating for this goal.[1] In this movement, which is supported by *Democracy Without Borders*, Oded Gilad and Dena Freeman are well-known activists and thinkers. We are privileged to publish their work, which brings the movement's thinking up to date and shows how the need for a democratic world federation is just as important in the 21st century as it was in the early days. There is no question that this book will be one of the most important resources on the subject for some time to come.

Oded and Dena do not mince words, which is refreshing and probably necessary. The book is written in a chatty and easy-to-access style. It puts complicated ideas that are usually only discussed in high-level academic and policy circles into a form that can be understood by the general reader. This style of course emanates from the fact that the chapters in this book are slightly edited transcripts of videos published by the authors on YouTube. Those videos increase the reach beyond this book's readership and makes it easy to spread the content. This is key because the issues addressed on the coming pages and in the videos should not be restricted to a small group of experts. It is high time that they are discussed by everyone, because they are fundamental to our shared future on this planet.

Andreas Bummel
Democracy Without Borders

Note

1 Reprinted on pp.168ff.

Introduction

Why is it that humanity can't get its act together to solve the climate crisis, to deal rationally and effectively with pandemics, or to curb the power of multinational corporations? How can we come together to make a more equal, free, just and sustainable world for everyone? In this book, which is based on a series of video lectures which we published on YouTube, we try to answer these questions. In the process we propose a different way to look at the world and to make sense of it, a way that is radically different from the approach taken in most mainstream analyses.

We argue that at the root of most of the world's problems you can find the great algorithm or political operating system that goes by the harmless name of 'the international system'. People accept this system as just a given thing that is back there in the matrix, and don't have a clue about what's so wrong about it, and what could or should replace it. In this book we take a clear look at the 'international system', and at the problems that it causes. We argue that many of the problems that we currently face, whether it's climate change, pandemics, or inequality, are ultimately caused not so much by local factors, but by the shape of the world order, and in particular, the nonsensical political division of humanity into some 200 separate nation states.

Divided like this, we cannot come together to solve the increasing number of truly global problems. Instead of taking a holistic view about what is best for humanity, and for our planet, our politicians are locked into a zero-sum game, with each one working from a narrow national perspective, rather than trying to think what is best for the world as a whole. They constantly try to get what is best for their own country, and do not care if in the process they lead the world into crisis and destruction.

While politicians like to tell us that 'there is no alternative', we believe that there are alternatives. Of course there are. There are many different ways that the world could be organised, and we need to start discussing them and debating them.

At the moment we have a global economy, and a global ecology, but for some reason our politics is stuck at the national level. Most

importantly, democracy is stuck at the national level. That means that
the people of the world have no say in decisions that are taken at the
global level. It also means that there is no-one, and no political body,
that is trying to find solutions to global problems that are good for
everyone, and for our planet. The recent COVID pandemic is just the
latest example of this, with rich countries looking out for themselves, while leaving those in poor countries to suffer and die. What
they don't seem to realise is that this selfish nationalistic approach
will never get rid of COVID and that a wider, global approach is
necessary.

To solve the challenge of the COVID pandemic, and a host of
other global problems, we need to shift from international competition to global cooperation – from a system of global oligarchy to one
of global democracy. Only in that way can we come together to solve
global problems in an effective, just and sustainable way, and to create
a world where the benefits of our work and our technology are shared
more equitably among the whole the humanity. The only way to do
this, to really make a global democracy, is to add a small, democratic,
layer of federal government at the global level. Then instead of having
decisions taken in secret by a small group of governments at the G20
or at the International Monetary Fund, we will have open and transparent parliamentary processes at the global level, where the democratically elected representatives of the people of the world will sit together and debate the best way forward.

What we need is a radical re-organisation of the world system. We
argue that the current international system is simply out-dated, unjust and unsustainable, and that we need to move towards a global
system, and most importantly, one that is democratic and that will
bring about the will of the people. There is widespread support for
democracy at the national level. Now it's time to bring it also to the
global level.

Outline of the Book

The chapters in the first section provide a new framework for looking at
the world, one that is global, rather than international. We look at the
history of the evolution of democracy and show how global democracy
is the obvious and necessary next stage. We outline how the current

system of what's called 'global governance' works, or doesn't work, and present the alternative vision of a democratic world federation.

The second section looks more closely at specific issues, such as human rights, climate change and economic inequality, and shows how these issues cannot be solved in the current international order. These are all fundamentally global problems, and all the good-hearted attempts to solve them through the current international order, or through non-governmental organisations, sadly do not work. That's why after seventy years of so-called human rights, most people still do not have these rights. And why after decades of climate agreements and protocols and treaties we still have rapidly increasing levels of carbon dioxide in our atmosphere and steadily increasing global warming. And that's why with all the wealth and abundance in our world, there is still shocking poverty and inequality. This section explains why that is, and points the way to global democracy as the solution.

The third section looks at the history of the idea of global democracy and world federation through the lives and ideas of six key world federalist thinkers. These men and women, from Africa, Asia, Latin America, Europe and the United States, all came to the conclusion that the world needed to be organised as a democratic world federation in order to solve particular problems that troubled them. Rosika Schwimmer wanted to find a way to end war, to give women equal rights, and to end the plight of refugees and state-less people. Albert Einstein and Hideki Yukawa wanted to secure peace and abolish nuclear weapons. Josué de Castro wanted to find a way to end world hunger, while Jawahlarlal Nehru and Kwame Nkrumah wanted to create a world system in which poorer countries, the former colonies, would not be dominated by the richer ones. All of them wanted a world that would be more peaceful, more equal and more just. From their different countries, their different cultures, and their different political backgrounds, they all came to the conclusion that the best way to organise the world was as a democratic world federation. The final chapter in this section then looks at the history of the World Federalist Movement, the transnational movement promoting world federation that started in the 1940s and continues to this day.

The final section begins to look at how we can move to make this radical idea, a democratic world federation, a political reality in the

21st century. What are the steps for the world to move towards global democracy? We look at possibilities for world citizenship and a world parliament and we outline the many campaigns and activities that are currently taking place to push the world in the right direction. Most importantly, we show how you can get involved and play your part in making the world truly just and democratic.

Section I
Developing A Global Framework

1. Federalism and World Federalism

The core argument of this book is that in order to bring about global peace, justice and sustainability, we need global democracy. We argue that world federalism, organizing the world as a democratic political federation, is the most simple and straightforward way of achieving global democracy. So in this chapter we start by taking a closer look at the concept of 'federalism'. What is it? And why is it interesting to consider applying it to the whole world?

What is Federalism?

Federalism is a form of political organisation where governance is split into at least two levels. It's a form of what we can call 'multi-level governance'. Instead of having one centralised state, federal systems have a power-sharing arrangement between at least two levels of government: the central state, which governs the entire country in relation to issues of importance to everyone; and regional states, or provinces, which govern certain types of policy, usually of immediate relevance to the people who live there.[1]

The central state might make policy about international trade, or defence or citizenship, for example, while the provincial states might control local health or education policy, or cultural matters.

All federations are different and arrange the different policies, or 'competences', that exist at each level according to their own needs. So for example, in the US and Germany, there is one main language spoken across the whole federation, while in Switzerland and Ethiopia different languages are spoken in different regional states. Or to take another example, environmental protection is mainly controlled by the central government in Malaysia, while in Nigeria it is mainly controlled by the regional states. All federations are different, and there is no 'one size fits all'. As a very general rule of thumb, when it comes to economic policy, left wing politicians tend to want it to be more controlled at the central, federal level, as this allows more redistribution between states and thus fosters greater economic equality. Those on the right, in contrast, tend to want it more controlled at the local level, as this means most economic matters stay within the local state and there is no redistribution from richer states to poorer states.

Most federations operate according to the principle of 'subsidiarity', meaning that power to decide on an issue is given to the lowest level that is able to appropriately deal with that issue. This is because federal systems are against the centralisation of power, and prefer to have as much power as possible at the lower levels. But as the previous example about economic policy shows, it is not always the case that devolving power to lower levels will allow issues to be governed better. For some issues, it is important that they are governed at the central level.

Federations will usually have a constitution which says which things are governed at the central or federal level, and which at the local or regional level. So as a general framework it is very flexible and can be adapted to all sorts of different contexts and situations. And obviously, when designing a federation it is very important to look at all the details carefully and decide on the design in a democratic way.

The History of Federalism

It is interesting to have a quick look at the history of the idea of federalism, and how it emerged, because this can give us some useful insights into what kinds of problems federalism solves and why it might be worth considering as a possible future political structure of the world.

The idea of federalism first arose in Europe in the 18th century, around the same time as the idea of the centralised state was beginning to emerge. Before that there were no states in the modern sense. Instead there was a complex system of many different kinds of governance arrangements, which overlapped at different scales and in different areas. Power was divided between feudal lords, empires, free cities, the Catholic church, and others, and there were often competing claims to authority in any one place.

Somehow this complicated system lasted for many hundreds of years and only began to change after the Treaty of Westphalia in 1648, when the idea began to emerge that it would be better to have separate, fully sovereign states, where the central government controlled all the power within that state. Over the next hundred or so years modern states evolved, with strong centralised governments.[2] In many cases larger, strong, states were created by joining together several smaller states or kingdoms. For example the modern states of Italy and Germany emerged after the unification of several smaller states and kingdoms.

It was around this time, and during this process, that the idea of federalism began to emerge – as a critique of the centralised state model and as a more flexible alternative. In many cases, small states and cities did not want to be swallowed up into larger states, but instead wanted to retain some of their autonomy. They also wanted to preserve local cultures and languages.

During this period there were many discussions about the pros and cons of different scales of governance, and the pros and cons of unification or separation. For many people the idea of federalism offered a good balance: some unification and some separation; some governance at a higher level, and some at a lower level. It seemed to combine the advantages of uniting into a big and strong state, whilst also allowing a fair degree of local autonomy and the ability for local culture and local languages to flourish.

However, despite all these discussions, no federations were actually created in Europe at this time, and instead centralised states dominated the new political landscape. But not very long after, the first federation was indeed formed – not in Europe, but in the newly independent United States of America. The US Constitution of 1787 created the first federation, uniting the 13 former British colonies into one overarching political unit, whilst allowing each individual state to retain significant power and autonomy. Seeing the success of the American model, many other countries soon followed suit. Argentina became a federation in 1853, Canada in 1867, Brazil in 1889, Australia in 1901, Austria in 1920, India in 1949, amongst many others.

What is a Confederation?

Now you might have heard of the term 'confederation' and you might be wondering if federation and confederation are the same thing? The answer is that they are not. There are some very important differences between the two.[3]

A confederation is a union of equal, sovereign states that have signed a treaty to give some very limited power to the centre. All decisions must be agreed unanimously, and the member states can leave the union at any time. Furthermore, a confederation unites the states as collective actors, as the country as a whole. It does not give any rights or responsibilities to individuals, who remain citizens of their particular state but not of the confederation.

A federation, in contrast, is one over-arching political unit in which there is a system of divided powers, such that a central government and local provinces or states each have different policy responsibilities. A federation is a more permanent structure than a confederation, and it will have a constitution that determines which decisions are taken at which level. In a democratic federation, decisions are taken by a democratic majority.

Very importantly, a federation is not only a union of states, it is also a union of individuals. Citizens of a federation have certain rights and responsibilities granted to them by the central federal level. These might include voting rights, the requirement to pay taxes, and so on. Therefore, while confederations have only one legislative chamber, where all the states are represented, federations always have two chambers, one where states are represented and one where individuals are represented.

Before the United States became a federation, it initially tried to be a confederation. The Continental Congress of 1781 elaborated Articles of Confederation that gave only very limited power to the central government – to declare war, make treaties, and maintain army and navy – while the states remained largely separate and sovereign. But this system did not work very well. In particular there were many economic problems concerning differences of economic policy between the states making it difficult to support a common currency and make debt repayments after the war. So a few years later, in 1787, they changed their minds and decided instead to unite more deeply and form a federation.

Other confederations that have existed in history have also failed to survive into the modern era, such as the United Provinces of the Netherlands, which collapsed at the end of the 18th century; the Swiss Confederation, which collapsed in the mid-19th century; and the short-lived German Bund (1815-66), which also collapsed in the mid-19th century.

The European Union, or EU, is currently an unusual hybrid, with elements of both federation and confederation. It started off as an economic confederation, but over time has added elements that are typical of federations, such as a constitution and individual rights. But it still retains many elements of a confederation, such as the right of exit, the system of making treaties between the states, and the need to make major decisions unanimously. It is possible that it will eventually evolve fully into a democratic federation, or it may continue in some kind of hybrid form for a long time. In the meantime it is an interesting political laboratory for those of us interested in looking at different ways that states can integrate.[4]

Why are Large Countries Often Organised as Federations?

Today, around thirty of the world's 195 countries are federations. This may not sound very many, but since many of these federations are very large countries, together they account for some 40% of the world's population. In other words, almost half the world's people are today governed under a federal political system.

Furthermore, when we look at which states choose a federal structure and which choose a centralised structure, we find overwhelmingly that the larger the country the more likely that it is to be a federation. In fact seven of the eight largest countries by area are federations – the United States, Canada, Brazil, Australia, Russia, India, and Argentina. The only exception is China, the third largest, and the only one organised as a centralised unitary state.

The reason that large countries choose federalism is because federalism is an excellent form of political organisation for large and complex societies. It offers a good balance between centralised governance and local autonomy, and it also enables different peoples and ethnic groups to live side by side as equal citizens. These are also reasons that federalism might be a good political structure for the world as a whole.

From World Confederation to World Federation

If we look at the world as a whole, at the global level, we see that today it is basically organised as a very weak confederation, with the United Nations at the centre. UN member states retain their full sovereignty and can choose, if they want, to enter into treaty-based agreements with other states with regard to common global problems, such as peace and human rights. However, there is no power above the states to enforce their compliance with the treaties, and indeed states can pull out of treaties at any time. So, as other confederations have found, it is virtually impossible to make and enforce binding common decisions.

Furthermore, while states are represented in the General Assembly and other UN bodies, there is no chamber that represents individuals, and the UN is not able to grant individuals any rights or responsibilities, despite many resolutions to this regard. Thus the UN is rather powerless and remote from most peoples' lives. The global confederal system has also proved quite ineffective in solving common global problems, such as climate change, biodiversity loss, and economic inequality, amongst many, many others.

That is why we think that the way forward to a more effective, more democratic and more just form of global governance is to move from a global confederation to a global federation.

The vision of world federalism is federation both upwards and downwards. At the global level the world would come together as a federation of states, with a constitution, a parliament, and individual rights and responsibilities. At the same time, at the local level member states would be able to reorganise themselves into federations of mini-states. So power would shift both upwards and downwards. And crucially, there would be no centralised, all-powerful, world government.

Instead, there would be a few key issues that would be governed at the global level. Climate policy seems the most obvious example. But we could also consider human rights and certain aspects of economic policy, and certain elements of health policy. Putting these at the global level would enable us to improve redistribution from richer states to poorer ones, to reduce inequalities and to create a more just world. Things like education policy, religious matters, language and cultural policy would stay at the state level, or perhaps devolve further down to the sub-national state level. But clearly, they would not be governed at the global level.

So a world federation would allow a very high degree of diversity, while bringing us together on certain key matters that affect us all, and enabling us to make decisions about them in a just and democratic way.

Notes

1 See also Levi, Lucio. 2008. *Federalist Thinking*. Maryland: University Press of America.

2 Croxton, Derek. 1999. The Peace of Westphalia of 1648 and the Origins of Sovereignty. *The International History Review*, 21, 3: 569-591. Gustafsson, Harald.1998. The Conglomerate State: A Perspective on State Formation in Early Modern Europe. *Scandinavian Journal of History*, 23,3-4, 189-213.

3 Glencross, Andrew. 2007. *Federation/Confederation*. International Encyclopedia of Political Science. papers.ssrn.com/sol3/papers.cfm?abstract_id=2119924

4 For more on the EU as a hybrid federation-confederation, see Fiorentini, Riccardo and Guido Montani. (eds). 2015. *The European Union and Supranational Political Economy*. London: Routledge, particularly Part II: Europe between Confederalism and Federalism.

2. A Democratic World is Possible

Some people say it's crazy to talk about global democracy, when even on the national level democracy seems to be receding and in crisis in so many countries, and when walls and fences keep growing longer and higher between countries. But supporters of global democracy point to that same reality, but view it with a completely different interpretation. The crisis, we say, is not of democracy as such, but of national level democracy – the democracy that, by definition, ends at the border of the state. This democracy is in crisis because the powers that challenge it are fundamentally global – global corporations that are far larger than states so they can easily evade taxation and regulation, global environmental problems that today no body is accountable for addressing, and staggering global inequality. And all of these feed into secondary problems, such as the strong migration pressures from poor to rich countries. National borders can be quite effective at blocking desperate people from moving between countries. But they offer no help at all at addressing the root causes that make these people desperate in the first place. So the real question should be: how can we seriously expect nation state level democracy to function properly when it's so much smaller than the problems that it faces?

National Level Democracy Cannot Solve Global Level Problems

Within democratic states, governments have a range of effective tools to address poverty and inequality, such as taxation of the richer people and then redistribution to everyone, providing infrastructures, or education, or healthcare, or welfare of some sort. But at the global level these tools simply do not exist as yet. There is no institution that has either the democratic legitimacy or the democratic power to use such tools globally. And that is a huge problem because we have serious global issues that without proper funding simply cannot be addressed.

Today the top 1% and the global corporations can pick and choose where to pay taxes and they often end up paying nowhere. Therefore money is piling up in their accounts, giving them great wealth and driving the shocking inequality we see in the world today. But we need their tax money. If there were some taxation and redistribution at the global level, then the whole world would be much better off. Furthermore, the huge wealth that these elites can currently amass gives them huge political power. They can buy our national politicians and undermine our national level democracy. And this is exactly what is happening. So in order to make our world more just and fair, and to save our national level democracy, we need global democracy, that framework of a democratic state, at the federal level of the world.

Which Comes First, Global Solidarity or Global Democracy?

Some people argue that before we can start speaking about building democracy at the global level, we need first to focus our efforts at nurturing greater feelings of global solidarity, generosity and compassion. Without these, they say, global democracy cannot evolve. The problem with this approach is that in our modern era, when societies are very large and diverse, it is impossible to truly realise solidarity, generosity and compassion unless the different groups of the society share also an inclusive and democratic political framework.

If we look at the best examples of the most solidaric nation states, where the feelings of communal fraternity and solidarity are arguably stronger than those that exist on the global level, it is clear to everybody that even here these moral sentiments by themselves are not enough to sustain justice in society. It is self-evident to us that preventing the strong within those countries from harming or exploiting the weak cannot be left only to the voluntary good will and the high moral sentiments of the strong, or to the invisible hand of the market. Instead it is clear that the framework of the democratic state, with a democratic justice system and laws, and regulation, taxation and redistribution, is required to make a just society. It is not possible to rely on the 'moral goodness' of the strong. Of course not! It is also necessary to have laws which define appropriate behaviour and which apply to everyone equally, and which can be enforced.

If such a democratic framework is necessary even within the most solidaric of nation-states, so much more so is it vital and necessary at the global level, where the population is many times larger and much more diverse. This is why we cannot postpone working for a shared global democracy. Without it, the important values of solidarity and generosity and compassion will remain locked in the box of 'charity' of the strong, that make them feel good with themselves, rather than a system of true justice for all.

Would Global Democracy Lead to a Centralisation of Power?

Another question that I often hear from those who are sceptical about global democracy is 'shouldn't we fear that a federal state at the global level might lead to too much concentration of power in the hands of the few?' And again, it is exactly the other way around. We need that framework of a federal democratic state at the global level precisely in order to prevent the concentration of power that plagues our world today, and is, indeed, the major cause of injustice in the world.

This concentration comes in two forms. First is the concentration of state power in the hands of so many undemocratic national governments. When they oppress their own peoples, there is currently no power above them that can hold them accountable for the injustices that they inflict. Second is the huge concentration of economic power in the hands of a small global elite of super-rich individuals and global corporations. To be able to regulate them, to tax them and to hold them accountable for the injustices that they cause, we need nothing short of democratic state, with the tools of a democratic justice system, that will work on the same level that they work on. And that level is the global level.

Now there are many good things about the market system and many good things about capitalism. But in order to function correctly and benefit society, the market needs proper state regulation. This is necessary to keep it in check and to prevent market failures, such as the formation of private monopolies or cartels that actively stifle the competition that is at the heart of the market system. At the moment it is fashionable to say that the state is bad. And it is true that many of today's monopolies are often protected and enabled by national level governments, with obscene patent laws and other measures. But the problem is not that government is bad, but rather that it has been rendered undemocratic and ineffective. When state power is divided between separate national governments it becomes very easy for the global corporations to influence, and indeed dictate, the national laws that they want. With global corporations, but only national level governments, we have the ridiculous situation that the corporations are much bigger and stronger than the governments that are supposed to regulate them. This is the crux of the problem.

Even so, despite these unfavourable conditions, national governments still manage to impose some measure of limits and regulation on global market powers for the benefit of their populations. If democratic government could extend beyond the nation state level and work at the same level as the global market, it could be much more effective, just and successful.

Isn't the United Nations a Kind of Global Democracy?

Finally, there is the outrageous claim that we don't need to talk much about global democracy, because we already have the United Nations, and so many other international organisations, like the World Bank and the World Health Organisation. These institutions, some people say, allow the representatives of all the world's countries to work together peacefully to promote the common interests of humanity. But do they?

The problem with this rosy fairy tale is that all these institutions are fundamentally undemocratic.[1] Democracy has two fundamental components – the demos, the people, and the kratos, the government. In the words of Abraham Lincoln, 'democracy is the government of the people, by the people and for the people'.

So the first question with regards to the UN and all the other so-called 'international institutions', is 'who is their demos?' Who has the right to vote in them? And the answer is that in all of them, the right to vote is reserved exclusively for governments. Not 'governments that have been democratically chosen', not 'governments who do not oppress their own citizens', but simply 'governments'. That is the rule of the international system, this is how it works.

When you look at the General Assembly of the United Nations, you see a big conference hall that is full of humans. And yet, humanity is absent there. It has no say and no representatives in that room. People in so many countries, who are not less human than you or us, have no say as to who will be sitting in that room and voting, often against their will, and yet in their name. This means that the very terms 'United Nations' or 'international institutions' are the worst forms of fake. Rather than 'inter-national', the correct adjective to describe them is 'inter-governmental'. If we understand the word 'nation' to mean the citizens of a country, the people themselves, then the fact that whole nations are not being asked what they want, shows how these institutions are fundamentally undemocratic as far as the demos is concerned.[2]

If you look for the kratos, the government element in those institutions, the situation is even worse. You see, inter-governmental organisations are just organisations that governments can choose to join if they like. They generally only do so if it serves their interests and if it does not threaten them. Governments don't have to join, and they don't have to stay, and they don't have to comply with any resolution that they don't like. The UN organisation is not 'supra-governmental' or above the governments, it is only 'inter-governmental'. It's just a link between governments that depends entirely on their voluntary agreement. So, there is no kratos, or government element, in those institutions. Which means that they are not democratic also from that perspective.

The true role of these institutions is to provide nothing but a façade of legitimacy, legality and democratic representation to a global system of governance that actually has none of that. They are just a cover for a global system of government of the people, but by the elite and for the elite. That is what we have in the world today. But we need something completely different. Something truly democratic.

We, humanity, deserve to recognize ourselves as a demos, that can and should share a federal human kratos – a government of the people, by the people and for the people of the world. We need to come together and put global democracy at the top of our priorities, because without it all the other causes and goals cannot be really reached. Real global democracy is, quite simply, the key to solving so many of the problems that inflict humanity today.

Notes

1 See also Archibugi, Daniele and Raffaele Marchetti. 2009.. Democratic Ethics and UN Reform. In *The Ethics of Global Governance*, edited by Antonio Franceschet. Boulder: Lynne Rienner Publishers.

2 See also Valentini, Laura. 2014. No Global Demos, No Global Democracy? A Systematization and Critique. *Perspectives on Politics*, 12, 4: 789-807.

3. The History and Future of Democracy

We think that what the world needs is global democracy. But we have heard that many people are disillusioned with democracy and think that it doesn't work. While other people very much support the importance of democracy at the national level, but think that it is impossible at the global level. So in this chapter we will take a look at the history of democracy, and the possible futures of democracy, and try to answer both these points.

The Emergence of Democracy in the Nineteenth Century

If we look at the political systems of most European countries at the start of the 18th century, we see that they had a system of decision-making where the wealthy, land-owning elite got to make decisions for the whole of society – a kind of 'democracy of the elite' if you will. There were governments and parliaments, but on average only 2% of the adult male population had a vote. Eligibility to vote was based on how much land one owned. So the landed gentry, the smally minority of around 2% who lived in great opulence and in large mansions, got to vote, while the vast majority of the people – the serfs and workers and farmers, the 98% – lived in shocking poverty and had absolutely no say in how their society was governed. It is not surprising that the elite decision-makers made decisions and policies which benefitted the elite, and which were not good at all for the masses. Thus the rich got richer and the poor got poorer, and rates of inequality soared.

Things only began to change with the industrial revolution. First of all, serfs and farmers started to move away from the countryside to become factory workers in the towns. Here, conditions were often even worse and people began to agitate for improvements. In the towns they met other people from different areas and began to develop a national identity, rather than a purely local one based on their village. They began to think of their society on a larger scale, not just of the feudal manor. And they began to want a say in how this society was run.

Secondly, the new industrial entrepreneurs who were running the factories and making lots of money were often not from the landed gentry, and thus even though they began to become wealthy they were not eligible to vote because they did not own land. They too, wanted a say in the running of society.

But why should the landed elite listen to either of these two groups? They had all the power and had nothing to gain by sharing it with anyone else. Thus throughout the 18th century and into the early 19th century there were strikes and protests and demonstrations and even violent revolutions in virtually every European country, as the masses tried to persuade the elites to share their power. The primary call was more democracy, for the right to vote and to have a say in how society was run. This was seen as the key to improving all the other problems in society.

Over the course of the next 100 to 150 years government after government lowered the threshold of how much land you had to own, or how much money you had to have, in order to be eligible for the vote. This carried on, step by step, until by the early 19th century the vast majority of European countries now let all males over the age of 18 vote.

A subsequent struggle was continued by the women, as they too, demanded the right to vote. The suffragettes chained themselves to railings, ran in front of race horses, blew up post-boxes and used all sorts of techniques to get their voice heard. And eventually they too were successful.

By the mid-20th century the impossible had happened – the elite had given the vote to everyone and there was universal suffrage in virtually every European country. The struggle had been long, but it was successful. The disenfranchised 98% now got their right to vote.

Increasing Democracy, Decreasing Inequality

In the years after World War Two, most people voted for Labour governments, with leaders from the Trade Unions who represented the workers, and who put in policies that led to the creation of much more just and equal societies. These new, democratically elected governments institutionalised the welfare state which provided free education and healthcare to everyone, which improved public infrastructure and public services, and which stepped up welfare services to the unemployed and disabled.

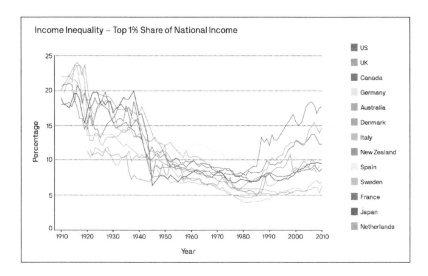

As an indicator of how much better society got now that there was democracy, let's consider how rates of economic inequality changed during this period. French economist, Thomas Piketty, has made an incredibly detailed study of levels of inequality during the 20th century[1], and some of the results of his work are summarised in the graph above. The graph starts on the left hand side in 1910, and we can see that there is a very high degree of inequality in all the western countries. But as the 20th century progressed, and states became more democratic, the levels of economic inequality began to decrease. In most countries, there was a really quite dramatic drop in economic inequality in the late 1940s, after the Second World War and the creation of the welfare state. During the decades of the middle part of the century, from the late 1940s all the way up until around 1980, there was a reasonably low degree of economic inequality in most of these countries, as democracy prevailed. Then things start to change, and we see a sharp increase in inequality that continues up to 2010, where the graph ends, but indeed this increase continues until today.

Coming Together Behind a Shared Vision of a Democratic and Just Global Society

Before we consider why the graph suddenly changes direction around 1980, let's reflect for a moment on what happened in the 19th century. Workers and farmers managed to unite together in a common protest against the elite. This may sound simple, but at the beginning of this period these people were very diverse and separate and knew little about each other and had no sense of themselves as a common group, as 'workers' or 'the proletariat' or what have you. A coal miner from the north of England, say, did not feel any sense of unity with a machine worker from the west of England. And neither of them would have considered that they had anything in common with a seamstress from anywhere in England. But during the course of the 19th century these disparate groups came together, learnt about each other, and began to see that despite their differences they were indeed positioned in a similar way in the national economic system. Their differences – of trade, of gender, of location, or whatever else – became largely irrelevant in their common struggle. By recognising their unity, and coming together in joint political action, they succeeded in bringing about what many people would have said was impossible.

If you were a serf living at the beginning of the 18th century, working the lands of your feudal master, while he enjoyed a life of luxury and opulence, and got to vote in a parliament which kept things as they were, and some visionary came up and told you that in the future everybody would be able to vote, and that there would be a democratically elected government that would bring about a more just and fair society, would lower rates of inequality, and would provide free education and free healthcare to everyone.... Well, you would probably have laughed and called that person a naive idealist. 'The elites won't give up their power', you'd say, 'it's not possible'. 'It's just a fantasy'. And indeed, that sounds quite reasonable. But if everyone had thought like that, nothing would have changed.

But instead, a few brave souls started to imagine a better society, and started to share this vision with others. And as the vision inspired people, they began to get active. Leaders emerged to help organise them. They used the new technologies of the day. They were creative. They were determined. And eventually, they were successful.

The situation is in many ways rather similar to the situation today regarding global democracy. To many people global democracy seems like a great idea, but a kind of idealist and impossible fantasy. 'The global masses are too diverse and separated,' you say, 'What does a factory worker in Bangladesh have in common with a agricultural worker in Kenya? Or with indigenous peoples in Latin America? How could they possibly all come together in a common struggle?' Well, it's already starting to happen.

'And in any case, how could we create a unified global society, we're all just too diverse?' Well, history is the story of diverse people recognising their unity and coming together. In the age of the internet and mobile technology, we can surely do it too. 'Oh but the elites will never give up their power,' you say. Well, they won't voluntarily. But they have given up power before, and there is no reason why they won't do it again. It's up to us to create the right conditions so that they choose to do so. The path to success is not clear or obvious, but neither was it at the beginning of the 19th century. It's up to us to start now and work it out as we go along, just as they did.

So, this is what the history of democracy tells us about the possibility of democracy at the global level. It *is* possible, if we want it, and if we are prepared to struggle for it.

But what about the other question which we mentioned at the beginning? Is democracy any good? It doesn't seem to be working very well now, even at the national level. Do we *want* global democracy?

So let's go back to Piketty's economic inequality data for the 20th century. From the beginning of the century all the way through to around 1980 rates of economic inequality were decreasing as the degrees of democracy were increasing. But around 1980 this pattern changed, and rates of economic inequality started to rise, and they have continued to rise right up to the present day. In fact, rates of economic inequality at the beginning of the 21st century are at almost the same high levels they were at the beginning of the 20th century. So what happened? There was democracy in most countries considered here throughout all this period, so why did inequality suddenly start to increase? Why did democracy lead to more equality up until 1980, but then to more inequality after 1980? Did democracy somehow stop working?

A Subtle Process of De-Democratisation

Well, the question of whether there has been democracy throughout all this period is actually a bit complicated. The answer is kind of yes and no. You see, in the period between roughly 1950 and 1980, each country had its own economy, and the economies of different countries were only slightly interconnected. There was trade between countries, of course, but at quite low levels. Most businesses operated in just one country and were regulated by the government of that country. So during this period the government and the economy operated on the same scale. And thus the democratically elected government of a country could regulate the economy of that country so that it functioned for the benefit of everyone who lived in that country. So this was a period of real national level democracy, and this functioning democracy led to relatively low levels of economic inequality inside nation states.

While this situation was very good for most people, it wasn't so great for the elite. They had to pay taxes, and follow regulations, and they found that this began to limit the amount of profit that they could make. And so, in 1975 a group of elites from Europe, America and Japan, called the Trilateral Commission, came together to discuss the problem and to try to find a solution. Their resulting report was called 'The Crisis of Democracy'. The crisis, they argued, was that there was *too much* democracy! Or in their words, 'an excess of democracy'. Citizens were beginning to participate too actively and were demanding too many government services. This was making it all rather difficult to do business profitably. The solution, they claimed, was therefore to limit democracy.[2]

The report didn't specify exactly how democracy should be limited, but the elites could draw some ideas from the work of British-Austrian economist, Friedrich Hayek. Hayek had written quite explicitly that democracy needed to be limited in order for 'the economy to function optimally', or as we might say, so that the elites could make big profits. He argued that while a certain amount of democracy was a good thing for society, most economic matters should be carefully bracketed out of economic control. He contended, in particular, that governments should not have the right to raise taxes for the purpose of redistribution and he argued strongly against any notion of 'social justice'.[3]

Hayek, and other neoliberal economists, figured out several ways to bring economic matters out of democratic control, while still leaving the basic structures of democracy in place. The most fundamental way was to expand the economy beyond the borders to the state. In a globalised economy, no state would be able to control and regulate the economy, and thus much of the economy would escape democratic control.

And indeed, since around the beginning of the 1980s, western governments have implemented policies to enable economic globalisation. They have removed capital controls and tariffs and duties and made it easier and easier for capital to flow across borders and for national economies to integrate into one big global economy.[4] This is what we generally call 'globalisation', or more precisely, 'neo-liberal globalisation'. At the same time, however, government and regulation has remained at the state level. It has not globalised, to match the economy. And thus in this way, much of the economy has now escaped state regulation and democratic control, just as Hayek suggested and predicted.

Governments now find it very hard to tax elites or big corporations, for example, because they can simply move their money outside of the country, ideally to a tax haven, where it can sit in secret. This has greatly helped the elite to make big profits.

There are also many other ways that parts of the economy have been quietly removed from democratic oversight. For example, central banks have been given independence to make monetary policy, in many cases outside of democratic government control. Monetary policy hugely affects economic inequality, but now in many countries there is no longer any democratic say in how it is set. Another example is that in many countries round the world, particularly poorer countries in the global South, the World Bank and the IMF have encouraged governments to draft new constitutions which insulate certain key economic and financial matters away from parliamentary oversight, and thus remove them from democratic control. And whole rafts of undemocratic 'global governance' arrangements have been created which govern key areas of the global economy without any input from democratically elected parliamentarians and without the majority of the worlds' peoples knowing anything about them.

Put all these things together, and you will see that there has been a long and subtle process of economic de-democratisation taking place since the 1980s. The structures of democracy still exist – political parties, elections, and so on – but it has been hollowed out. Economic matters, in particular, have been largely removed.[5]

This explains two things. Firstly, it explains why rates of economic inequality started to increase from around 1980 onwards, and why the correlation between democracy and equality seemed to break down at that point. The economy was largely de-democratised. Most of the regulatory tools that governments can use to limit inequality, such as taxation and redistribution, became ineffective, or much, much less effective than they had been in the previous years. It also explains the sense that many people have these days that democracy is somehow not working. That's because in certain key areas, it's not.

But that doesn't mean that democracy as a system of governance is no good. On the contrary, it shows that neoliberal economic globalisation has undermined national democracy. If we have a global economy, but national level democracy, then that national level democracy will not be able to function properly, at least in respect to economic matters.

Re-Democratisation Through Global Democracy

So what should we do? If we want democracy, proper democracy, then we have to organise things in a way that puts democratic government on the same scale as the economy. Only in that way can the economy come under democratic regulation and control. Only in that way can we have real, functioning democracy, and not the hollow sham that we have now.

To put it really simply, there are two options: either we reduce the scale of the economy back to the national level, or we expand the scale of democratic government up to the global scale. Or in other words, we can choose between de-globalisation or global democracy. These are our two options if we want real and functioning democracy.[6]

In our high-tech and hyper-connected world, we don't think that retracting back into our small nation states is a serious option. The world is interconnected, people are interconnected, the ecology is interconnected, the climate is interconnected. What we need now is political interconnection. This will provide a way for the voice of the people to be heard, a way for the many to govern the world, and its resources, for the benefit of everyone. And it will provide a way in which humanity can come together to solve global problems. If we want to do all this, *and* save our national democracies, then we need global democracy. It is the best option, and it *is* possible. This, is the future of democracy.

Notes

1 Piketty, Thomas. 2017. Capital in the Twenty-First Century. Translated by Arthur Goldhammer. Cambridge: Harvard University Press.

2 Crozier, Michel, Huntingdon, Samuel and Joji Watanuki. 1975. *The Crisis of Democracy: On the Governability of Democracies to the Trilateral Commission.* New York: New York University Press. web.archive.org/web/20120309011043/-http://www.trilateral.org/download/doc/crisis_of_democracy.pdf

3 See Hayek, Friedrich. 1982. *Law, Legislation and Liberty.* London: Routledge; Hayek, Friedrich. 1973. *Economic Freedom and Representative Government.* London: The Institute of Economic Affairs. iea.org.uk/wp-content/uploads/2016/07/-upldbook507.pdf

4 For example, see Perraton, Jonathan, Goldblatt, David, Held, David and Anthony McGrew. 1997. The Globalisation of Economic Activity. *New Political Economy*, 2, 2: 257-277; Schwartz, Herman. 1994. Globalisation; The Long View. In *Political Economy and the Changing Global Order*, edited by Richard Stubbs and Geoffrey Underhill. London: Macmillan; Neilson, Jeffrey, Pritchard, Bill and Henry Wai-Chung Yeung. 2014. Global Value Chains and Global Production Networks in the Changing International Political Economy: An introduction. *Review of International Political Economy*, 21,1: 1-8.

5 Freeman, Dena. 2017. *De-democratisation and Rising Inequality: The Underlying Cause of a Worrying Trend.* Working Paper Number 12. International Inequalities Institute, London School of Economics and Political Science, London, UK. eprints.lse.ac.uk/101847/

6 See also Freeman, Dena. 2020. *Can Globalization Succeed?* London: Thames & Hudson.

4. Is Globalisation the Problem?

Contemporary globalisation has many problems. It drives widening economic inequality, creating a world where a handful of billionaires own more wealth than half the Earth's population combined. It leads to the erosion of democracy at the national level, as global capital overwhelms national governments and ends up dictating policies and practices. And it makes it virtually impossible to solve pressing global problems, such as climate change, environmental degradation and biodiversity loss, because there is no decision-making body at the global level, able to make rules and regulations for the whole world and ensure that they are enforced. We are certainly not the first to highlight these problems. Academics and activists have been pointing out these issues for at least twenty years. But the trouble is, they have not offered any plausible solution. They have simply vented their frustration with the current system.

The Anti-Globalisation Movement

For example, in 1999 a huge group of some 40,000 activists came together to protest outside the Seattle meeting of the World Trade Organisation (WTO), where governments were meeting to discuss further integration of the world's economies. The activists were against the policies and approach of the trade organization and the neoliberal form of globalisation that it produced. They demanded a globalisation that would benefit everyone on the planet, not just the wealthy elite. All well and good, but what would that look like? They were not sure.

This big demonstration kicked off the so-called 'Anti-Globalisation movement'. Over the next several years they organised large protests outside nearly every meeting of the World Bank, International Monetary Fund (IMF), WTO, G20, and several other international organisations. At the local level they organised a range of protests and demonstrations in many countries, particularly across Africa, Asia and Latin America. They cried 'our world is not for sale', and rallied together under the slogan 'another world is possible'. But what did this 'possible other world' look like?

In 2001 they established the World Social Forum – named to contrast it to the meeting of elites in Davos at the World Economic Forum – and different activists and social movements from around the world came together to discuss what kind of world they wanted to build. The first meeting in Porto Alegre in Brazil, brought together over 12,000 people, a wide-ranging mix of human rights activists, indigenous peoples, environmentalists, feminists, anarchists, farming peoples, civil rights activists, trade unionists, students, religious groups, anti-sweatshop campaigners, and many more. Coming from different countries and cultures, speaking different languages, they somehow found a way to sit down to speak to each other, and to listen to each other. But while these discussions were exciting, and in many ways very important, they failed to come to any real conclusions.[1]

The World Social Forum began to meet every year, in different countries round the world, and over time the Anti-Globalisation Movement began to re-define themselves. They were not against globalisation per se, but they were against the particular form of neoliberal globalisation that was happening then, and indeed now. As they developed transnational networks and built solidarity beyond their own countries, they realised that they were actually pro-globalisation. They realised that they were all part of a shared global society in so many ways. They just wanted a different kind of globalisation, one that was more just and equal and not dominated by billionaires and trans-national corporations and elites. They began to call this 'globalisation from below'. And instead of the 'anti-globalisation movement' they began to call themselves the 'anti-corporate globalisation movement' or the 'alter- (or alternative) – globalisation movement', or increasingly, 'the global justice movement'.

But what did 'globalisation from below' or 'global justice' actually mean? Still there was no clear articulation. Many of the activists in these movements suggested small-scale local solutions, such as eco-villages, cooperatives and so on. But while these are fine in their own right, they are clearly not a model for a large-scale globalised society. The groups could not find a global vision which they could all come together behind. They could not find a model for a just and sustainable globalised world. So in the end they became more of a talking shop. There were hours and hours of discussions, but no concrete plans and no collective actions towards political change. Thus after ten or fifteen years this movement lost momentum and in many respects fizzled out.

Right Wing Movements for Nationalism and De-Globalisation

But the problems of contemporary globalisation did not go away. In fact they intensified and got worse. After the financial crash of 2008, and the subsequent bailing out of the banks with public, tax-payers money, many governments implemented punishing austerity measures, cutting public spending on health, education and welfare. Unsurprisingly, this led to economic inequality surging even further. Even in the rich countries of Europe and America, more and more people slipped into poverty and struggled to get through the month. Food banks opened up as better-off individuals stepped in with charity to help the poor, while the state did little. The feelings of anger, frustration and powerlessness increased and spread to wider and wider sections of society.

In response to this, a very different type of movement emerged – right-wing, populist nationalism. People like Donald Trump in the US, Jair Bolsanaro in Brazil, and Viktor Orban in Hungary rode the wave of discontent and came into power. These politicians also argued that globalisation was the cause of many of today's problems. But they offered a very different, and seemingly more simple solution: 'if globalisation is bad, let's de-globalise. Let's go back to nationalism. Let's put up trade barriers to protect our economies, let's put up walls and immigration barriers to keep out foreigners, let's look out for the interests of our own people first, and to hell with everyone else'.

This blunt, racist, selfish approach has found a lot of support with many people. But history has shown us that nationalism, xenophobia, racism and increasing competition between states has only led to conflict and war. This is very similar to what happened in the run up to World War Two. The recent aggressive stance of the US under Trump, the growth of anti-Islamic sentiment and the moves of several nationalist governments to limit the rights of ethnic minorities certainly does not bode well.

But this narrow nationalist thinking is problematic in so many other ways too. First of all, in the age of the internet, air travel, global production chains, is it really possible to 'go back to nationalism'? We don't think so. And indeed, most of these populist nationalists still support global business and global investment. It is mainly the cross-border movement of people they wish to stop, much less that of capital.

But even if it were possible, do we really want to close ourselves up in narrow, inward-looking nation states? Do we not want to connect with our brothers and sisters around the world? And most importantly, do we not want to find a way to solve common global problems? Climate change is accelerating at a rapid rate and threatens to have huge and dramatic impacts on our lives and our eco-systems in the coming years. Do we really want to put our heads in the sand and ignore this? Do we want to pretend that pointless, unenforceable treaties are going to make things better? Or do we want to find a way to come together as a whole, so that we can democratically solve our shared problems?

Another Kind of Globalisation is Possible

The choice is not between globalisation as it is now, or de-globalisation. That's a false choice. Neither of these is a good option. The way forward is to build a different kind of globalisation. And in our view, while 'democratic globalisation from below' is all well and good, it needs to be combined with 'democratic globalisation from above'. We need to build the right structure of globalisation and in this book we outline what we think this means.

Crucially, it means getting decision-making at the right level to solve the problem, with global problems being solved at the global level. And just as crucially, it means building democracy fundamentally into the system at all levels – local, national and global.

In our view, a democratic world federation offers a vision of a more just and democratic form of globalisation. We think it offers the best chance for creating a type of globalisation that gives everyone a voice and that unites humanity to be able to work together to solve shared global problems, and to bring about justice and solidarity.

It's a vision that activists and thinkers from Africa, Asia, Latin America, Europe and the US have come up with again and again throughout the 20th century – from Nehru to Nkrumah to Einstein – and which offers a real alternative to the current international system.

The vision of course needs refining. The details need to be worked out. How would a world parliament work in practice? How would a united global Ministry of Environment tackle climate change? Who would sit on the Global Tax Body to decide on a fair system of global taxation and redistribution? Which issues would be decided at which level of government? All of this requires discussion, debate and fine-tuning. And if activists and academics and politicians can come together to focus on these questions, then we can do this. Another world *is* possible. First we have to imagine it. Only then we can build it.

Coming Together Behind a Shared Vision of a Democratic and Just Global Society

To make it happen we need a massive world movement of citizens who call for global democracy – who publish articles in newspapers and blogs to spread the idea, who write to their members of parliament and tell them this is what they want, and who come out to the streets to make their voice heard. We need a 'great convergence' of NGOs and social movements. Everyone who cares about human rights and refugees and climate change and inequality and a host of other issues that can only be solved at the global level, should come together to focus on changing the system, because only with real global democracy can any of these issues truly be solved.

We need campaigns, petitions, and social media activity. We need new political parties that stand in local and national elections with the promise that if elected they will pursue change in international organisations in order to bring about global democracy. These parties could then connect with other similar parties in other countries, and work together to forward the same vision. Maybe we also need new tools – ways to instigate forms of online voting, parallel decision-making systems, and yet other things that no one has thought of yet. There are many possible ways forward. Right now, the most important thing is that we start to come together behind this shared vision of a just and democratic world order.

What's clear is that it will probably take a serious struggle to bring about the radical social and political change that we seek. Democracy has never been freely given; it has always had to be won. That's because it is fundamentally about challenging the power of elites and spreading power more equally in society. As we discussed in chapter 3, it took massive political struggle throughout the 19th and early 20th centuries for democracy to be won at the state level. Now it's time for us to continue to the next stage. The struggle to bring about global democracy may be biggest and most important political struggle of the 21st century.

Note

1 For more on the World Social Forum see Patomäki, Heikki and Teivo Teivainen. 2004. The World Social Forum: An Open Space or a Movement of Movements? *Theory, Culture & Society*, 21,6: 145–154; Teivainen, Teivo. 2002. The World Social Forum and G lobal Democratisation: Learning from Porto Alegre. *Third World Quarterly*, 23, 4:621–632; Santos, Boaventura de Sousa. 2007. *The World Social Forum and the Global Left*. Coimbra: Centro de Estudos Sociais. eg.uc.pt/bitstream/10316/11086/1/The%20World%20Social%20Forum%20and-%20the%20Global%20Left.pdf.

5. Love is all you need. Or is it?

When we speak to people about the vision of a global democracy, they often associate it with John Lennon's song 'Imagine', that also describes a world of unity and peace. But while we of course like that song and its message, some important distinctions need to be made.

In the song, Lennon takes what are arguably the major things that people have been fighting over throughout history – countries, religions and private property – and invites us to imagine a future in which we will no longer believe in them and will no longer uphold them: Imagine there's no countries, and no religion too, and no possessions. Instead, he says, we could then just be living our lives in peace, and in brotherhood, sharing all the world. Or in one sentence: 'All you need is love'.

You Can't Love All the People, All the Time

The problem with this sweet approach, however, is that even if we could somehow make all of these things disappear one day, which is doubtful, it's just too likely that we, imperfect human beings, will already find something else to disagree on and to fight over. And think about it, we are not really built to just love all the people all the time, especially when the strong are exploiting and harming the weak, or the environment. We don't want to love them. What we want is a functioning democratic justice system that will hold them accountable and make them stop.

If we want to be serious about things like peace and justice and sustainability, then romantic and childish cliches about love and brotherhood are not really helpful. What we really need is nothing short of the framework of the democratic state, but applied on the level that includes all the parts of our global society, the global weak and the global strong, together. The democratic state is a basic, indispensable requirement for peace and justice.

It is such a necessity because it enables us to address the two basic tendencies, or you can call them 'defects', of human society. First, is the tendency of the strong to harm the weak, and second is the tendency of people and groups to split into mutually hostile camps.

The first tendency starts with a simple fact of life: humans, either as individuals or as groups, are not equal in their power. There is always side A that is physically or otherwise stronger than side B; whether it's the adult and the child, the average man and the average woman, the majority and the minority, and so on. Whenever one side is stronger, sadly-what often happens is that this side uses their advantage for their own interests. So we see, again and again, situations where the strong exploit, or oppress, or otherwise harm the weak. Perhaps not always, but way too often.

For those occasions, in order to help the weak and protect them from the strong, we have to have a third, neutral party, which is stronger than both sides and which belongs to both of them. And that is the democratic state which is built on three basic principles:

A. Everyone has the same fundamental rights. These rights are not dependent on anything else, such as physical strength, and thus the weak have these rights too.

B. The government of the democratic state is the only one that has the right to use violence, and can only do so if and when it's necessary to protect its citizens.

C. In order to make sure that the government itself will not misuse its power against the people, the people have the ultimate power over the government – through elections, and a web of checks and balances, and constitutional separations and limitations, which all check the power of the government.

In this way, the democratic state can be there for the weak, and in case of injustice it can intervene through the courts or the police or other authorities. Thus, if side A and side B have a dispute which they can't work out, they are invited to turn to the third party, the state's court, where both of them can try to explain why they are right according to the law. It will be the impartial judge or jury who decides who is right, and the respective strength of each side will be irrelevant.

With regard to the second issue that we mentioned – the repeating tendency of people and groups to split in to mutually hostile camps – we can also see that the democratic state offers an excellent solution. Rather than ignoring this basic tendency, or telling everyone that they should just love each other all the time, democracy suggests diverse ways to channel this tendency into non-violent and even constructive forms of disagreement and social group dynamics.

If some people have new and different ideas about how society should run, for example, democracy says: 'great, go ahead and start a new organisation or movement or a political party'. In a democratic society it's OK to disagree with other people. You can discuss and even argue with them, on the streets, on the media and in the parliament. This is how we can get new and better ideas and decisions. And yes, you are free to hate other people. The only things that you are not allowed to do is to break the law or to use violence. The latter is the special prerogative of the state.

Real Love is a Shared Global Democracy

So to sum up, democracy recognizes that the most valuable asset of humans, as imperfect social creatures, is their ability to interact and cooperate, to split and join, and to change their minds. And it offers a framework for them to do it in a safe and peaceful and fair manner. This is why it is indispensable for large-scale human society. The naïve argument of some anarchists, who claim that we could get along just fine without a state, is simply not true. This might have worked for when most people lived as small groups of roaming hunters and gatherers, but it is not relevant for today's large-scale and complex societies.

With the powerful modern technologies that we have today, how people live on one side of the planet can have enormous consequences for people living on the other side. This is why in order to have peace and justice and sustainability, we need to have that mechanism of the democratic state, at the very global level. That is the level of our ecology and of our economy, and it also needs to be the level of our democracy.

The kind of love that we really need in the world is sharing an all-inclusive global democracy. And that is what we need to imagine.

6. What is Global Governance?

We hear today a lot about 'global governance'. It sounds reassuring, as if the world is somehow being governed even though there is no global government. But what does contemporary global governance actually look like? How is our world actually being governed, and by whom? Moreover, is this form of governance good? Or effective? Or just? Or democratic?

The current system of global governance is very messy and complicated, if it can be considered to be a system at all. It is more like a rather messy collection of different organisations, networks and committees that operate on different bases and which overlap and often contradict each other.[1] Broadly speaking, there are three different types of global governance arrangements: state-centred, multi-stakeholder, and private, which we can look at in turn.

State-Centred Governance

This is the most well-known form of global governance. It consists of various international organisations or clubs where governments come together to negotiate and make decisions. The United Nations is the key example here. Almost all the governments of the world's states have a seat in the General Assembly and the various other committees and councils which carry out the UN's work.

This is also arguably the most democratic of all the global governance arrangements, because each UN member state has one vote. So in theory at least, richer and poorer countries have the same power. In practice, of course, rich and powerful states have all sorts of ways to persuade poorer and weaker states to vote in particular ways. But even if the UN is the most democratic of the international organisations, that is sadly not saying much, as it is not very democratic at all.

Firstly, the 'one state, one vote' formula ignores the fact that states vary hugely in terms of their population. The small island state of Tuvalu has a population of around 12,000 people, while India has a population of almost 1.4 billion people. And yet both countries have the same one vote. This doesn't really seem right. Perhaps a system of weighted voting, according to the number of people per country, would be more appropriate?

Even more problematic is the fact that individual citizens do not have any say at the UN, only their governments do. And in many cases governments don't really represent the views of their citizens. So while the UN Charter talks of 'We the peoples...', really it should say 'We the governments...'

Having a second chamber, like a parliament, which directly represented world citizens, in parallel to the General Assembly which represents country governments, would make the UN far more democratic and connected to the people.

There are many other problems with the UN, from its lack of enforcement capability to the way that it is funded. But bad as the UN may be, other international organisations are even less democratic.

Take the World Bank and the International Monetary Fund, two organisations that play a very important role in global economic matters. In these organisations again only governments are represented, but this time it is not 'one state, one vote', but rather votes are apportioned according to the amount of money the country contributes to the organisation. So, it is more like 'one dollar, one vote'. The result is that these international organisations are completely dominated by the rich and powerful countries. The US, UK, France, Germany and Japan combined control over 35% of the votes. The US alone has 15.88% of the votes. Since some major decisions require an 85% majority, this means that the US effectively has a veto on those decisions.

So perhaps it is not surprising that these organisations often give loans to poorer countries and then add on all sorts of strings and conditionalities that in effect mean that in many cases it is the World Bank or the IMF that effectively dictates the economic policy of these countries. And of course, they dictate policies that benefit the rich countries and tend to cause increasing poverty and inequality in the countries that receive the loans. They would act very differently if all countries had an equal say in defining their policies and actions.

Climbing further down the democracy ladder we come to 'clubs' of governments. These are arrangements of a relatively small number of governments who come together in a rather ad hoc way, without an official organisation, to make decisions on global affairs. A key example here would be the G20, in which leaders of 20 powerful countries meet together in summits to make decisions which effect the whole world. Or the G7, in which case it is leaders of just seven countries. Who chose these countries? Who gave them power to make decisions for the rest of the world? Why don't other countries get a say? Who even knows what they really discuss behind closed doors? The whole arrangement is deeply secretive and undemocratic, and leads to global policies which favour the richer countries and go against the interests of the poorer ones.

Another form of state centred global governance is what are called 'trans-governmental networks'. These are issue-specific networks where particular government agencies from different countries share information or work together in a fairly loose network form. There are dozens and dozens of these networks and they carry out very important elements of global governance, but most people have never even heard of them.[2] In most cases their members are only or predominantly from the richer countries and across the board they are highly secretive, with decisions taken behind closed doors and rarely made open to the public. Many of them operate in the economic and financial sectors, such as the Basel Committee on Banking Supervision, the Financial Stability Board, and the International Competition Network. It is deeply undemocratic that secretive unelected and unaccountable officials are quietly making policies on issues such as banking, finance and competition, and many, many other matters that effect all of us.

So much for state-centred global governance. Some parts are more democratic than others, but overall it is highly secretive and highly undemocratic.

Multi-Stakeholder Governance

Is the situation any better when we look at the second form of global governance arrangement, namely multi-stakeholder networks? Unfortunately, the situation is even worse.

In state-centred arrangements the key actors are ministers and government officials, who at least in some countries have been democratically elected by the citizens of their countries and are accountable to them. So they have some right to claim that they represent the people. But in multi-stakeholder networks there are many different kinds of actors or 'stakeholders'. Alongside government officials, you will generally find NGOs, transnational corporations, and other business representatives taking part in the discussions and voting on the decisions. Why is this bad? Well, if we look at it from the point of view of democracy, we have to ask, 'who elected these people? 'who do they represent?' With NGOs it is rather problematic. No-one elected them. And it is very hard to see who they represent – their financial donors? their activist supporters? While many NGOs do fantastic work and indeed try to make the world more fair and more just, it does not make sense from a democratic point of view that they should be making decisions on our behalf, rather than elected representatives.

With transnational corporations and business organisations the situation is even worse. Who do they represent? Here the answer is clear. They represent their shareholders. And they are duty-bound to stand up for their interests and to make as much profit as possible for them. So how can corporations possibly be tasked with making decisions for the whole of society? They are, by definition, legally bound to think about what is best for their shareholders – a generally small group of wealthy elites – rather than what is best for society as a whole.

Furthermore, they have huge budgets to attend meetings with large teams of lawyers and large teams of consultants and can easily outweigh the smaller teams of people from the NGOs and even from the states.

So in many cases, multi-stakeholder networks end up being a thinly veiled form of corporate rule – with business representatives making decisions which benefit their shareholders, while claiming that they are doing what is good for society in general.[3]

In the past few years there has, unfortunately, been a trend towards more and more 'stakeholder governance', and it is making global governance even more un-democratic. There are now dozens and dozens of multi-stakeholder networks, such as the World Commission on Dams, the Alliance for Water Stewardship, or the Global Alliance for Vaccines and Immunization (GAVI), where states, companies and NGOs ostensibly try to come together to solve problems. But despite the fancy logos and the upbeat press releases, these networks have not really solved any of these problems, but have instead instituted market-oriented 'solutions' which somehow just happen to make their member companies richer, while having little or no impact on the intended problem.

GAVI is a good example – the Global Alliance for Vaccines and Immunization. You'd think they would be rushing to waive patent rights and to quickly get the world vaccinated against COVID-19, wouldn't you? Well, instead of doing that they created COVAX, short for 'COVID-19 Vaccines Global Access Facility', with the WHO and two other multi-stakeholder networks, the Vaccines Alliance and CEPI, the Coalition for Epidemic Preparedness Innovations.

What does COVAX do? COVAX pools together money from richer governments and gives it to big pharmaceutical companies to help them develop COVID vaccines. The idea is that this will speed up the development of new vaccines and enable them to be quickly manufactured on a large scale. COVAX is also supposed to help distribute vaccines to poorer countries, by supplying enough vaccines to vaccinate 20% of their population. This may all sound good at first sight, but if you think about it for a moment, it basically functions to gives public money to private corporations to develop vaccines. It then allows these corporations to sell the vaccines back to governments at whatever market price they can negotiate. In this way governments essentially pay for the vaccines twice, they pay for their development and then they also for their purchase. And the amount of vaccines distributed to poorer countries is woefully small.[4]

Isn't this simply an embarrassment? An example of what kind of system gets established when private companies are in the driving seat? If we really wanted to distribute COVID vaccines quickly and equitably round the world and avert the huge global crisis we are currently in, we would have firstly insisted that the companies sell their vaccines at cost price, or with a very small profit. Secondly, we would ensure that patents are waived during the pandemic crisis, and that knowledge and skills about how to manufacture the vaccines are actively transferred to as many countries and companies as possible. That way global production could be massively ramped up, and of course, prices kept down. By doing this, far more people would have access to COVID vaccines far more quickly, and the pandemic would be ended more rapidly for everyone. But then the pharmaceutical companies wouldn't have made such big profits. Today their directors and shareholders have made billions. This is precisely the problem of letting private companies get involved in global governance under the guise of 'multi-stakeholder governance'. You might think that it can't get any worse. But unfortunately, it can.

Private Governance

A third type of global governance arrangement that is growing rapidly, is private governance – governance arrangements that are openly run by private companies, without being dressed up as multi-stakeholder arrangements or anything else.[5]

You may have heard of SWIFT, the Society for Worldwide Interbank Financial Telecommunication, and you may have used it when you transferred money to another country. It has developed technical standards and coding systems for banks all over the world. But did you know that it is a private corporation? Owned by 2,500 banks? And did you realise that it is developing these standards and guidelines independently from national and intergovernmental regulation? We have a system in which the banks make their own rules without any governmental oversight. After all the banking crashes of the past few years, do we really think nothing can go wrong?

Another example of private global governance is ICANN, the Internet Corporation for Assigned Numbers and Names. This is a private non-profit organisation which manages the centralized domain name system (DNS) to control the routing for the vast majority of global Internet traffic. With the huge power of the internet, does it make sense to have it governed by a private corporation? Wouldn't it be better if there was state-based oversight and regulation, by democratically elected global representatives?

Even more worrying is the growing system of privately run global courts and arbitration tribunals that is beginning to form the main enforcement mechanism for trans-border business relations, both between companies, and between companies and states. You see, as more and more companies are doing business across state borders, they have realised that they need some form of global enforcement mechanism to ensure that they and their partners keep their agreements. And in contrast to the area of human rights law, which we discuss in detail in chapter eight, these companies will not accept some wishy-washy voluntary system of 'recommendations'. They want a system of binding international business law that is backed up by global courts. But rather than have a state-based system of global courts, where we can ensure that judges are chosen fairly and that democratically created law is applied appropriately, what has happened is the creation of a number of private tribunals, with judges overwhelmingly from the private sector, making decisions behind closed doors, and very often favouring private companies over states.

Furthermore, there has to be something very wrong with our overall global governance system if we allow companies to set up private global courts and tribunals to enforce business law, but we say it is impossible, or unfeasible, to set up global courts to enforce human rights law. Why the difference? Why does business law have more power than human rights law? Could it be because companies are increasingly taking part in global governance, making the decisions and setting up the systems?

What Do You Prefer: Corporate Rule or Global Democracy?

Is this the type of global governance that we, the people of the word, want? Wouldn't it be far, far better to have a global democracy? So that we can have a say in what structures and laws are made at the global level? Wouldn't that allow us to build a much better system of global governance, or global government, in which the rules and laws empower us, the people, and not just the elites and the corporations?

Notes

1 For more on global governance see Koenig-Archibugi, Mathias. 2003. Mapping Global Governance. In *Governing Globalization: Power, Authority and Global Governance*, edited by David Held and Anthony McGrew. Cambridge: Polity Press, Cambridge.

2 For more on transnational networks see Hale, Thomas and David Held. 2011. Mapping Changes in Transnational Governance. In *Handbook of Transnational Governance: Institutions and Innovations*, edited by Thomas Hale and David Held. Cambridge: Polity Press.

3 For an excellent critique of stakeholder governance see Gleckman, Harris. 2018. *Multistakeholder Governance and Democracy: A Global Challenge*. London: Routledge.

4 See also Correa, Carlos. 2021. *Vaccination inequalities and the Role of the Multilateral System.* SouthViews, 224. www.southcentre.int/southviews-no-224--19-july-2021/

5 Hall, Rodney and Thomas Biersteker. *(eds). 2002.The Emergence of Private Authority in Global Governance.* Cambridge: Cambridge University Press; Knill, Christopher and Dirk Lehmkul. 2002. Private Actors and the State: Internationalization and Changing Patterns of Governance. *Governance,* 1: 41-64.

Section II
Problems of the Current 'International' System

7. Global Apartheid

In recent years more and more academics, activists and statesmen have been using the term 'global apartheid' to describe the world system, drawing an analogy between the infamous system of white minority rule in South Africa and the international order we live in today.[1] To many, this analogy can sound shocking and outlandish, but actually it is extremely accurate. Understanding this leads us to challenge the story that we are being told about the world, and also points to the type of systemic change that we need.

The essence of the argument is that the key element of the apartheid formula is a system of economic integration combined with political segregation. This is what underlay the apartheid system in South Africa, where blacks and whites were integrated into the same economy but politically segregated, and it is what underlies our existing world order, in which humanity as a whole is economically integrated in the global market, but politically and legally segregated into separate nation states.

The Apartheid System in South Africa

To understand the analogy and the similarities, let's start with a quick review of how this formula was applied in South Africa. There, the economic integration meant that whites and blacks played different roles, but in the same economy. The whites were the owners and managers of businesses, while the blacks had to do all the dirty hard work for a lousy payment. But they were both part of the same business or corporation.

The gap in their status and their different roles in that integrated economy resulted from the second part of the apartheid formula, which was their political segregation into separate legal systems. White people, only, were counted as citizens of South Africa, and their rights were protected by the rule of law and they could participate democratically in the national decision making. The blacks, in contrast, were politically excluded. And the way in which they were excluded is of particular importance. The white government declared ten remote areas as 'states' of the blacks, each supposedly belonging to a different tribe. Each black person in South Africa, regardless of where they actually lived, was deemed to be no longer a citizen of South Africa, but a citizen of one of those new fictitious 'homelands'. By this cunning move, the blacks of South Africa suddenly found themselves with the status of foreigners in their own country, with no citizen rights. Instead they found themselves under a strict regime of movement control and surveillance, and a constant risk of deportation.

The white government tried to tell the world that these so-called 'black homelands' were self-governed and autonomous nation states. They even tried to brand them as 'Bantu-states', where the word 'bantu' means 'people' in some of the local African languages. But everyone knew that these were nothing but puppet states, whose corrupt black leadership had to obey the white government, or be removed and punished. Cynically, people started calling them 'Bantu-stans'. The word 'stan' means 'state' or 'land' in many Asian languages. And just as everyone knew that at that time, during the Cold War, Kazakh-stan or Uzbeki-stan were not controlled by the Kazakh people or the Uzbek people but by the Soviet Union, so it was clear that the Bantu 'states', or the Bantu-stans, were engineered and controlled by the whites.

Ridiculous as the Bantustans were, they were extremely efficient in fulfilling their true purpose, which was to legally divide and rule the black population. In this way, the white minority enjoyed the best of both worlds. By integrating with the blacks only economically, the whites made sure that they wouldn't have to do all the hard work in the mines and the fields, or even clean their own homes. And by excluding the blacks politically, the whites got to have a democracy just for themselves.

Global Apartheid

Now, when we zoom out to the global level. what do we see? We have huge global economic integration, in the sense that financial markets are almost completely integrated and the economic activities of multinational corporations span the entire Earth. Almost every single product that we wear, that we eat, that we use, relies on this global economic integration. Like in South Africa, people around the world play very different roles and get very different compensation for their work in that economically integrated system. And for most people, what determines their place on the ladder, to a great degree, is not their personal talent or diligence, but their nationality, and on which side of the border they happen to stand.

If they are citizens of some western country (which is just a nicer way of saying 'mostly white country') most chances are, statistically, that they stand much higher on the global social-economic ladder than most of the citizens of the non-European, non-white countries.

It is true that there are many important exceptions, but on average, and in comparison to the majority of the world's people, white people enjoy much better education, health services and public infrastructures, and their environment is much less polluted and their working conditions are by far superior.

Take for example the border between the state of California in the USA, and Mexico. On the Californian side of the fence, it is not legal to pay a worker less than $13 an hour. That is the minimum legal wage. On the Mexican side, the minimum wage equals just US$1 per hour. What a difference! It means that even for doing exactly the same work, just by being on Californian soil a worker will get a salary that is thirteen times bigger than his fellow worker who happens to stand on Mexican soil.

Despite the huge economic integration of the world, and the ecological unity of the Earth, national borders legally and politically divide humanity to some two hundred separate jurisdictions. In this way the rights and liberties of people who work in the same economic system, even in the same business or the same corporation, can 'legally' be entirely different.

In other words, in the international system, what determines your place on the ladder, at least formally, is not the colour of your skin or the shape of your eyes or nose, but the colour of the passport that you have, or the colours of the flag under which you happened to be born.

Racism, Past and Present

Today we think that racism is inherently wrong, that it is a bad thing to treat a person differently just on the account of something as superficial as the colour of their skin, that tells you nothing about the inner worth of that person, then how can it be right to treat people differently just on the account of the nationality that is written on their papers? Isn't that even more superficial? Can that field in the identity card, or the colour of a person's passport, tell you anything about the inner worth of that person? Or can the soil that the person is standing on, on either side of a fence, justify treating the person with such a different set of laws? Of course not.

There were some dark times in the 19th and early 20th centuries, at the peak of European colonialism and imperialism, when many in the global white elite of the day thought that the nonsense of racism and white superiority were backed up by the serious science of biology. A time will come, hopefully sooner rather than later, when nationalism – the idea that you it's OK to treat people with entirely different sets of laws and rights just according to their 'nation', whatever that word means – will be as discredited and delegitimized as racism is nowadays.

But has racism really disappeared today? Why is it that even though race is no longer the official criterion for segregation, so many of the world's elite are white? Surely, this is not just a coincidence. It is, rather, another good reason to use the term 'global apartheid'. Because the current world order is still, fundamentally, a racist one. Only that unlike the racism of the colonial age, which was direct and blunt and official, the new racism that governs the world today is hidden by the seemingly innocent division of humanity into supposedly sovereign nation states. And also by the fact that within the white states, non-white minorities have, at least legally, the same rights, and some are doing really well.

But when we zoom out to the global level we see that, just as the creation of the 'Bantu-States' in South Africa did not really liberate the blacks there, but rather deepened their oppression, so on the global level the creation of nation states across the whole world, after the fall of colonial empires, did not end the rule of the white minority over the world's people, but instead actually enabled it to continue. It did not mend the racial segregation of humanity, but allowed it to persist. What we have now is the same old racist hierarchy, but under a different cover. It may be slightly more sophisticated, but it is no less cruel, oppressive, and unjust.[2]

The Answer to Global Apartheid is Global Democracy

It's high time we realised that nation states are our global Bantustans, whose supreme purpose is to isolate the democracies of the global white elite from the 'threat' of the participation of the non-white majority of the world's people, the world's 'demos', the main victims of this senseless and heartless system.

The answer to global apartheid is global democracy – a federal level of government of humanity, by humanity, and for humanity. We need to move from a system of economic integration plus political segregation to a system of both economic and political integration. That means uniting all the world's people, no matter the colour of their skin or the place they happened to be born, into one unified democratic system. Then we can all be equal citizens of this earthly home on which we live together.

Notes

1 For example, Alexander, Titus. 1996. *Unravelling Global Apartheid: An Overview of World Politics.* Cambridge: Polity Press; Benedicto, Ainhoa Ruiz, Akkerman, Mark and Pere Brunet, 2020. *A Walled World: Towards a Global Apartheid.* Barcelona: Centre Delàs d'Estudis per la Pau; Besterman, Catherine. 2020. *Militarized Global Apartheid.* Durham: Duke University Press. Bond, Patrick. 2001. *Against Global Apartheid: South Africa Meets the World Bank, IMF and International Finance.* UCT Press.

2 See also Chimni, B. 2004. International Institutions Today: An Imperial Global State in the Making. *European Journal of International Law*, 15, 1: 1-37.

8. Human Rights

Let's have a look at human rights. Human rights, in theory, are rights that all people have, just because they are human. So, irrespective of nationality, race, religion, gender, language, geography, colour, or any other distinguishing feature, all people, in theory, share these same rights. Sounds good, right? But because our world order is 'international, rather than 'global', there are some problems.

First, we need to consider, what are rights? Well, rights are essentially principles of entitlement that are created by a society. Rights are generally created by laws or statutes, and to be effective they have to be enforced by a legal and judicial system. In most cases, rights are therefore created and enforced by states. So, for example, in many states citizens have the right to vote. If anyone tries to forcibly stop a citizen from voting, that citizen can appeal to the police or to the court system to restrain the person trying to stop them from voting and indeed to punish them. Or in many states, citizens have the right to private property. So if someone else trespasses on your property, or steals your property, you can go to the police or the courts and seek redress.

If there were no police, or no courts, then these rights would be rather meaningless, because you would have no way to defend them. And this is exactly the problem with international human rights. These are rights that supposedly apply to everyone, everywhere. They are fundamentally global rights. And as such, to be effective they require a global system of enforcement, some kind of global police force or global court. But neither of these exist. Therefore there is no way to defend, or enforce, human rights. So they end up being theoretical, or aspirational, at best – but not real rights.

The International Human Rights System

But hang on, you say, there's the Universal Declaration of Human Rights, and a whole system of international human rights law. Surely that makes human rights real? Well, let's take a look.

The whole idea of human rights arose primarily after the Second World War, and in particular in response to the holocaust, where the Nazi government actively murdered its own citizens if they happened to be Jewish, homosexual, or have some other trait not considered to be 'perfect Aryan'. After the war, it was therefore considered important to set up a system through which citizens would be protected from abuses by their own governments. So in 1946 the newly established United Nations set up the UN Commission on Human Rights to devise such a system. The Commission established a Drafting Committee of lawyers and philosophers under the chairmanship of Eleanor Roosevelt, and in 1948 they adopted the Universal Declaration of Human Rights.

The declaration lists thirty human rights. It includes the right not to be tortured, the right not to be enslaved, the right to be considered innocent until proven guilty, the right to education, the rights to food and shelter, the right to freedom of expression, and many others. So far so good. But as you might have noticed, many people today are sadly still tortured, still enslaved, still deemed guilty without proof. And vast numbers of people, do not have access to education, adequate food or shelter, or the ability to safely express themselves. So what went wrong?

First of all, the Universal Declaration of Human Rights is a 'declaration', not a 'treaty'. It is an aspirational document, but it has no legal force whatsoever. If the creators had wanted to really bring about these rights in the whole world, they would firstly have written a treaty. Because treaties, in contrast to declarations, at least in theory, are legally binding on those states that ratify them.

Secondly, they would have created some kind of global enforcement mechanism to back up these rights and make them defendable. This was in fact the original idea. Right at the beginning, during the second session of the Commission for Human Rights in 1947, Australia introduced a draft resolution to establish an International Court of Human Rights to oversee violations of the proposed covenant (or treaty) of Human Rights. A Working Group composed of Australia, Belgium, Iran and India was established to work out the details of the court: How would it function? Where would it be located? How many judges would there be and how would they be chosen? Should it be new court or part of the already existing International Court of Justice (ICJ)? But while this group were working out all the details and things seemed to be progressing well, another group of countries stepped forward and opposed the whole idea. This second group included big powers such as the US, China, and Russia. They managed to derail the whole process so that in the end the idea never got off the ground. And unfortunately, that effectively was the end of human rights, in any real sense of the term.

What happened instead was a long, drawn-out process of creating so-called 'international human rights law' with lots of different treaties, but basically no meaningful enforcement system. There are now nine core human rights treaties, which are supposedly legally binding. In addition, there are dozens of declarations, which are only aspirational documents, rather like voluntary normative guidelines.

So how do these treaties work? First the text is negotiated by states. This generally takes several years. Then, once the text is agreed, states are invited to sign, and then to ratify, if they want to. Many states choose not to sign or ratify these treaties. In that case the treaty simply does not apply to them. A state is only legally bound by the treaty if they ratify it.

As we might expect, there is a wide range in the number of ratifications for different treaties, as states pick and choose the treaties which they feel might be beneficial to them and avoid the treaties which might limit their powers in particular key areas. The International Covenant on Civil and Political Rights, for example, has been ratified by very many countries. But the International Convention for the Protection of All Persons from Enforced Disappearance has been ratified by far fewer states. And the International Convention on the Protection of the Rights of All Migrant Workers and Members of Their Families has even fewer ratifications. So international law does not automatically apply to all states. This is the first problem.

The second problem is that even if states do sign and ratify a treaty, such that in theory it is legally binding for that state, there is no enforcement mechanism. If a state abuses the rights of some of its citizens, these citizens have no global police to turn to, and no global court to turn to. Basically, there is nothing they can do. And thus, many states continue to abuse many of these rights, even when they have signed and ratified the relevant treaties.

Instead of setting up a court or some other type of proper enforcement system, the UN Human Rights Council, as it is called now, has a number of different 'mechanisms' through which it 'monitors' the implementation of these treaties. There are various different mechanisms: 'Charter mechanisms', such as the Universal Periodic Review, and 'Treaty mechanisms', such as Treaty Bodies. But in most cases, what these boil down to is a process in which each state presents a report about its human rights performance, and then the Human Rights Council, through one of these 'mechanisms' offers its 'recommendations'. None of this is legally binding or enforceable in any way, and other than perhaps being a little bit embarrassing for the states presenting their reports, it is a largely pointless exercise. Some people may argue that it is better than nothing, and that is probably true. But it is far, far short of what a real global human rights system could be.

One thing is clear, if we wanted a properly enforceable human rights system we would not have designed it this way. We would have instead followed the earlier suggestion of having a global Human Rights Court. What we have is a system that, to the untrained eye, makes it look like we take human rights seriously, when actually we don't.

Attempts to Improve the International Human Rights System

There have been some recent attempts to push states to start taking human rights more seriously. In particular, there were two initiatives which aimed to create global courts which would be able to enforce human rights.

In the 1990s a large coalition of NGOs came together, spearheaded by the World Federalist Movement, to push for the creation of an International Criminal Court that would hold national leaders and other individuals accountable for the worst human rights abuses, such as genocide and war crimes. Some states were in favour of this idea, while others were against. After several years of discussion and negotiation, the Rome Statute of the International Criminal Court (ICC) was adopted in 1998 and in 2002 the court was established in The Hague, in the Netherlands.[1]

This marked a big step forwards, as this court is the first global court that can hold individuals, rather than states, accountable. However, it is far from perfect. One of the most serious problems is that the court can only rule over individuals from states that have signed and ratified the Rome Statute, or who commit crimes within the territory of a state that has ratified the Rome Statute. Unfortunately, many states, including the US, have not ratified the statute, with the result that there are big gaps in the jurisdiction of this court.

A second attempt to beef up the human rights system took place shortly after that, but this was less successful. In 2008 Switzerland put the idea of a global Human Rights Court back on the table. They drew up a detailed proposal of how it could function and tried to initiate discussion and debate. However, whilst academics and NGOs were very much in favour, most states were against it, as they did not want to have any limit placed on their powers. And thus again, the idea did not get off the ground.[2]

So we see the difficulty of trying to create a global rights system, within an international state system. The two just don't sit together. States that would have their powers limited by enforceable global human rights law, have to be the ones that choose to create such a law and appropriate enforcement bodies. And of course, they don't.

Human Rights Require a Democratic Global Level of Government

If we are serious about human rights then we need a truly democratic global system, where we, the citizens of the world, can vote to create binding global human rights law with a global court to enforce it.

At the moment, in the current 'international order' or 'global confederation' that we have, this is not possible, as we individuals do not have a say or a vote with regard to what happens at the UN or at the global level more generally. If we had real global democracy and a democratic global federation that united all the world's citizens, then we could all come together and vote to create a system that would really protect our human rights.

Notes

1 For more on the Coalition for the International Criminal Court see Glasius, Marlkies. 2006. *The International Criminal Court: A Global Civil Society Achievement.* London: Routledge.

2 For more on the Swiss proposal see Scheinin, Martin. 2009. Towards a World Court of Human Rights: Research Report within the Framework of the Swiss Initiative to Commemorate the 60th anniversary of the Universal Declaration of

Human Rights. www.eui.eu/Documents/DepartmentsCentres/AcademyofEuropeanLaw/CourseMaterialsHR/HR2009/Scheinin/ScheininClassReading1.pdf. About the idea of a world court of human rights more generally, see ICJ. 2011. Towards a World Court of Human Rights: Questions and Answers, Geneva: ICJ. www.icj.org/wp-content/uploads/2013/07/World-court-final-23.12-pdf1.pdf; Trechsel, Stefan. 2004. A World Court for Human Rights? *Northwestern Journal of International Human Rights*, 1,1: 3-20.

9. The Climate Crisis

Ever since scientists started warning us about the enormous danger of man-made global warming, it was clear that this is a problem of such a scale, a global scale, that solving it would require some kind of human collaboration and organisation at a level that is way above the local nation state. However, the attempt to solve it through international institutions and agreements has proved dangerously ineffective. The past three decades have been a very long time to pull the breaks on greenhouse gas emissions. Yet despite all the fancy meetings and summits, conventions and reports, protocols and panels, the rate of greenhouse gas emissions in the world has not fallen, or even flattened, but has continued to soar. Today it is more than 65% higher than what it was in the late 1980s, when national governments started negotiating what they were willing, or not willing, to do about it.

This colossal failure of the international system to deal with the climate crisis contains therefore a really important lesson for anyone who is worried not just about the climate, but about the ability of humanity to respond to any of the global threats and challenges that we are increasingly facing.

Climate and Justice

At the very heart of the climate crisis is basically a simple problem of injustice. Science tells us that when people burn fossil fuels – coal, oil and gas – it will eventually harm other people, mainly by intensifying extreme weather events, such as droughts, storms, heatwaves and floods, and raising the levels of the oceans. We also know that the billions of poor people in the world, precisely those who use the least fossil fuels and therefore are least responsible for this problem, are the ones who are going to suffer the most, because their communities are the least equipped to face these disasters.

In an ideal world, high inner morality and good social norms would have been enough to make everyone use only clean energies and refrain from causing harmful pollution. But unfortunately, in reality, we know that in order to prevent injustice we cannot just leave it to the potential harm-givers to decide freely whether they want to harm other people or not. There must be some system, a justice system, to hold accountable those who harm others. The justice systems that we have today within our nation states are based exactly on this principle. Victims can take those who harm them to court, sue them, and receive compensation. And the fact that this system exists also serves to deter others from causing similar harms in the first place. Yet while greenhouse gas in the atmosphere do not stop at national borders, and the harms they inflict apply globally, our existing justice systems are still confined to the very narrow territory of the nation state. This makes it almost impossible for those harmed by climate change to sue those that cause it.

The Problem with International Agreements

The problem with the international system is that rather than challenging the principle of national sovereignty, that divides humanity to completely separate jurisdictions, it sanctifies this division and reinforces it. The very cornerstone of the international order is the idea of the 'international agreement', the notion that states can come together to solve a common problem, if they 'agree' to do so. If some governments do 'not agree' – if they prefer to allow their citizens and corporations to pollute the entire world and harm all of humanity for their personal profit – well, according to the explicit rules of the international system, they can. And so they do.

This is why the United Nations Framework Convention on Climate Change, which all governments signed back in 1992 in the so-called first 'Earth Summit' in Rio, did not contain any binding measures against the emissions of greenhouse gases. The Kyoto Protocol of 1997 was also a voluntary agreement, so the greatest polluter, the United States, did not join it. Canada did join, but then withdrew from it after finding a new giant reservoir of fossil fuels, the tar sands. The developing countries weren't covered in the protocol at all. In 2009 in Copenhagen the great Conference of Parties came again to a dead end. And in 2015, in the Paris Agreement, governments agreed to set for themselves their own voluntary targets for emission reductions, knowing that if they choose very low targets, or if they don't meet those targets,

or if they pull out from the agreement completely, then there is no justice system above them to hold them accountable.

Not surprisingly, the targets that they chose for themselves were so
unambitious that even if they all meet them it is expected that global
warming will still exceed 3°C beyond the preindustrial natural baseline.
To understand how dangerous that would be you need to realise that
in the Ice Ages, tens of thousands of years ago, the world was on average
only 3°C cooler than what it was just a 150 years ago, when we started
burning coal. This means that making the Earth 3°C warmer puts us at
risk of huge environmental changes. It could mean losing all the ice in
the world. If that happens sea levels will rise by as much as seventy me-
ters, sending entire cities and states deep underwater. That would be a
very high price to pay for maintaining the freedom and the sovereignty
of national governments to do whatever they like, regardless of how
their decisions affect and harm us, the rest of humanity.

Publicly naming and shaming those governments can feel good,
but it is dangerously far from the bare minimum that we really need.
As long as their decisions have power over our lives and our future,
we need nothing less than a right to vote those decisions down.

'No Emission Without Permission! Global Democracy Now!'

Before the American revolution of 1776, the settlers told the British
government: 'if you want to tax us, and have power to decide how we
live our lives, then you need to let us be represented in your parliament, our parliament, so that we can take such decisions together'.
Their slogan was 'No taxation without representation'. Today, the reality of the global climate crisis should make us realise that what we
need now is a kind of a global revolution, a conceptual and institutional revolution, that will tell every polluter and every national government in the world one very simple thing: decisions that affect only
yourselves, that's your business, decide as you will. But any decision
whose impact goes beyond your borders to affect the lives of people
elsewhere, you have no right to take these decisions alone. The most
that you can do is to bring them as proposals to be approved by a
higher federal institution at the global level, in which all the humans
who may be affected by your proposed actions will have an equal say
in whether or not to approval them.

This means that above all the national parliaments and governments and courts, and above all the multinational corporations, we should have one federal world parliament that will allow all of us to take part in legislating a global rule of law and a global justice system. This global rule of law should then be enforced by the world federal executive branch, the federal government of humanity, by humanity and for humanity. These are not just clichés. This is our planet and our future, so then it must also be our choice. Our slogan should be 'No emission without permission! Global democracy now!'

We are so used to the current system and so immersed in it, that it can seem hard to imagine our world organised as a democratic world federation. But this is the only real alternative to the anarchic international system that currently divides us today. Nothing less will do. In a reality where we have one global market system, and one global ecological system, national independence is a myth, a pie in the sky, that has to go, and be replaced with a new, democratic, institutional system fit for global interdependence. It will enable us to finally come together to solve not only the climate crisis, but also plenty of other injustices and inequalities that currently plague and endanger our world. For example, we could set up a global tax system so that we can start taxing fossil fuels globally, in order to reduce global greenhouse gas emissions. Until then, national restrictions on emissions, if there are any, are just incentivizing polluting industries to go off-shore, to countries where the governments are too weak or corrupt to do anything.

Can Climate Change be Solved in the Current International System?

While many green activists agree that a global justice system would be a very desirable thing, for many it sounds too big and too ambitious. They fear that achieving it will require huge amounts of time and energy, that we simply don't have. They argue that the danger posed by climate change is so great that we just have to find an immediate solution within the current system. But is that realistic? We have already wasted more than three precious decades trying to deal with climate change through our current international order. Is there really a chance that in the coming years things will somehow work differently?

Many climate activists hope that as the scientific evidence on global warming continues to pile up, even the most ardent deniers of the problem will finally get it. And then, just out of sheer self-interest, in order to protect themselves and their children, they will be ready to give up on fossil fuels and leave them in the ground. But will they? The amount of all the fossil fuels that have been found, but are still in the ground, is almost 4 times larger than the amount of all the fossil fuels that humans have used since the beginning of the Industrial Revolution. These proven reserves are worth a lot of money, to a lot of powerful people and national governments who own those resources. It will be very hard for each of them to voluntarily give up their share of the loot.

You see, even when they realise what those fuels are doing to our climate, as long as there will be no one to force all of them to give up the resources that they own, too many of them will choose their own self-interest over the common good. This is the classic 'prisoner's dilemma'. Each one will think, 'Since those other people will probably care only for themselves and their children then, well, sorry, so should I. Now is not time for a moral high-ground, now is the time to take this dirty money and find a literally high ground where my children can live safely. And then surround it with a high wall with landmines around it and machine guns, to stop all those damn climate refugees from coming in.'

If we want the owners and shareholders of fossil fuels to leave them in the ground, we cannot leave it to them to decide about it themselves. We have a stake in what happens, and we must have a voice, and a vote. 'No emission without permission! Global democracy now!' That's the key.

What about Market-Based Solutions?

In the absence of a global justice system, some green activists say that the best way to ensure that at least some of the fossil fuels are left in the ground would be just to not buy them. So they make the effort to reduce their own consumption, by riding bicycles and taking the bus, and travelling less on airplanes, and so on. And they work hard to convince their cities and states to move to green energies. That's all well and good. Except that when some people start to use less fossil fuels, there is then more supply than demand, and so the global prices start to go down. And when the prices go down, other people in the world start using them more, because it's cheap. So even if you manage to get your country to reduce its consumption, it ends up encouraging other people in the world to use more! This is yet another pitfall of voluntary, local action in a globalised world.

One good thing that voluntary, market-based action did help to achieve, however, is the big reduction that happened in the prices of renewable energies in the past couple of decades. It was the voluntary decision of several governments to subsidize clean energies that boosted their mass production, which then led to a fall in their prices. All of this has led over the past twenty years or so to a sharp increase in the use of clean energies, at the average rate of almost 15% every year. This is indeed a very good trend, and it should remind us of the importance of governmental interventions in the economy.

But when we look at the larger picture, we see that it's really not fast enough. In fact, clean energies' starting point was so low, that despite this rapid growth over two long decades, by around 2020 they still make up less than 5% of global energy usage. Fossil fuels, on the other hand, still supply 85% of the world's energy. Their share is so large, that while their rate of growth in those two decades has been slower, less than 2% a year, it has led to an increase in net production that is by far larger than that of the renewable energies combined. This is why the rate of greenhouse gas emissions has continued to rise, rather than fall. Extrapolating these trends into the future shows that clean energies may only become the major source of energy in around twenty or twenty five years' time. This should make us very worried, because that might be too late for our climate.

Debunking the Arguments of the Fossil Fuel Industry

As long as national governments are divided and competing with each other, it is super easy for the fossil fuels interest groups to divide and rule them – to buy politicians, to buy media, to even buy academics, in order to make sure that their business will not be under any real threat. To check the power of this global industry, the worlds citizens need to have their own united federal government that will be able to do the job.

Because even if the green hopes come true, and somehow by voluntarism alone clean energies will replace fossil fuels in time, humanity is still going face the huge challenge of dealing with the effects of the warming that has already been injected into the climate system during all these long decades of inaction. We might, and might not, be saved from the worst scenarios of sea level rise, but extreme storms and droughts and floods are still expected to get worse and wreak havoc on hundreds of millions of people. Helping these victims from this injustice must not be a question of voluntary' charity', that those who got rich by using fossil fuels might give and might not. It has to be funded by a global tax system. And that can only be imposed by a federal global government.

In order to defend their industry, the fossil fuels lobby came up with two influential arguments. The first argument was that putting a tax on fossil fuels in order to reduce their consumption would actually make the poor suffer the most, because they would not be able to afford even the small amount of energy that they need. The second was that the people of the rich nations of the world, who got rich by consuming so much fossil fuel, do not have the right to tell the poor to avoid those same fuels that are necessary for their development. This, apparently, is not 'fair'.

Our children will find it hard to believe that anyone really believed these arguments. The right way to help the poor, of course, is not to let them also pollute and harm others as we did. No! The right way to help them is to subsidize clean energy for them. To put a tax on pollution, to start taxing the richest 1%, and then we have enough money to help all of us, including the poor, to make the transition to a low-carbon world. We need to tax the harm-givers, and use the money to help their victims cope with the disasters that they did not cause. That would be a much more fair, and sensible, approach.

But in the anarchic international system that we currently have, in which humanity is legally separated and divided, doing this is extremely difficult. That is why in order to solve the climate crisis, and bring about real global justice, we must unite together in one global democratic system.

10. Economic Inequality

Among the most pressing issues in today's world are poverty and inequality. While a small group of billionaires live in astonishing abundance and opulence, with houses and servants and yachts and diamonds and wealth that most of us can't even imagine, around 700 million people live in extreme poverty, defined by the World Bank as living on less than $1.90 per day. A shocking 1.8 billion people, roughly a quarter of the world's population live on less than $3.20 per day and fully half of the world's population, some 3.3 billion people, live on less than $5.50 per day. Let that sink in for a moment – half of the world's population live on less than $5.50 per day.

In our rich and abundant world, how is that possible? And how is it possible that, as Oxfam recently reported, just eight of the world's richest individuals own more than this 50% of humanity combined?[1] What have we done, how have we organised our global society, to make this reality possible? And most importantly, what do we want to do about it?

While there are many different causes of both poverty and inequality, one of the most important causes, which people often ignore, is the fundamental structure of the world system. And most critically, that the economy is largely global, while democratic systems of regulation and taxation are only located at the national level. This makes it virtually impossible to regulate the global economy and make it work for the benefit of everyone.

There are two basic problems here. Firstly, the scale-mismatch between the global economy and national regulation and taxation creates all sorts of loop-holes which allow elites and big corporations to escape regulation and avoid paying taxes. And secondly, the lack of democratic structures at the global level to make decisions regarding global economic matters means that there is no means for the worlds people or their representatives to come together to decide, on democratic terms, to change the system to one that is more effective and more just. Let's have a look at some examples to make this clearer.

National Tax Systems in a Globalised World

The tax system is an obvious place to start, because taxation and re-distribution has been the main tool by which most governments seek to reduce inequality and balance out their societies. But since around 1980 economic inequality has risen so sharply that we might wonder what happened to this system and its ability to address inequality?

Well, most national tax systems were developed between around 1930 and 1960. This was a time when most economic and business activity happened within national borders and rates of international, or cross-border, business activity were very low. So the systems were designed to focus almost entirely on taxing income and profits created within a country, and then the government used that tax money on public services in that country, and on redistribution between the rich and the poor within that same country.

However, in the 1980s economic globalisation got going and governments decided to allow capital to flow in and out of their countries much more easily. Financial markets began to integrate more closely, and businesses started expanding their operations and their marketing to include other countries. But the tax systems didn't really change.

As elites and corporations found that they could pick and choose which country to operate in, they often chose countries which had lower rates of corporate taxation. So suddenly countries found themselves all competing against each other to attract corporations to their countries, each one lowering the corporate tax rate more than the last one. In this situation it is not surprising that from 1980 to 2010, corporate tax rates fell dramatically in almost all countries – from around 40% to roughly 25%. What this means is that over this period governments got less tax money from corporations and thus had less money from this source to invest in society and redistribute to the poor. Instead, the corporations got to keep more of their profits for themselves and their wealthy shareholders, and the tax burden was shifted more and more to the middle classes. This obviously was a major contributor to increasing inequality.

Furthermore, as corporations expanded and started operating in many different countries they found that in the international system, where regulation takes place only at the national level, there wasn't a legal structure which they could use to set themselves up as a global corporation. Instead, in each country they worked in, their operations had to be established as a separate, legal company in that country, and according to that country's rules and regulations. So instead of becoming 'global corporations,' they became 'trans-national corporations' – networks of related but separate companies operating in different countries. So Shell, for example, or Unilever, or any other big corporation you might think of, is legally not one big corporation. It is in fact a network of Shell Netherlands, Shell UK, Shell Nigeria, and so on. Each one is legally its own separate company. But of course, this is a bit of a myth. Because these corporations are in fact run as one big, global corporation, following the strategy and direction of the headquarters. But it's a very useful myth. Useful for the corporations, that is. Because, amongst other things, it provides them with a way to legally avoid paying a lot of tax.

Here's how it works. Imagine a transnational corporation, let's call it STONE. STONE has headquarters in France, and two subsidiaries – the mining company STONE (Nigeria) and the consulting company STONE (Luxemburg). If STONE (Nigeria) buys advisory services from STONE (Luxembourg), the executives in the STONE headquarters in France can decide how much they should pay. Since this money will never leave the STONE corporation, they could choose to set the cost far higher than the actual market cost, and in this way they can covertly move money from Nigeria to Luxembourg, without anyone knowing.

Why would they want to do this? Well, if Nigeria had a corporate tax rate of, say, 30% and Luxembourg had a corporate tax rate of 5%, that would be a good reason. And if they could set up a third subsidiary in the Cayman Islands, or some other tax haven where the tax rate is zero, and then find a way to move all the profits over to that company, well, that would be even better. You get the picture. This practice is so common that it has even got its own name, 'transfer mispricing'.

To get an idea of how much this happens, let's recall that there are around 100,000 transnational corporations today. And between them they carry out about two-thirds of total world trade. Around half of the international trade that they carry out is trade between two different subsidiaries of the same corporation. So that's around a third of total world trade. And while not *all* such intra-firm trade is carried out in this way in order to move money from A to B in order to avoid paying tax on it, an awful lot of it is.

It has been estimated that some $138 billion of potential tax payments are lost this way, every single year. That's a lot of money. A lot of money that should have been public money – money that states could have used to build schools, provide healthcare, support the poor – but instead has become private money, forming the increased profits of a small group of the already-wealthy elite.[2]

The unbalanced international system – with a global economy, but with regulation and taxation only at the national level – creates all kinds of other similar loop-holes through which the elites and the transnational corporations can find ways to legally avoid paying taxes. But if we had a democratically elected layer of government at the global level, then these loopholes could be closed and this could all be sorted out.

A Global Tax System

First of all, it would make it possible to treat transnational corporations as what they really are – *global* corporations. They could be legally registered as one business entity, and then regulated and taxed as such, at least partly at the global level. Secondly, it would be possible to agree a common rate of corporate tax for the whole world. Then there would be no benefit in shifting money from A to B, because it would all be taxed at the same rate anyway. This would also mark the end of tax havens, because they also would have to have the same tax rate. And then it would be possible to tax the global corporation as the one entity that it actually is.

Setting thing up in this sensible way, with the regulation and taxation taking place on the same scale as the business operations, would solve so many problems of tax avoidance, and thus force the elite and the corporations to pay their fair share of tax, just like everyone else. And with more tax money, states could invest more in society, making it better for everyone.

If some tax money were collected at the global level, though a global tax body, say, then the democratically elected global layer of government could also decide what to do with that money. Perhaps it would go to the government of the state where the tax money arose, perhaps it would be redistributed to a poorer state more in need, or perhaps it would be used to pay for efforts to solve common global problems, such as climate change. Most likely it would be used for a combination of all of these things. The result would be a reduction of economic inequality, both in countries and between countries, and also the creation of a fund to finance the provision of global public goods.

We could go a step further. Everything that we've discussed up to now has been about closing the loopholes and making the current international tax system work. But what if created an extra layer of taxation and redistribution at the global level? If we had a global tax body, and a democratically elected global layer of government, then we could decide to implement some new global taxes, with the aim of reducing inequality, curbing harmful behaviours, and providing global public goods.

There are various proposals in this regard. French economist Thomas Piketty, who has carried out some of the most detailed studies of economic inequality to date, has suggested a global wealth tax, in order to bring down today's shocking rate of inequality. According to his calculations, a tax of just 1% on all wealth could raise $1.56 trillion, a really huge amount of money that if transferred to the so-called 'developing countries' could truly end poverty and completely change the world. Or if we only wanted the tax to kick in for the very rich, he suggested an alternative model of a tax of 2% on wealth above Euro 4 million, (so if you own less than Euro 4 million, then you wouldn't have to pay any of this tax at all). Designing it this way would raise Euro 500 billion, still a very large sum of money that could significantly reduce inequality and do a lot of good in the world.[3]

Another suggestion is a global financial transaction tax. This was originally proposed by American economist James Tobin in 1970s, who suggested putting a small tax on currency trading. Ideas have developed since then and the current idea is to put a tiny tax of 0.1% on traded shares and bonds, and of just 0.01% on derivatives. This tax would raise money from the financial sector, a sector which is particularly under-taxed and over subsidised, and which is the place where most of the super-wealthy hold their money. Having such a tax would slow down speculative trading, which would be a good thing in its own right. It would also raise a lot of money, probably around $300 billion per year, predominantly from the wealthy. This money could then be redistributed to the poor or invested in global public goods, such as the fight against climate change.[4]

Yet another idea is a global tax on natural resources. This could both de-incentivise the unnecessary use of finite natural resources and raise money for redistribution and for global public goods. One idea is to have a small tax, of just 1%, that companies would have to pay when they extracted natural resources, such as oil, gas, and minerals. It is estimated that $300 billion per year could be raised by a 1% tax on oil alone.[5]

And there are many other possibilities. But the point is this: we have the tools to deal with economic inequality – they are taxation and redistribution. We just need to have them functioning at the right scale, and that is the same scale as the economy, the global scale.

The contemporary *international* political system, combined with the *global* economic system, has led to a situation where our national level systems of taxation and redistribution fail to work effectively. And this is one of the main reasons that inequality has soared so much since globalisation got underway. If we could build a democratic global system of taxation we could both fix our national systems and get them to work again, and also develop a whole new global level system of taxation and redistribution. Doing this is the best way that we can think of to reduce economic inequality and create a more balanced and fair world, and one in which 26 of the world's richest individuals do not own more than 50% of humanity combined.

What about International Development?

But hang on, you say, don't we deal with poverty and inequality through 'international development'? What about the Millennium Development Goals (MDGs)? And the Sustainable Development Goals (SDGs)? And all the aid that governments give? And all the NGOs doing development work to help the poor in Africa, Asia and Latin America? Isn't that more important? Well, let's take a look.

First of all, the results speak louder than any arguments. Despite all these efforts, there is the shocking poverty and inequality that we have described. So all these 'development' activities don't really seem to be working.

Secondly, let's look at how much money is actually given to the developing countries in government aid. It is about $134 billion per year, and trending downwards. Do you remember how much money is lost each year due to transnational corporations using clever schemes to avoid paying tax where they should? It is about $138 billion per year, with an awful lot of it being due to developing countries. So if we could just stop these clever tax avoidance schemes, that would be pretty much just as effective as giving all this aid. As it is, the two pretty much cancel each other out.

Furthermore, do you know how much money is needed to fully implement the SDGs? Before the SDG framework was put in place, the World Bank estimates that this requires around $1.4 trillion per year. This is way above the amount of development aid currently given. So you might wonder how anyone actually plans to implement the SDGs then? Well, the honest answer is that they don't really. There are vague hopes that the private sector investment may fill the gap, but the private sector invests in order to make a profit, not to help society, so this doesn't work. In any case, there is no sign of them stepping in with anywhere near this sum of money. But remember Piketty's wealth tax? Just a 1% on global wealth would raise $1.56 trillion per year. Bingo! Done!

But perhaps the biggest flaw with the SDGs is that it puts the responsibility for poverty alleviation with each government. Each country has its own goal and is supposed to work out how to get there on its own. So the SDGs are fundamentally 'international' and not 'global'. Instead of looking at the world system as a whole, seeing how it fosters poverty and inequality, and then trying to change that system to something more just and democratic, the SDG framework focusses the attention on each individual country, as if it existed in a vacuum, and looks at what can be done in that country, and only inside that country, to alleviate poverty and inequality. And while of course there are always small changes that can be done inside a country, this framework completely distracts people and NGOs and development organisations from the core global problems that are the main drivers of poverty and inequality.

A few years ago we attended the High Level Political Forum on Sustainable Development at the United Nations in New York. This is the annual meeting in which governments are supposed to report on their progress to date on reaching their targets for the SDGs. It was the most bizarre, and pointless, meeting that we have ever attended. Imagine all these state representatives, in their suits and ties, taking around five minutes to present what they had done – they had built some hospitals, they had drafted a new environment policy, they created a re-training scheme for the unemployed, and so on and so on. All things that governments do anyhow, for the benefit of their population. Then people got to ask one or two questions and everyone clapped politely, and then on to the next country. This went on for a whole week and then everyone went home. Nothing, absolutely nothing, was discussed about the world order, and fundamental global issues, such as tax, but also sovereign debt, international trade rules, and various other features of the world system that make things phenomenally hard for the developing countries.

Sadly the notion of 'development', rather like the notion of 'human rights', has just become a smokescreen to make it look like we are doing something about poverty and inequality and injustice, when actually we are not. The international politics of social justice has sadly become a theatre, a farce, a fake. Look carefully, and it all falls apart. Don't be fooled!

If we really want to bring about global justice, if we want human rights, and if we want to reduce inequality and create a fairer world, then we need a layer of democratically-elected government at the global level, and a set of global institutions, like a global tax body, and a human rights court, which will enable the people of the world to make human rights and economic justice a reality. There really isn't any other way.

Notes

1 Oxfam. 2017. *An Economy for the 99%*. Oxfam Briefing Paper. oxfamilibrary.openrepository.com/bitstream/handle/10546/620170/bp-economy-for-99-percent-160117-en.pdf?sequence=1

2 See Crivelli E, De Mooij R, Keen M. 2016. Base Erosion, Profit Shifting and Developing Countries. *FinanzArchiv: Public Finance Analysis*, 72,3,: 268–301; ActionAid.

2013. *How Tax Havens Plunder the Poor.* www.actionaid.org.uk/sites/default/-files/publications/how_tax_havens_plunder_the_poor_2.pdf

3 Piketty, Thomas. 2017. *Capital in the Twenty-First Century.* Translated by Arthur Goldhammer. Cambridge: Harvard University Press.

4 Patomäki, Heikki. 2007. Global Tax Initiatives: The Movement for the Currency Transaction Tax. Geneva: United Nations Research Institute for Social Development; Patomäki, Heikki and James Tobias. 2001. *Democratising Globalisation: The Leverage of the Tobin Tax.* London: Bloomsbury; Raffer, Hunibert. 1998. The Tobin Tax: Reviving a Discussion. World Development, 26, 3: 529-538; Stecher, Heinz. 1999. *Time for a Tobin Tax? Some Practical and Political Arguments.* Oxfam Policy Paper.

5 Pogge, Thomas. 2002. *World Poverty and Human Rights.* Cambridge: Polity Press; Pogge, Thomas. 2010. Eradicating Systemic Poverty: Brief for a Global Resources Dividend. *Journal of Human Development*, 2, 1: 59-77.

11. Migration and Refugees

In 2013 a small boat overloaded with some five hundred people set forth from Libya, heading towards Italy. Most of its passengers had already travelled long distances before they got on the boat, coming from Eritrea, Somalia and Ghana, and each of them had paid around $3,000 in order to board the small and rickety boat. Several women who could not afford to pay the fee were raped, and anyone who argued found themselves tied up and beaten up. What drove these people to pay so much money to get on this dangerous little boat in such awful conditions?

They, like many other people, were fleeing from dictatorial regimes, persecution, poverty and hopelessness. They were willing to leave their families and their homes, pay their entire life savings, and endure bad treatment and dangerous conditions, for the chance to set foot on European land, where they could apply for asylum, receive refugee status, and start a new life.

The group of people on this particular small boat were not in luck. As the boat was nearing the Italian island of Lampedusa it got into trouble and eventually sank. More than 360 people lost their lives.

Italian Prime Minister Enrico Letta called the event 'an immense tragedy'. António Guterres, then the United Nations High Commissioner for Refugees, commended the Italian Coast Guard for their quick reaction to the disaster. The International Organisation for Migration decided that it was time to start tracking the number of people dying on migratory routes. But no-one, absolutely no-one, decided to do anything serious about the underlying problems that lead to this kind of migration.[1]

Since then, upwards of 40,000 people have died trying to reach other countries, with more than half of them dying while trying to cross the Mediterranean Sea. The International Organisation of Migration has indeed been busy collecting data since the 2013 tragedy, and if you look at their website you can see gruelling numbers of how many migrants have died by drowning, how many by dehydration or hyperthermia, how many by starvation, how many died by being shot, and so on. It paints a detailed picture of huge, huge suffering. And yet hardly anything has been done about it and migrants continue to try to reach Europe and America and continue to die in the process. What's going on here? Why are people so desperate to leave their own countries? And why do they have to endure such dangerous journeys in order to reach safe havens?

Push Factors

Well, many people are desperate to leave their native countries because they live there in awful conditions. They may be persecuted as an ethnic minority or as a political dissident or as someone with the wrong kind of sexuality. Or they may have found themselves pushed off their land by a large infrastructure project, or a mine, or a plantation. Or perhaps their home area became uninhabitable due to storms or flooding caused by climate change. Or maybe they just realised that there was no way for them to escape grinding poverty in their country, as there were no jobs and no opportunities for them or their children. All people want to live a secure and decent life, and thus many of them would have looked to the rich countries of the world, to Europe and to America, where people seem to live in freedom and comfort and abundance, and they would have thought, 'I want that too. Let me try to get there'.

The problem is that in today's international system, where all countries are sovereign and borders stop people moving freely between countries, this is often just not possible. And certainly not 'legal'. And yet thousands of people are so desperate that they try anyhow. And thus we have today what is framed as a major 'problem' with refugees and migrants, which the international community is trying to do something to 'solve'.

How the International System Addresses Refugees and Migrants

Let's take a look at what the UN actually does regarding refugees and migrants. In 1950 the United Nations General Assembly created what to this day is its main agency for helping refugees, the United Nations High Commission for Refugees, and in 1951 governments signed the Refugee Convention, which forms the backbone of so-called 'international law' with regard to refugees. That same year they also established the Provisional Intergovernmental Committee for the Movement of Migrants from Europe, to deal with the migrants and displaced people in Europe after the Second World War. This organisation would in 1989 become the International Organisation for Migration and in 2016 formally take a place in the UN system.

International law distinguishes between 'refugees' and 'migrants'. Refugees are defined as people who flee their countries due to fear of persecution and violence, and it is agreed, in theory, that they should be entitled to asylum or protection in other countries. Migrants, on the other hand, is a much broader term, which also includes those who have left their countries due to economic reasons, seeking a better life for themselves elsewhere. According to international law, while states ought to offer support to refugees, they have every right to refuse entry to migrants.

This distinction is, of course, very problematic for several reasons. Firstly, economic or ecological problems, such as extreme poverty or environmental disasters such as a drought or a flood, can be just as life-threatening as violent persecution. And indeed, many people have repeatedly proposed to update the refugee definition and expand it to recognise economic destitution and environmental causes. But to date this has not happened.

Even worse, the decision of who is a migrant and who is a refugee is left to individual states and their border control agencies. Many governments almost blankly reject asylum applications and deport the applicants without any serious investigation, while others choose to take their time and be extremely slow on checking the applications, leaving asylum seekers hanging in limbo for years without knowing their legal status and without proper state protection. And migrants are often locked out completely.

Now your mind might tell you that this makes perfect sense but, your heart, well, might feel that there is something wrong here. The first problem has to do with the fact that in our modern world, the ancient concept of *asylum* seems like a very primitive way to bring about justice. In ancient days, the asylum was a sacred place, like a temple, an altar, a church or a mosque, where people would be protected from those who wanted to harm them. But inside our states today we do not have such systems. Instead, we have modern justice systems, with a police force and laws and courts that protect people from the harm of others. So, why do we accept this strange asylum system at the global level?

Why not create a system of real, binding international law that would protect citizens from abuse or persecution by their state? Some of the ideas are there in the various Human Rights Conventions that we discussed in chapter eight, but as the increasing number of refugees shows, these ideas are not being put into practice.

How could we make human rights real? Well, as we discussed before, that requires a world system in which everyone would become world citizens, in the real sense of the term, with a world government and a world parliament and world courts to guarantee our real human rights. But instead, we carry on in the same dysfunctional international system, in which the international agencies have no power to force countries to do anything, and thus refugees often find themselves stuck in camps and transitory situations for years upon years upon years. The UN High Commission for Refugees, instead of overseeing International Refugee law, spends most of its time and resources providing humanitarian assistance to directly help refugees in distress, mainly in the poor countries. This just sticks a plaster on the situation and makes it easier for governments to shake off any of their responsibilities to the people. Instead of letting more people in, they simply make a small donation to the UNHCR to buy some tents and set up refugee camps in poor countries.

And what about migrants? Why are there so many of them? And why is it apparently OK to keep them out? Well, in short, the reason that millions of people migrate to other countries is because of the shocking inequality that exists in the world today. National borders try to fence people into poor countries, where they must remain against their wishes, while the people in rich countries enjoy the products of their labour and are themselves free to travel around the world as they wish.

As inequality has increased steadily since the 1980s, so has the rate of international migration. According to the UN there were 173 million people living outside their country of origin in the year 2000, 221 million in 2010, and by 2020 the number had increased to 281 million people. Today international migrants make up around 3.6% of the world's population.[2] And this figure of course, does not include all the migrants that die on route, and the millions and millions of others who sorely wish to migrate but lack the courage or resources to do so.

It seems obvious that the fundamental way to deal with the issue of migration is to deal with the issue of inequality – to make the world more just and fair, so that people can live a decent life wherever they are. We've discussed this issue in chapter ten, and our view is that the only way to truly deal with massive inequality is to build democratic global organisations to deal with economic issues, such as tax, debt and trade, so as to balance out the world economy. In short, this requires a democratic federal layer of government at the global level.

But in the meantime countries are not making much of an effort to deal with inequality. Far from it. Instead, the rich countries are putting up ever higher fences and barriers to stop migrants and refugees from getting in. The so-called 'international community', dominated by the rich countries, is developing pointless declarations and compacts which seek to give the impression that they are doing something to help migrants and refugees, but instead are keeping things as they are and retaining the status quo.

At the end of 2018 representatives of many governments came together and signed another declarative agreement, called the 'Global Compact on Migration'. While this was supposedly aimed to help migrants, it in fact did nothing of the sort. Instead, the Compact explicitly re-affirmed country's sovereign rights to determine their own immigration policies, and decide themselves who to let in and who to exclude. As the European Commission and several governments have been quick to emphasise, the Compact will have no legal effect whatsoever on national legal systems.[3] In other words, it's another piece of pointless theatre at the international level, to try to make ordinary people believe that something is being done, while in fact, nothing is.

A Unified World for All

If we are serious about ending the root problems that cause people to migrate and seek refuge, if we are serious about tackling poverty, oppression and the climate crisis, then we cannot leave those things to be handled by separate sovereign governments. Each one only thinks about its own interests, and none of them think about the greater whole. Instead, we have to take some of their powers and push it up to a supra-national level, and create a global authority that exists *above* states. Only such an authority, democratically elected by the world's people, can look holistically at global problems and find just and appropriate solutions.

Only in a world federation, with world citizenship and open borders, will the problems of refugees and migrants be solved. Only in a democratic world federation will people be able to live and work wherever they want. And only in a democratic world federation will human rights become real and meaningful, will poverty be eliminated, and economic inequality be reduced to a more reasonable level.

The time has come for the citizens of the world to re-think the stories we have been telling ourselves and to face up to the bitter truth that today the international world order exists for the very purpose of separating the world's peoples, disempowering them, and bolstering inequality so that the rich can make their billions whilst ignoring the suffering of so many people, and indeed of our ecology, our climate and our planet. It's time to look for a new model of world order, one that can foster justice and equality. We believe that a democratic world federation is the only real answer.

Notes

1 Italy Boat Sinking: Hundreds Feared Dead off Lampedusa. www.bbc.com/news/world-europe-24380247; Lampedusa Boat Tragedy is 'Slaughter of Innocents' says Italian President. www.theguardian.com/world/2013/oct/03/lampedusa-boat-tragedy-italy-migrants.

2 World Migration Reports 2000, 2010, 2020. International Organisation of Migration. worldmigrationreport.iom.int/wmr-2022-interactive/

3 www.eeas.europa.eu/node/53761_en

Section III
Key World Federalist Thinkers

12. Rosika Schwimmer: A Feminist's Struggle for World Citizenship

In this chapter we look at the life and thought of Rosika Schwimmer, a major world federalist thinker. Schwimmer was a leading women's rights activist and peace activist before she developed her ideas about the need for a democratic federal world government. For her, a democratic and all-inclusive world government, with women serving in office as well as men, was necessary in order to move away from what she saw as the patriarchal and militaristic world system and to bring about true and sustainable world peace. Moreover, she believed that the future world government should be directly elected by the world's people and accountable to them, rather than simply being a unity of states. In this way, she believed, it would be possible to grant world citizenship to everyone and thus guarantee the rights of women and minorities and refugees and all other people who could not count on their own national governments to grant them rights and freedoms.[1]

Rosika Schwimmer, 1914

Early Life

Schwimmer was born on 11th September 1877 in Budapest, then capital of the Austro-Hungarian Empire, to a middle-class, secular Jewish family. She attended primary school in Budapest and then her family moved to Transylvania, where her father worked as an agricultural merchant, and she continued her education in a local convent school. She was a talented linguist and by the time she left school she could speak English, French, German, and Hungarian, and was able to read Dutch, Italian, Norwegian, and Swedish. In 1894, when Schwimmer was 18, her father lost his business and went bankrupt, and the family returned to Budapest.

Schwimmer found that she needed to work. She started to work as a governess, and then she took other short-term jobs as a bookkeeper and as a correspondent clerk, and then as a journalist and as a translator. But in all this she found it extremely hard to find a proper job that paid a wage that she could actually live on. This was because at this time it was not considered appropriate for women to be economically independent, and thus jobs for women tended to be short-term, part-time and very lowly paid. As a very independently-minded young woman, Rosika found this appalling. She fervently believed that every person was equal and should have the same rights and opportunities, and be paid the same for the same work. So she set about trying to change things.

Working to Improve Women's Rights

In 1897 she started working for the National Association of Women Office Workers where she started to collect proper data about women's wages and work conditions. Once she had put together the picture for Hungary, she wanted to compare that with the situation of women workers in other countries, so she started writing to international feminist organisations to collect statistics on women's working conditions there. In the process of corresponding with other feminist organisations she came into contact with several leading figures in the international feminist movement – people such as Aletta Jacobs, Marie Lang and Adelheid Popp – who encouraged her in her work, and opened her eyes to women's activism happening in other countries. Young Rosika started to mature into a serious women's rights activist.

In 1903, at the age of 26, she co-founded the Hungarian Women Workers Association, as an umbrella association to bring together all the various organisations working on women's issues in Hungary.[2] In the next year, she attended the inaugural conference of the International Woman Suffrage Alliance in Berlin, Germany. There she spoke about labour conditions of women industrial workers in Hungary, and listened to other women activists talk about the situations in their countries, and she met many of the leading feminists from the international movement. She returned home energised and inspired. Following that, set up the Hungarian Association of Feminists, along with her colleague Vilma Glucklich. This organisation was considered very radical at the time, as it set out to work for gender equality in *all* aspects of women's lives, including education, employment, access to birth control, and reform of laws governing married women's socioeconomic status and inheritance rights. During these years Rosika further developed her ideas about women's liberation, arguing for example that housework should be done by women's collectives, rather than separately in every household, as this would free most women for more interesting and rewarding pursuits. And most importantly, she initiated the campaign for women's right to vote – a campaign which would ultimately gain its objective in 1920.

In 1907 Schwimmer had a very public argument with a prominent professor who sought to limit women's access to higher education and insisted that educated women were like 'female monsters' who destroyed families. Schwimmer argued against him, claiming that women had the right to be educated just like men, and that that would not make them 'monsters'. Indeed, she pointed out, this professor's own wife had enjoyed an excellent education and she both had a family and was not a monster! This public debate led to Schwimmer becoming a well-known figure in Hungary. She gained a considerable following, even though the male-dominated press constantly criticised her and her organisation. The criticisms did not deter her. She proudly smoked, drank wine, and wore colourful, comfortable loose-fitting dresses without a corset. She described herself as a 'very, very radical feminist'.

She started to go on lecture tours around Europe, arguing for women's rights and particularly the right to vote. She was a great speaker and she won over audiences with her energetic personality, piercing intelligence and biting satire. She quickly became widely known as one of the most inspiring and influential feminist campaigners in Central Europe.

A few years later she moved to London and became the press secretary of the International Woman Suffrage Alliance. This was a crucial moment in the history of the British women's suffrage campaign. Many prominent suffragists, led by Emmeline and Christabel Pankhurst, had started the tactic of direct action in the last few years, smashing windows, sabotaging the mail, and defacing public monuments to publicize their cause. One suffragette, Emily Davison, had dramatically rushed onto the Derby race course, snatched the bridle of the King's horse, and been trampled to death, becoming a martyr to the cause of suffrage. Schwimmer was against such tactics because as well as being a feminist, she was also a very committed pacifist. And she was against using violence for any cause.

Feminism and Pacificism

In these years before the First World War there were many feminist campaigners who agreed with Schwimmer, and did not partake of the more violent methods used by Pankhurst and the other suffragettes. But as soon as the war began, many of these feminists forgot about their abhorrence of violence and quickly supported the war effort. Many even thought that it was necessary to put the whole issue of women's rights temporarily to the side in order to give their efforts to supporting the war. Other women's rights campaigners, particularly those in the US, wanted to solely focus on getting women the vote, and not get involved in 'stop the war' campaigning. Schwimmer, however, was unusual: she believed that rights for women and world peace were inseparable issues and pledged herself to advance both, despite the war.

Schwimmer had always been an ardent pacifist and pacifism ran deep in her family. One of her uncles, Leopold Katscher, had founded the Hungarian Peace Society, and she had grown up amid discussions about how a world parliament and a world court were needed so that states could solve their differences in a legal way, just as individuals do, without resorting to violence and war. In August 1913 she attended the 20th Universal Peace Congress in The Hague, where international peace activists came together to develop and promote these kinds of ideas.

However, peace was not on the cards at this time and a few months later the First World War broke out. Schwimmer, a native of Austro-Hungary, was still living in London, and with Austro-Hungary and Britain on opposite sides in the war, she suddenly she found herself in enemy territory and unable to return home. Then the British government branded her as an 'enemy alien' and she was forced to leave the country. But where should she go? She managed to get to the United States, and there she continued her activism for both women's rights and for peace, and increasingly, emphasised the connection between these two things. She travelled around America with other feminists, giving talks about the need for women to have the right to vote and thus have a say in choosing the government, because if women were to vote they would surely not vote to go to war. For Schwimmer, both pacifism and feminism were fundamentally political issues. And so the work that needed to be done, she believed, was to change the political situation. As such she strongly opposed a lot of the non-political activism which was taking place at the time. She was very critical, for example, of all the charitable relief work that both feminist and pacifist organisations were carrying out during the war. As she said,

'The problem with war relief was that it narcotises so many good people into believing everything is done if we care for the victims, while we don't care to prevent as much as possible the making of new victims.'[3]

She fervently believed that this kind of activity was just 'charity' and that in the long-term it prolonged the unjust political situation by putting a plaster on it so that it didn't seem so bad. Instead, Schwimmer wanted herself and other women to get involved in *politics* – to form new processes and structures which would bring an end to war, rather than simply acting as nurses and relief workers to help the needy in what she saw as the patriarchal, militaristic world.

In 1915 Schwimmer helped to create the Women's Peace Party, and became the organisation's International Secretary. She began to devote all of her energies to opposing the war and urging a peaceful settlement, and she issued a proposal calling for the neutral nations to meet and formulate a plan for mediation. At the Hague Congress of Women held later that year, Schwimmer convinced the conference to send representatives to meet with leaders of both neutral and belligerent nations and encourage peaceful mediation. She argued,

'When our sons are killed by millions, let us, mothers, only try to do good by going to the kings and emperors, without any other danger than a refusal!'[4]

Jane Addams led the delegation to the belligerents, and Schwimmer took responsibility for meeting with leaders of the neutral countries. She met with US President Woodrow Wilson and Secretary of State William Jennings Bryan, and tried to convince them to convene a United States–sponsored neutral mediation conference to try to end the war. But they were not convinced.

Schwimmer did not give up. She tried a different tactic. She managed to secure a meeting with Henry Ford, of the Ford Motor Company, the leading American automobile manufacturer, who was publicly against the war, and successfully convinced him of the need for a meeting of neutral states to discuss how to end the war. Ford in turn approached President Wilson and personally asked him to establish such a Neutral Mediation conference, and even offered to finance it. Again, Wilson again declined.

Still Schwimmer did not give up. If the governments wouldn't do it, she thought, then the people should do it. So she persuaded Ford to finance an unofficial international mediation conference, which she would organise. And indeed, the Ford Neutral Mediation Conference took place in Stockholm on 8th February 1916, with Schwimmer serving as Expert Adviser. To get publicity for the event, Schwimmer arranged for the American delegation, which included Ford, to sail to Stockholm on what became known as the 'Peace Ship'. However, the press again ridiculed Schwimmer and her activities, and in the end the whole thing was unfortunately a bit of a flop.

From Joy to Despair

At the end of the war the Austro-Hungarian Empire collapsed and the new democratic Republic of Hungary was formed. Schwimmer returned home. One of the first things that the new Prime Minister did was to table a bill giving literate women over the age of 24 the right to vote. The bill was passed by parliament, and for the first time in Hungary women's suffrage became a reality. Schwimmer was ecstatic. The war had ended, she and millions of other women had gained the right to vote, things were changing.

The new prime minister was so impressed with Schwimmer that he invited her to become a member of his National Council of Fifteen, and also to serve as Ambassador to Switzerland. She was delighted to accept, and she became one of the world's first female ambassadors. But the good times were very short-lived.

Just five months later Hungary's democratic government was overthrown by Béla Kun's Communist regime. In a sharp turn of events, Schwimmer was re-called to Hungary, her passport was confiscated and she was barred from leaving the country. Then things got even worse. The Communist regime was in turn overthrown by the fascist and antisemitic regime of Admiral Nicolas Horthy. In the period known as the 'White Terror' they began to purge and kill the Jews and rumour had it that Schwimmer was on the list.

Schwimmer fell into despair. The death and suffering that she saw all around her hurt her deeply, and the fear for her own life and that of her family weighed her down. In a letter that she wrote to her friend and feminist activist in the US, Lola Maverick Lloyd, she wrote that her whole family were contemplating collective suicide. While Schwimmer and her sister supported the idea, her parents were against it, and thus it did not happen.

Becoming a Refugee and Experiencing Statelessness

In the end she and her family managed to find a way to get out of Hungary. In 1920 loyal friends and peace activists succeeded in smuggling them out on a steam boat on the Danube River and they arrived safely in Vienna. Suddenly Schwimmer found herself as a refugee, living in a foreign country with no rights, and being financially supported by her feminist friends and colleagues.

The following year, in 1921, at the age of 44, and with the help of her American friend Lola Maverick Lloyd, she secured permission for herself and her family to emigrate to the United States. She renounced her Hungarian citizenship and set sail, arriving on 26 August 1921.

A few years later, in 1924 she applied for US citizenship. However, in the application form there was a question which asked whether the applicant would take up arms and fight in defence of the country. As a committed pacifist, Schwimmer wrote 'no'. This led to her being called for questioning and for interviews, and ultimately being denied US citizenship.

Schwimmer was shocked. She appealed in court and started a legal battle which would go on for the next five years and go all the way up to the Supreme Court. But in 1929 she finally lost the battle, as the Supreme Court judges voted by a majority of 6 to 3 to deny her citizenship. One of the judges that had voted in her favour did point out that as a woman over 50 she would not be allowed to take up arms even she if she wanted to, but this argument somehow failed to persuade the other group of all-male judges. And thus at age 52, she found herself a stateless person, permitted to stay in the US, but unable to work, and again, unable to vote.

This whole drama got her to start seriously thinking about the issues of statelessness and what could be done to help individuals who had been denied citizenship. She had little sense of allegiance to any one nation, but felt connected to the whole of humanity. She wrote, 'I have no sense of nationalism, only a cosmic consciousness of belonging to the human family'[5]. But how could she make this almost spiritual sense into a political reality?

The Need for World Citizenship and World Government

In 1924 she had started to develop her ideas about the need for a world government – a federal level of government that would be above national governments, and that would both end the need for war and organise joint action on common problems, and also provide a type of global citizenship to all peoples of the world, including those that did not have any national citizenship.

This world government, she believed, should be totally different from the League of Nations, which was not only powerless and ineffective, but was also based on patriarchal and militaristic principles and run solely by men. The future world government needed to be fundamentally egalitarian, and have women serving alongside men as Presidents, representatives, diplomats, political strategists, and so on.

In the next few years she continued discussing these ideas with her friend and fellow peace and women's rights activist, Lola Maverick Lloyd, who also shared her radical feminist, pacifist and internationalist views. Lloyd had spent years criticising the League of Nations as being fundamentally undemocratic. While others criticised the League for its lack of enforcement power, or because of its limited membership by only some states, all very valid criticisms, Lloyd criticised it from a different angle. She found the organisation problematic because it was dominated by states, and was closed to the input from non-governmental organisations or from ordinary citizens. As the 1920s progressed, Lloyd was beginning to come to the conclusion that the League of Nations was un-reformable and that instead a whole new world government needed to be created, directly elected by the people and directly accountable to them.

These two women were far more radical than most of the activists in either the feminist or the pacifist movements at this time, and they increasingly took to developing their ideas together.

They increasingly focussed on the notion of *world citizenship*, in which all people of the world would have real legally-protected rights granted by a world government, irrespective of the situation of their own state or national government.

In 1934, as Hitler consolidated power in Germany and began persecuting Jews and other German citizens, Schwimmer wrote,

'The establishment of world citizenship and world passports is a fundamental necessity, and the key to physical safety. This is essential not for Germans only, but for all others who are without a country, without rights anywhere, without that minimum of safety which is the birthright of the most miserably citizen in any civilised country.'[6]

She argued that world passports could be created by the League of Nations, rather like the Nansen passports that they had issued in the 1920s to serve as identity papers for stateless refugees from countries undergoing massive civil war, such as Russia, and later Armenia and Turkey. But these new world passports could go even further and give real rights of world citizenship.

As the 1930s progressed Schwimmer and Lloyd became increasingly focussed on the idea of a democratic world government as the only way to bring about the long-term end of war and to protect women's rights and the rights of all minorities, refugees and stateless people. They read about the various other world government and world federation plans that were circulating at the time, but criticised them all because they did not emphasise the direct democracy of all world citizens. Most of them focussed on uniting states, and many of them preserved all sorts of structural inequalities, of race, of ethnicity, and of gender. Their model was fundamentally egalitarian, all-inclusive and linked directly to the people. And as we discuss more in chapter 22, their idea of world citizenship was truly radical.

They tried to convince other feminist and pacifist organisations, in particular the Women's International League for Peace and Freedom, in which they had both long been active. But their ideas were too radical for most of the people in these circles and they did not find much support.

Instead, as tensions increased again in Europe, the Women's International League for Peace and Freedom got bogged down in a long ideological debate about whether they should stand against fascism and Nazism and try to stop violence from developing, or whether they should remain neutral. Schwimmer and Lloyd were extremely frustrated when the organisation chose to stay neutral. Just staying neutral was not going to stop war. To do that it was necessary to change the world order, and to create a democratic world government.

The Campaign for World Government

And so in 1937 they set up a new initiative, the Campaign for World Government. They firmly believed that ordinary people did not want war. And thus they figured that if there was a truly democratic world government, that followed the wishes of the majority of the world's people, then this was the best possible chance of avoiding war.

Schwimmer's experience of being denied citizenship by the US, and being denied the right to vote for many years because she was a woman, and Lloyd's experience with the League of Nations, led them to emphasise a number of elements which were not in other world federation plans that were circulating at the time. In particular was the focus on individuals and their rights within the world federation. While other models focussed on bringing together states and developing the bureaucracy of the federal government structure, Schwimmer and Lloyd's vision emphasised that it should be individuals – men and women, of course – who directly voted for their representatives to the world government, and not states. And they also emphasised that the federal level of world government should be able to give real rights and responsibilities to *all* individuals, so that they would become world citizens in a real and serious sense of the term.

They published a small booklet, titled, *Chaos, War or a New World Order: What We Must Do To Establish the All-Inclusive, Non-Military Democratic Federation of Nations*, which set out their ideas.[7] The central idea was that a World Constitutional Convention should be convened, with delegates from every country, in order to draft a World Constitution for the new democratic federal world government. Ideally, governments should organise this process. But if they did not, then ordinary citizens should organise it themselves. In either case, they insisted that delegates should be ordinary people, not members of government or of the armed forces or navy. The World Constitution should outline the framework of a global level federal structure, with a World Parliament, which would regulate certain areas of political, economic and social cooperation between nations.

Beyond this, they also offered their own suggestions as to what might be in the World Constitution. They envisioned a federal structure similar to the US or Switzerland. The highest level, the world government, would only govern on matters related to the welfare of the whole world. Other matters would remain the responsibility of the national governments. People would be citizens of the world, with rights and responsibilities granted by the federal government, as well as citizens of their respective states. As such they would have a world passport and be able to travel freely and to reside in any country.

They also suggested that there should be a World Parliament, with representatives elected directly by the people. They proposed that each country would elect ten delegates so that all the different groups and minorities in a country could be represented. The delegates from one country would not be expected to agree on all matters or to vote together as a bloc. Instead, it was expected that they would find ideological allies from other countries and would more likely vote according to ideology, rather than nationality.

They proposed that the Parliament should set up a number of Commissions to deal with particular global problems. For example, they proposed an Economic Commission, which would gather all the unused war and defence budgets, because now armies and navies and weapons would not be needed, and then to spend this money on the employment of people in efforts for the improvement of the world and its citizens. They also suggested a Financial Commission to regulate global finance and to establish a uniform monetary system, a Trade Commission to remove tariffs and duties and establish a global free trade area, and a Raw Materials Commission to regulate the production and consumption of raw materials in an equitable manner at the federal level, so as to remove the economic push to go to war for colonies in order to get access to those raw materials. And alongside this, they also proposed a Commission to Create International Law, and global courts to enforce it.

Having published this booklet with their ideas, they formally set up the Campaign, with an office in Chicago focussing on national activities within the US, led by Lloyd, and an office in New York, focussing on the international campaign, led by Schwimmer. Between 1937 and 1939 they were active lobbying congressman and persuading them to raise resolutions in the US Senate and House of Representatives calling for the US government to convene a World Constitutional Convention. However, when the Second World War broke out they shifted tack and focussed more on trying to convince the US President to convene a Conference of Neutral States, which would find a way to bring about the end of the war and guide states towards peaceful coexistence and world federation.

In 1943 Lola's daughter, Georgia Lloyd, then a recent graduate in Political Science from the University of Chicago, she took over the reins of the Chicago office. In 1944 she participated in discussions about the nature of the future United Nations and developed her vision of what it should look like, and in 1945 she attended the United Nations Founding Conference in San Francisco as an accredited Non-Governmental observer.[8]

Meanwhile Schwimmer, and her friend and colleague Edith Wynner, ran the New York office.[9] In 1945 Wynner travelled to London to meet Henry Usborne and to help him develop his ideas about how to create a world government. Earlier that year Usborne had become a Member of Parliament for the Labour Party. In his maiden speech in the House of Commons he had said,

'I believe that there is only one hope of permanent peace, and that it lies in world government. Until we have world government, as distinct from world leagues or confederations, we cannot guarantee world peace... We must therefore do something now and take some positive steps in that direction.'[10]

Now he sat down with Edith Wynner to develop ideas for what exactly those steps might be, and together they developed a plan to organise a World Constitutional Convention that would draft a World Constitution.

A World Constitutional Convention

In 1947 Georgia Lloyd, Edith Wynner and Henry Usborne all attended the Montreux Congress, the important congress in Switzerland which led to the formation of the World Movement for Federal World Government (WMWFG), later to become the World Federalist Movement, or WFM. Usborne presented the plan to hold a World Peoples' Convention to draft a World Constitution, and it was accepted by the Congress as one of the possible strategies to bring about a federal world government.

The following year, in 1948, he set up the Peoples' World Assembly Movement and started to prepare for the Convention, which he proposed should take place in Geneva in 1950. He and his colleagues reached out to parliamentarians and activists in as many countries as possible and sought to arrange the democratic election of delegates to the Convention.

As we discuss in more detail in chapter 18, the Peoples' World Convention did indeed meet in Geneva in December 1950, with some five hundred delegates from forty seven countries. But it was not a huge success. Despite the lengthy discussions they did not succeed in drafting a World Constitution or in agreeing a clear way forward. By then the Cold War had started and many people had stopped believing that a world federation that included both America and the Soviet Union would be possible.

Usborne did not give up hope, but he did decide to change tactics. He moved away from the idea of a World Constitution Convention and instead in 1951 he set up the World Association of Parliamentarians for World Government, to bring together parliamentarians from different countries to discuss the need and shape of a future democratic world government, and to work towards it a bit more slowly.

But as Usborne changed directions, another world government activist stepped up to continue the call for a World Constitutional Convention. In 1950 Henry Philip Isely joined the Chicago branch of the Campaign for a World Government, then run by Georgia Lloyd, and published a pamphlet entitled, 'The People Must Write the Peace', calling again for a Peoples' World Constitutional Convention and in 1958 they launched the World Committee for a World Constitutional Convention.

In 1961 Isely and some colleagues decided to set up the World Committee as a separate organisation, and they established headquarters in Denver, Colorado, and in 1966 they changed the name to the World Constitution and Parliament Association. By this time the World Federalist movement had moved away from the idea of a World Constitutional Convention and decided to focus more on the project of reforming the UN into a viable future world government. But nonetheless, the World Constitution and Parliament Association worked throughout the 1960s to try to gather support from national governments to hold a World Constitutional Convention.

However, after several years they had only managed to get five governments on board. And so, like Schwimmer and Usborne before them, they decided that if the governments would not do it, then the people should do it themselves. In 1968 they held the first session of a Peoples World Constitutional Convention, in Switzerland, with some two hundred delegates from twenty seven countries and 5 continents, and established a drafting committee to produce a draft Constitution of the Federation of Earth. In 1977 they organised a second session of the Peoples World Constitutional Convention, this time in Austria, where the draft was debated and amended and finally agreed. The document was then sent to the UN General Assembly and to all national governments, in the hope that it would be signed and ratified. Unsurprisingly, the document did not receive any ratifications. But nonetheless, the group continues to today, calling for the ratification of the provisional Earth Constitution and for the creation of a World Parliament.[11]

To date over 150 proposed World Constitutions have been drafted, many by ordinary people and some by high-powered thinkers such as Professors of Chicago University. While none of these World

Constitutions have come into force, they and their drafters all owe a debt of inspiration to Rosika Schwimmer and Lola Maverick Lloyd, and the work of the Campaign for World Government.

Inspiration and Legacy

In 1948 Rosika Schwimmer was nominated for the Nobel Peace Prize. However, she died in August that year, at the age of 71, before the committee had completed its deliberations. No Peace Prize was awarded that year. Schwimmer's vision of a world federation and a democratic world government was inspired by her years as a women's rights campaigner and as a peace activist. It was also born as a result of her experience of statelessness, and her awareness of the refugees and other people who also found themselves without national citizenship and thus without rights and safety. These experiences drove her to develop a particular vision of world federation that directly linked the world government to the world's people, and created a form of world citizenship with real and enforceable rights. Her ideas inspired thousands of people to think about how the world order should be designed and to participate in writing World Constitutions. They also overflowed into the post-war human rights movement (see chapter 8) and campaigns for refugees and stateless persons (see chapter 11). While with hindsight we may realise that there are many stages to go through before the world's people, or their representatives, can sit down together to draft a world constitution, there is much in her ideas and methods that can still inspire us today.

Notes

1 Szapor, Judith.2019. 'Good Hungarian women' vs. 'Radicals, Feminists, and Jewish Intellectuals': Rosika Schwimmer and the Hungarian Women's Debating Club in 1918–1919. *Women's History Review*, 28:6, 895-913; Wenger, Beth. 1990. Radical Politics in a Reactionary Age: The Unmaking of Rosika Schwimmer, 1914-1930. *Journal of Women's History*, 2, 2: 66-99; Threlkeld, Megan. 2018. 'Chaos, War or a New World Order?' A Radical Plan for Peace and World Government in the 1930s. *Peace and Change*, 43,4: 473-497; Wernitznig, Dagmar. 2015. 'It's a Strange Thing Not to Belong to Any Country, As is my Case Now': Fascism, Refugees, Statelessness and Rosika Schwimmer, 1877-1948. *Rivista Telematica de Studi Sulla Memoria Femminile*, 27: 102-108; Wernitznig, Dagmar. 2017. Out of her Time? Rosika Schwimmer's Transnational Activism after the First World War. *Women's History Review*, 26:2, 262-279

2 Szapor, Judith. 2017. Hungarian Women's Activism in the Wake of the First World War. From Rights to Revanche. London: Bloomsbury Academic.

3 Schwimmer's comments in a letter to Mrs Illingworth, cited in Werntiznig, Dagmar. 2016. Living Peace, Thinking Equality: Rosika Schwimmers' (1877-1948) War on War. In *Living War, Thinking Peace (1914-1924): Women's Experiences, Feminist Thought and International Relations*, edited by Bruna Bianchi and Geraldine Ludbrook. Newcastle: Cambridge Scholars Publishing, p126.

4 Speech by Rosika Schwimmer at the International Congress of Women, 1915.

5 Schwimmer's statement quoted in the Brief submitted by the US Government to the US Supreme Court in US v Rosika Schwimmer, October 1928, pp2-3, cited in Wenger, Beth. 1990. Radical Politics in a Reactionary Age: The Unmaking of Rosika Schwimmer, 1914-1930. *Journal of Women's History*, 2, 2: 66-99.

6 Schwimmer, Rosika. 1934. The German Crisis and World Citizenship: The Problem of Exile Grows More Acute the World Over. *Polity* 2, 12: 207, cited in Threlkeld, Megan. 2018. 'Chaos, War or a New World Order?' A Radical Plan for Peace and World Government in the 1930s. *Peace and Change*, 43,4: 473-497, p490.

7 Lloyd, Lola Maverick and Rosika Schwimmer. 1937. Chaos, War or a New World Order: What We Must Do To Establish the All-Inclusive, Non-Military Democratic Federation of Nations. Chicago: Campaign for World Government.

8 Georgia Lloyd Papers. New York Public Library Archives archives.nypl.org/-mss/1787

9 See also their book, Wynner, Edith and Georgia Lloyd. 1949. *Searchlight on Peace Plans: Chose your Road to World Government.* New York: E.P. Dutton and Co.

10 Usborne, Henry. 1950. World Government. Debated in British Parliament on Friday 28 July 1950, Hansard record hansard.parliament.uk/Commons/1950-07-28/debates/a09ccc95-cd51-4923-a023-fc3805eafb4e/WorldGovernment

11 Martin, Glen. 2011. The Earth Federation Movement: Founding of a Global Social Contract for the People of Earth. Institute for Economic Democracy Press. worldparliament-gov.org/history-of-the-earth-constitution/

13. Albert Einstein: A Vision of a Unified World

One of the interesting things about Albert Einstein, which few people today know, is that he was a passionate advocate of establishing a federal state of the entire world: a unified democratic political framework for all of humanity. The story of how he came to this thinking is not only fascinating, but also highly relevant for us today, considering the global challenges that we face.[1]

The story must begin with an understanding of the political background in which Einstein grew up. He was born in 1879, within the borders of a rather new political entity called the German Reich. This was a federation, a union of some thirty states and small kingdoms that were previously legally separated and competing: Prussia, Saxony, Bavaria, Württemberg and many other smaller ones. It was only eight years before Einstein's birth, in 1871,

Albert Einstein, 1921

that they all joined under one constitution, one parliament, and one strong Prime Minister, Bismarck. The federal unity of Germany made it very easy for Einstein's parents, for example, to move, when he was still a child, from the state of Württemberg to the neighbouring state of Bavaria, within the German Reich.

Over the course of his life, Einstein would see many more dramatic changes in the political landscape of Germany, Europe and the world, showing him how the existing political order at any given time and place is not something natural and eternal, but is instead a dynamic human creation, that people can always change and improve.

Early Life

Albert was born to a family of secular Jews working in the high-tech business of the time, which was electric power enlightenment: they built generators to light public events, big fairs and then even major city streets. Young Einstein was a keen student and he immersed himself in the books of science and philosophy, and in so doing came to increasingly doubt the nationalist indoctrination of the German school system. He hated the education techniques that sanctified dumb memorizing and blind obedience, whose purpose it seemed was to prepare good soldiers for the German army.

At the age of 17, fearing the prospect of being enlisted to that army after high school, he moved to Switzerland to study physics in the university, as Switzerland was known for its longstanding tradition of peace and neutrality. As he left Germany, in 1896, Einstein had to give up his German citizenship, and he remained an officially stateless person for five years, until he was eventually granted Swiss citizenship.

Scientific Brilliance

As we all know, Einstein did amazingly in his studies. In the year 1905, when he was only 26 years old, he made a huge scientific revolution. That year alone, he published four major articles that described his theoretical discoveries of the most fundamental laws that govern our universe, from the quantum theory about the bizarre behaviour of the tiniest particles, to laying the foundations of the mindblowing theory of general relativity, that explains the movements of even entire galaxies and light in space and in time. And as if that was not enough, he also revealed the rule that matter and energy are interchangeable, which explained, for the first time, the nuclear reactions that kindle our sun, and all the other stars in the universe. What an enlightenment!

Eight years later, in 1913, he was invited by the University of Berlin to be the Head of their very prestigious Physics Research institute. The following year he returned to Germany to take up that position, and also managed to get his German citizenship back.

The First World War and the Call for a Federation of Europe

But that same year, 1914, happened to be the year in which the dark clouds of the First World War gathered and thundered over Europe. Einstein found that he couldn't just ignore the war and shut himself in the academic ivory tower. Instead, he joined other leading scientists to write a 'Manifesto to the Europeans', courageously calling on them to refuse to go to this 'fratricidal war', as they called it, and instead come together to form a union of the continent. Only in such a union, they wrote, 'the terms of peace shall not become the cause of future wars.' In a piece titled 'My Opinion on the War,' Einstein wrote:

> 'I am convinced that it is possible, in the near future, to form a Supra-National organisation in Europe that will prevent European wars, just as now a war between (the states of) Bavaria and Württemberg is impossible in the German Reich.' [2]

The idea of a supra-national federation at the European level, or even at the global level, has been dreamt up again and again over the centuries by philosophers, statesmen and poets. Kant described it as the basis for 'perpetual peace', and Victor Hugo spoke passionately about a 'United States of Europe'. But, as we know, it would take the Europeans two devastating world wars with tens of millions of dead before they would finally start to take serious steps in that direction.

But when the First World War finally ended, the winners failed to rise to the grandness of the opportunity that they were given, and rather than creating such a union for the benefit of all humankind already then, they created just its pale shadow, the impotent League of Nations.

With regard to Germany, the winners applied a revengeful approach, that planted feelings of resentment in the German public. Throughout the 1920s, the Nazi party tried to enflame these feelings, but it had very little success so long as the German economy was on the path of recovery and reconstruction. It is notable that despite the many hardships, for the entire decade after the war, most Germans endorsed the new democratic system, and the Nazi party remained tiny and insignificant, on the margins of German politics.

Global Economic Crisis and the Rise of Nazism

But at the very end of that decade it all changed, with the crash of the New York Stock Exchange in the United States. Even then, the economy was already global, and the financial crisis quickly spread to many other countries, and Germany was hit particularly hard. As their economy plummeted, many Germans lost faith in democracy, and they became susceptible to the Nazi's message about restoring German prosperity, greatness and superiority over all the others. Because of that crisis, in the elections of 1930, the Nazi party suddenly soared from being a tiny minority group to being the second largest party.

Einstein, who by now had received the Nobel Prize in physics and gained international fame, publicly criticized not only the racist and militant politics of the Nazis, but also the anarchic structure of the international system, which he argued could not provide real peace, security or justice to anyone.

In a lecture he gave in 1931 he said:

'Anybody who really wants to abolish war must resolutely declare himself in favour of ... his own country's resigning a portion of its sovereignty to international institutions: he must be ready to make his own country amenable, in case of a dispute, to the jurisdiction of an international court.'[3]

But the Nazis' grip on power only grew stronger, and in 1933, while Einstein was on a long visit to the USA, they confiscated his property and revoked his German citizenship, and he remained in the United States of America for the rest of his life.

From Pacificism to the Atomic Bomb

The Nazi's increasingly blatant racist persecutions and war-mongering made Einstein change his mind about pacifism. Whereas, during the First World War, he had called on the Europeans to refuse to go to war, when it came to dealing with the Nazis he concluded that this was a monster that could not be tamed by peaceful means. Only military force could defeat them.

In August 1939, a month before the beginning of the Second World War, Einstein wrote a secret letter to US President Roosevelt.

He warned that Nazi Germany could take his ideas about nuclear energy and try to develop a new type of a bomb – a bomb that would be so destructive that it would give Germany a decisive strategic advantage. The USA, he suggested, should therefore try to develop such a weapon first, and use it as a deterrent.

This letter is a great example of how Einstein was far from being some naïve thinker who believed that 'all you need is love'. He did have the love of humanity in his heart, for sure, but for the love of humanity, in some extreme cases, such as when you stand against Nazis, you better also have an atomic bomb before they get it!

Two years later, at the height of the war, in 1941, when an American conscientious objector facing jail wrote to Einstein asking for his support, Einstein wrote in reply that there are two types of pacifism, 'sound' and 'unsound':

> 'Sound pacifism tries to prevent wars through a world order based on power, not through a purely passive attitude toward international problems. Unsound, irresponsible pacifism contributed in large measure to the defeat of France as well as to the difficult situation in which England finds herself today. I urge you to do your share, lest this country make the same mistake!'[4]

President Roosevelt took Einstein's advice and set up a military program to develop the nuclear bomb. But besides writing that letter, Einstein was not a part of that program.

After 6 years of horrendous world war, in May 1945, both Germany and Italy had finally surrendered. Only Japan, though battered and exhausted, refused to give up and continued to fight. Three months later, in August, soon after finally succeeding in developing the atomic bomb, US army aircrafts dropped one bomb on Hiroshima and another on Nagasaki in Japan, erasing the cities and causing the death of hundreds of thousands of civilians. Japan quickly surrendered.

After the bombardment of the two cities, Einstein remained publicly silent for a whole month. When he finally agreed to give a big interview to the Atlantic Magazine, he told the reporter:

> 'The only salvation for civilization and the human race lies in the creation of a world government. As long as sovereign states continue to have armaments and armaments secrets, new world wars will be inevitable.'[5]

The Need for World Government to Prevent War

At this time the idea of a world government was far more popular and better accepted than it is today. Earlier in the 20th century, peace activists had pushed for the creation of international law and a world court so that countries would be able to settle their disputes by legal means, rather than through violence and war. Their efforts had led to the creation of an international arbitration court in the Hague, in the Netherlands, and later to the formation of the International Court of Justice. But because no corresponding world parliament had been created, in order to legislate world law, and no world government had been set up, to enforce such world law, these 'international' courts had no real power and no democratic legitimacy. And thus, as we know, they failed to prevent both the First World War and then also the Second World War.

And so, the question on everyone's mind at this time was how to prevent a Third World War. The United Nations wasn't formed yet, and there was a giant question mark regarding the new post-war world order. It was already evident that the age of empires was quickly coming to an end, and many felt that it had to be replaced with representative democracy, not only on the national level, but also on the global level.

The American team of scientists who developed the atomic bomb felt a particular responsibility and great worry. They knew that if other countries also invested sufficiently in research, they could also develop nuclear arms, and that this would make the next war far more horrendous than the one just ended. Indeed, the next world war could be the very last.

In September 1945, just a month before the establishment of the United Nations, a few of these scientists, without consulting Einstein, published their own manifesto, calling for the creation of a 'council of nations' to supervise nuclear arms. Einstein fiercely criticized them, saying that a 'council of nations' would be entirely insufficient. The League of Nations had clearly been powerless to stop the Second World War, and he argued that having another similarly toothless institution would be pointless, and in the new nuclear reality, extremely dangerous. Just as a government was necessary at the national level to stop people in conflict from using violence against each other, he reasoned, so too it was necessary at the global level, in order to preserve peace and justice. On 24th October 1945 the United Nations organisation came into being. Two weeks earlier, Einstein together with several other notable thinkers, published a piece in the New York Times, fiercely condemning the proposed Charter, because it gave complete sovereignty to the member governments, without putting any power above them. In that sense, they wrote, it was comparable to the American 'Articles of Confederation', the document that first united the thirteen American republics that later became the USA. That confederation didn't work very well and was quickly replaced with the Federal Constitution of the United States of America. Similarly, they wrote:

'We must aim at a Federal Constitution of the world, a working worldwide legal order, if we hope to prevent an atomic war.'[6]

In interviews, Einstein warmly recommended a book that has just recently been published, titled *The Anatomy of Peace*. In it, his friend and writer Emery Reves presented concisely and convincingly the case for a federal world government.[7] This small book made it to the top of the bestsellers lists in the USA in March 1946, and stayed at the top for six whole months. It was translated into eighteen languages and its ideas about a world federation became extremely popular around the world.

Later that year, Einstein and few other leading physicists published a collection of essays called *One World or None: A report to the Public on the Full Meaning of the Atomic Bomb*. In his essay, Einstein wrote about the lessons that should be learnt from the failure of the League of Nations system. After the First World War, he explained, the international community had set up two institutions that resembled judicial and legislative branches of government. The first, the 'judicial', was the International Court of Justice, whose aim was to solve disputes and conflicts between states on the basis of international law. The second, the 'legislative', was the League of Nations organisation, where representatives of member governments could come together to peacefully negotiate the writing of that international law. When they all gathered in one big assembly room, it had the semblance of a kind of a world parliament. And what's more, one of their first resolutions was to make it 'criminal' to solve conflicts by war. Thus, he wrote,

> 'The nations were imbued with an illusion of security that led inevitably to bitter disappointment. For the best court is meaningless unless it is backed by the authority and power to execute its decisions, and exactly the same thing is true of a world parliament. An individual state with sufficient military and economic power can easily resort to violence, and voluntarily destroy the entire structure of supranational security built on nothing but words and documents. Moral authority alone is an inadequate means of securing the peace. [...]
>
> It is necessary that the individual state be prevented from making war by a supra-national organisation supported by a military power that is exclusively under its control. Only [then] can we have some assurance that we shall not vanish into the atmosphere, dissolved into atoms, one of these days.'[8]

This text also shows how Einstein's vision of a unified world was not a naïve utopia, but was rather based on hard realism. He was not satisfied with nice words and noble declarations, but instead wanted a supranational world government that would be able to keep states in order, prevent war, and belong to all the people of the world. He wanted nothing short of a federal world government, with proper checks and balances, and a proper rule of law.

Inspiration and Legacy

Einstein's main worry was the problem of war in a nuclear age. And it was this concern that led him to the conclusion that a federal world government was necessary. While his fears did not materialize, at least not yet, it is nevertheless evident that the dynamics of the Cold War, with its power politics, proxy wars, and mutual mistrust, took a huge toll on countless individuals and groups around the world. This terribly heavy toll could have been avoided if only Einstein's message had been heeded. If his moral and rational voice been listened to, we could have been living in a much more safe, just and happy world than the one we have today. Today, as we again face the possibility of global destruction, by nuclear war or by climate catastrophe, Einstein's vision and activism can be an inspiration to us all.

Notes

1 Baratta, Joseph. 2004. *The Politics of World Federation: United Nations, UN Reform, Atomic Control.* Westport: Praeger. Chapter 14: Albert Einstein on World Government, pp301-314; Nathan, Otto and Heinz Norden. 1960. *Einstein on Peace.* New York: Schocken Books.

2 Einstein, Albert. 1915. My Opinion on the War, cited in *Einstein on Politics: His Private Thoughts and Public Stands on Nationalism, Zionism, War, Peace, and the Bomb*, edited by David Rowe and Robert Schulmann. Princeton: Princeton University Press, p73.

3 Einstein, Albert. 1931. America and the Disarmament Conference of 1932, cited in *Einstein on Politics: His Private Thoughts and Public Stands on Nationalism, Zionism, War, Peace, and the Bomb*, edited by David Rowe and Robert Schulmann. Princeton: Princeton University Press, p248.

4 Nathan, Otto and Heinz Norden. 1960. *Einstein on Peace.* New York: Schocken Books, pp229-30.

5 Ibid.

6 Letter to the New York Times, 19th October 1945, signed by Albert Einstein, Owen Roberts, William Fulbright, Mortimer Adler, Charles Bolte, Cord Meyer, and Mark and Carl Van Doren. Cited in Baratta, Joseph. 2004. *The Politics of World Federation: United Nations, UN Reform, Atomic Control.* Westport: Praeger, p303.

7 Reves, Emery. 1946. *The Anatomy of Peace.* London: George Allen & Unwin Ltd.

8 Einstein, Albert. 1946. The Way Out. In *One World or None: A Report to the Public on the Full Meaning of the Atomic Bomb*, edited by Dexter Masters and Katharine Way. USA: McGraw-Hill Book Company, p76. oneworld.fas.org/-fulltext.pdf

14. Jawahlarlal Nehru: An Anti-Imperialist's Quest for One World

India's first Prime Minister, Jawaharlal Nehru, believed that the world should be organised as a democratic world federation. This chapter shows how he came to this conclusion from a very particular perspective: that of an anti-imperialist activist struggling for India's independence and seeking to formulate a post-imperial world order which would be just and fair for all.[1]

Early Life

Nehru was born in Allahabad in British colonial India on 14th November 1889, to wealthy bourgeois parents. His father was a prominent lawyer and stateman, and the young Nehru grew up in a luxurious and sheltered environment. He was educated at home by private governesses until the age of sixteen and then was sent

Jawahlarlal Nehru, 1936

to Britain where he attended the elite Harrow public school, before reading Natural Sciences at Trinity College, Cambridge. After that he trained to be a barrister at the Inner Temple Inn in London, and finally returned to India in 1912.

Young Nehru was a shy and sensitive soul, very much an idealist, and naturally supporting the under-dog. From his teenage years onwards he was against British colonial rule in India. He was shocked by the injustice and humiliation of being ruled by a foreign colonial power. It seemed to him to be just so obviously wrong. He passionately believed that India should become free and independent.

After he returned to India he started a career as a barrister. But soon his desire for Indian independence drew him into politics and he got involved in the Indian National Congress, where he quickly rose to prominence.

What Kind of Independent India? In What Kind of World?

The Congress, at this point, was mainly a conservative and bourgeois party, full of the Indian elite. They called for increased autonomy and local rule, but stopped far short of calling for independence from the British Empire. Nehru brought a more radical energy to it, and began to push it towards becoming more of an independence party.

At this time Nehru was essentially a bourgeois nationalist. His sole and main focus was extricating India from the British Empire and gaining independence. But a few events in the 1920s influenced him strongly and pushed him to broaden his views and consider both what kind of independent India he wanted to create, and where this independent India would sit in the world.

In 1920 Nehru spent two weeks at home with his sick mother in Allahabad. During this time some two hundred peasants marched fifty miles from the interior to the city, in order to raise awareness among the urban elite about their appalling living and working conditions. Nehru, always supporting the under-dog but never having really met any, went out to meet them and talk with them. He later accompanied them back to their villages and for the first time saw with his own eyes the grinding poverty of rural India.

While he had known about poverty in theory, this was the first time that he saw it close up, and the experience shocked him deeply. He later wrote in his autobiography:

'Looking at them and their misery... I was filled with shame, shame at my easy-going and comfortable life and our petty politics of the city which ignored this vast multitude of semi-naked sons and daughters of India, sorrow at the degradation and overwhelming poverty of India. A new picture of India seemed to rise before me, naked, starving, crushed and utterly miserable. And their faith in us, casual visitors from the distant city, embarrassed me and filled me with a new responsibility that frightened me.'[2]

Nehru began to think about social change as a core part of the struggle for independence. Could there be ways to create more equal societies, he began to wonder.

The League Against Imperialism

But the real turning point in his thinking came in February 1927, when he attended the Brussels Congress against Colonial Oppression and Imperialism. At this Congress, chaired by George Lansbury of the British Labour Party, representatives of working class and subject colonial peoples came together for the first time. Over 170 delegates attended, including those from thirty seven colonial territories. Delegates discussed their oppression under both colonialism and capitalism and shared their thoughts and stories.[3]

Nehru listened to speeches of delegates from other countries, such as Algeria, Palestine, China, Mexico, Cuba, Venezuela, and Colombia, and heard how similar their situations and struggles were.

He also broadened his thinking about imperialism as the heard the Latin Americas talk about the 'American dollar empire' and described how America acted like an imperial power even if it was not one directly, in the same way as the European empires.

Nehru began to see the struggle for independence from British imperialism as part of a multinational effort by the various colonies and dominions of Empire. He began to look at things from a more global perspective and came to the realisation that there was essentially a world level struggle going on, between the imperial powers on the one hand, and the anti-imperialists on the other. Seen this way, he reasoned that the anti-imperialists should work together and support each other.

It was here that he was also introduced more seriously to socialist thinking, and in particular, to Leninist ideas. According to Lenin, imperialism was a key part of capitalism, and imperialism could only be properly ended if capitalism was also ended and the world took on a socialist form of organisation that would foster equality instead of competition and exploitation. Whilst Nehru was not in favour of what was happening in Communist Russia by this time, and was very much a supporter of democracy, he still found much of interest in these ideas. He reflected on the appalling conditions that he had seen in India's rural villages and began to move away from his bourgeois beliefs and take on more socialist ideas.[4] By the end of the conference Nehru's worldview had changed considerably. He now saw the struggle for Indian independence as part of a broader struggle to change society, both in India and globally. Empire needed to be ended and replaced with free and equal states who could then join together in a world federation to bring about what he called 'World Union' or 'One World'. And this world union should be based on principles of democracy and equality that he believed would be manifested through socialist government and policies.

The Brussels Congress decided to form an organisation to facilitate continued discussion and cooperation. They called it the League against Imperialism, a name carefully chosen to mock the League of Nations. Nehru was elected to the Executive Council and continued to be actively involved in the organisation until 1930.

After the Brussels Congress Nehru returned to India energised and excited, and started giving talks to students and activists around the country, spreading his new ideas. In 1928 he gave a speech to students in Calcutta. He said:

'You have probably often condemned British imperialism because you suffer under it. But have you thought it is but a manifestation, certainly the most objectionable and aggressive manifestation, of a world phenomenon? And that this world imperialism is the direct outcome of a system of society which prevails in the greater part of the world today and is called capitalism. Your immediate problem and mine is to gain political freedom for our country, but this is only part of the problem facing us. So long as imperialism is not rooted out, mankind will be exploited and oppressed by a few. It may be that some of us may join the ranks of the exploiters, but that will not bring freedom to the many. We must aim, therefore, at the destruction of all imperialism and the reconstruction of society on another basis. That basis must be one of cooperation, and that is another name for socialism. Our national ideal must, therefore, be the establishment of a cooperative socialist commonwealth and our international ideal, a world federation of socialist states.'[5]

The Struggle for Indian Independence and for 'One World'

He also channelled his energy more and more into the Congress party and sought to push it to call more strongly for full independence. The Congress started to actively ask Britain to give India dominion status, and Britain's point-blank refusal only further enflamed the growing sentiment for independence.

Nehru began to be seen as the natural successor to Gandhi and in 1929 he became President of the Congress. He and Gandhi led the growing independence movement, and in the 1930s they initiated a program of civil disobedience against British rule. The British saw their power being challenged, and quickly arrested Nehru, and he spent from 1930 to 1935 mainly in prison.

As many political activists have found, being in prison is the perfect opportunity for reading, writing and developing your ideas. And Nehru used his time well, writing his first book *Glimpses of World History*. The book is a kind of world history from an Indian perspective, and it became extremely influential among a generation of Indian scholars and students. It shows a globalist outlook, seeing at the world as an inter-connected whole. At one part he writes:

'Our incursions into history have shown us how the world has grown more and more compact, how different parts have come together and become interdependent. The world has indeed become one single inseparable whole, each part influencing, and being influenced by, the other. It is quite impossible now to have a separate history of nations. We have outgrown that stage, and only a single world history, connecting the different threads from all the nations, and seeking to find the real forces that move them, can now be written with any useful purpose.'[6]

And he concludes that the progressive forces of the world, meaning the anti-capitalists and the anti-imperialists, must unite together to bring about a future of peace and cooperation in the form of a socialist world federation.

Once he was out of prison, Nehru travelled again to Europe and met up with many of his former colleagues from the League Against Imperialism. He delved more deeply into Marxist thought and also developed closer contacts with anti-imperialist movements in Africa and elsewhere. As the dark clouds of World War Two started to loom he turned his thinking to how to deal with the fascism that was rising in Europe and also to considering what a sensible post-war world order should look like.

In 1942, while Britain was preoccupied and weakened by the war effort, he and Gandhi put forward the Quit India resolution, again calling for Indian independence and setting that independence in the context of a future socialist world federation. In it, it says:

'The All-India Congress Committee ... repeats with all emphasis the demand for the withdrawal of the British power from India. On the declaration of India's independence, a provisional government will be formed ...[which] will evolve a scheme for a constituent assembly which will prepare a constitution for the government of India acceptable to all sections of the people. The constitution, according to the Congress view, should be a federal one. With the largest measure of autonomy for the federating units, and with the residuary powers vesting in these units....

The freedom of India must be the symbol of and prelude to the freedom of all other Asiatic nations under foreign domination. Burma, Malaya, Indo-China, the Dutch Indies, Iran and Iraq must also attain their complete freedom. ...

The Committee is of the opinion that the future peace, security and ordered progress of the world demand a world federation of free nations, and on no other basis can the problems of the modem world be solved. Such a world federation would ensure the freedom of its constituent nations, the prevention of aggression and exploitation by one nation over another, the protection of national minorities, the advancement of all backward areas and peoples, and the pooling of the world's resources for the common good of all. On the establishment of such a world federation, disarmament would be practicable in all countries, national armies, navies and air forces would no longer be necessary, and a world federal defence force would keep the world peace and prevent aggression.

An independent India would gladly join such a world federation and cooperate on an equal basis with other countries in the solution of international problems.' [7]

In response to the Resolution, and the protests that accompanied it, the British put Nehru back in prison, where he stayed until 1945.

Again he used this time to read and think. The early 1940s was a time when many thinkers were wondering how to build a sane global order that would stop the seemingly incessant wars and instead bring about peace. Many were thinking about some form of world federation, but there were important differences in details and design. Nehru read these writings with interest and was quick to critique those that he found insufficient. He had much praise for Wendell Wilkie's *One World*[8] for example, and also agreed with W. B. Curry's *The Case for Federal Union*[9] which argued for a world federation of all states in which all would lose the right to have an army, and thus defence budgets could be spent on development and improving conditions across the world. But he was deeply critical of Clarence Streit's *Union Now*[10], which seemed to propose a federation of the white, western states, with their colonies remaining as colonies. While for many in the US and Europe this seemed a reasonable idea, for Nehru, for whom the key driver towards a world federation was the creation of an equal and just system for all, this idea was an abomination.

He also pondered on the possible outcomes of the war. If Germany won, he thought, they would create a German-dominated European federation, with all the European colonies existing as colonies of this new federal state. If the allies won, then he considered:

'The only possible future is one of large federations of nations, or of a world federation, based on a different economy and on strict world control of production, transport and distribution. The present-day capitalist system goes. The British Empire ends. Small States cannot exist as independent units.'[11]

And regarding Indian independence, again he wrote:

'The independence that we seek has never been looked as isolation or the mere addition of a new national state to a crowd of others. We have always realised and looked forward to the world gathering closer together, and   functioning through federation or union, which we would gladly join.'

As we know, the allies won the war, but did not create a world federation. Instead, the present inter-state system emerged, with the United Nations at the centre.

Nonetheless, Nehru continued supporting the idea of a world federation. In 1947, when India was on the verge of independence and the drafting of the Indian Constitution was taking place, Nehru addressed the Constituent Assembly of India and again expressed the need for all nations to work towards building a world structure, which he called 'One World' in order for there to be peace among nations.[12] A few months later, on the 15th August 1947, India finally gained independence and Nehru became its first Prime Minister.

Trying to Reform the United Nations

Whilst Indian independence was of course a huge success and joy for Nehru, he also looked at the emerging international order with disappointment. He realised that without some kind of unifying federation, states would continue to compete with each other and go to war, and that extreme inequality would characterise the world for a long, long time.

Ever the optimist, he still believed that it was possible to move from it towards a world federation and he saw the newly formed United Nations as central to this process. While he was critical of the form that the UN had taken, he still saw it as a possible nucleus of a future world federation. In a speech to the Constituent Assembly of India that same year, discussing India's role at the UN, he said:

> 'The only possible real objective that we, in common with other nations, can have is in the objective of co-operating in building up some kind of world structure, call it 'One World,' call it what you like. The beginnings of this world structure have been laid down in the United Nations Organisation. It is feeble yet; it has many defects; nevertheless, it is the beginning of the world structure.
>
> And India has pledged herself to cooperate in that work.'[13]

And indeed, India under Nehru did try to strengthen the UN system so that it would have some real power. In the very first meeting of the General Assembly India raised the issue of the human rights of Indians in South Africa, where the South African government had recently passed the Asiatic Land Tenure and Indian Representation Act, which essentially segregated the Indian population and denied them certain basic rights. Appealing to the UN Charter, which South Africa had signed, India succeeded in getting a Resolution passed which said, 'the treatment of Indians in the Union should be in conformity with the international obligations under the agreements concluded between the two governments, and the relevant provisions of the Charter'.[14]

As we all know, this approach did not work and South Africa went on to create even worse and more draconian apartheid rules in the coming years. But it is interesting, nonetheless, that at the very start of the UN's history, India and indeed several other states believed that it was precisely the role of the UN to ensure that states treat all their citizens fairly and equally, according to the UN Charter.

Nehru was concerned about the many Indians who lived abroad, not just in South Africa, but in many other countries around the world. Who would guarantee their rights? India? Or their host state? He believed that the UN should guarantee their rights. And then people could move and live where they pleased, knowing their rights would be guaranteed wherever they were.

This thinking was behind India's active involvement in the early meetings of the UN's Human Rights Commission, where they pushed to make human rights real and enforceable, with a strong treaty and a world court to enforce it. But, as we discussed in chapter 8, they were sadly not successful.[15]

But even after these setbacks, Nehru remained committed to a strengthened United Nations as the centre-piece of a future federal world government. He wrote:

'World government is the only remedy for the sickness of the world.... [it could be]...an extension of the federal principle, a growth of the idea underlying the United Nations, giving each national unit freedom to fashion its destiny according to its genius, but subject always to the basic covenant of the World Government'[16]

How to Help Post-Colonial States in the Absence of a World Federation: The Non-Aligned Movement

As the emerging political reality took a different direction and the Cold War began to dominate international politics, Nehru turned to thinking about the situation of the various newly emerging post-colonial states in Africa and Asia. He knew that they would struggle in the competitive international system unless they found some way to work together.

As the Cold War developed and the world split into two big power blocs, Nehru developed the ideas of neutrality and non-alignment, and sought to create a third bloc of non-aligned countries who would not take sides in the new global power politics and who would instead support each other.

He affirmed five principles for good international conduct, known as 'Panchasheel', from the Sanskrit for 'five virtues', namely: mutual respect for other countries' territorial integrity and sovereignty; non-interference in another country's internal affairs; mutual non-aggression; equality and mutual benefit; and peaceful coexistence and economic cooperation.

These ideas were further elaborated at the Bandung Conference in 1955, attended by many newly independent countries from Africa and Asia, and came to be the core of the Non-Aligned Movement which was formed in the 1960s.

Throughout all this, however, Nehru remained committed to the idea of world federalism until his death in 1964. He had witnessed huge change in the world and he knew that further change was possible. He continued to hope that one day the now-independent countries of the world would finally unify into one democratic world federation.

Inspiration and Legacy

Nehru came to world federalism from a different perspective than many European or American thinkers. His vision of world federalism was inspired by a radical anti-imperialism and a desire for peace and cooperation between free and equal states. It was a particularly socialist vision of world federalism, calling also for a new and just world economic order which would reduce inequalities and balance out the world economy in a more fair and equitable manner.

Spending his formative years as a colonial subject, Nehru saw world federalism as more than a way to end wars. For him, it was fundamentally a way to bring about a just and inclusive global society.

It is a vision that can still inspire us today.

Notes

1 Nehru, Jawaharlal. 1976 [1935]. World Federation. In *Documents on Political Thought in Modern* India, Vol. II, edited by A. Appadorai. Bombay: Oxford University Press, pp804–805; Nehru, Jawaharlal. 1976 [1948]. World Government. In *Documents on Political Thought in Modern* India, Vol. II, edited by A. Appadorai. Bombay: Oxford University Press, pp810–811; Kumar, Suneel, and Gurnman Singh. 2012. Nehruvian Vision of Global Order and its Relevance in the Twenty-first Century. *South Asian Survey*, 19,2: 255- 267.

2 Nehru, Jawaharlal. 1951. *Toward Freedom: The Autobiography of Jawaharlal Nehru*. Boston: Beacon Press, p52.

3 For more on the Brussels Congress and the League Against Imperialism, see Louro, Michele. 2018. *Comrades Against Imperialism: Nehru, India and Interwar Internationalism*. Cambridge: Cambridge University Press.

4 Hazary, Narayan. 1965. Democratic Socialism and Jawahlarlal Nehru. *The Indian Journal of Political Science*, 26, 4: 100-105; Rathore, L. 1985. Political Ideas of Jawahlarlal Nehru: Some Reflections. *The Indian Journal of Political Science*, 46,4: 451-473.

5 Gopal, S.1972. Selected Works of Jawahlarlal Nehru, Volume Three, p206. Available at archive.org/details/HindSwaraj-Nehru-SW-03/page/n223/mode/-2up?q=federation

6 Nehru, Jawahlarlal. 1934. *Glimpses of World History*. Delhi: Asia Publishing House, p947.

7 The full text of the Quit India resolution adopted by the All-India Congress can be seen at archive.org/stream/in.ernet.dli.2015.130318/2015.130318.Gandhi-Nehru-And-The-Quit-India-Movement_djvu.txt

8 Wilkie, Wendell. 1943. *One World*. New York: Simon & Schuster.

9 Curry, W. B. 1939. *The Case for Federal Union*. London: Penguin.

10 Streit, Clarence. 1939. Union Now: A Proposal for a Federal Union of the Democracies of the North Atlantic. London: Jonathan Cape.

11 Quoted in Bhagavan, Manu. 2013. *India and the Quest for One World*. Basingstoke: Palgrave Macmillan, p66.

12 Nehru, Jawahlaral. 1947. 'Objectives of the Constitution'. In *The Penguin Books of Modern Indian Speeches: 1877 to the Present, edited by* Rakesh Batabyal. New Delhi: Penguin Books. pp382–385.

13 Nehru, Jawahlaral. 1947. Resolution in the Constituent Assembly regarding 'Aims and Objectives', cited in *The Political Philosophy of Jawahlarlal Nehru*, edited by M. N. Das. London: Routledge, p243.

14 Schifter, Richard. 1993. Human Rights at the United Nations: The South Africa Precedent. *American University International Law Review* 8, 2/3: 361-372. Billion, Jean-Francis. 2010. Fédéralisme et Décolonisation en Afrique Noire et aux Antilles. *Presse Fédéraliste* 147. www.pressefederaliste.eu/Federalisme-et-decolonisation-en

15 For more on this episode and on Nehru's views about world federation more generally, see Bhagavan, Manu. 2013. *India and the Quest for One World.* Basingstoke: Palgrave Macmillan.

16 Quoted in Bhagavan, Manu. 2013. *India and the Quest for One World.* Basingstoke: Palgrave Macmillan, p99.

15. Josué de Castro: World Federation to End World Hunger

This chapter looks at the life and thought of another important world federalist thinker, Josué de Castro from Brazil. De Castro was a doctor, scholar, activist and parliamentarian, who dedicated his life to addressing the problem of hunger.

In the early 1950s he was the Chair of the Council of the UN's Food and Agriculture Organisation, the FAO, but he came to believe that only a radical re-organising of the international system into a more just and democratic global order could ever truly solve the problem of hunger in the world.[1]

Josué de Castro, 1940

Early Life

De Castro was born in 1908 in the town of Recife, the main town of Pernambuco, one of the 26 states that comprise the federation of Brazil. That area in the North-East of Brazil was one of the poorest areas of the country and many of its inhabitants were the descendants of African slaves that had been trafficked during the colonial Atlantic slave trade. De Castro himself was born to a middle-class family of mixed European and indigenous Indian descent, and while relatively wealthy in the local context, he grew up very sensitive to the issues of race and of poverty, and ultimately of hunger.

His father was a small-scale cattle farmer, selling milk in the local markets, and his mother was a teacher in the local school. They separated when Josué was just four years old and he was mainly brought up by his mother. He used to play in the street with the poor, barefoot neighbourhood boys, and through them he learnt about the chronic, ever-persistent hunger that was present all around him. He was a sensitive boy and the suffering caused by hunger made a big impression on him. He later wrote,

> 'It was not at the Sorbonne or at any other savant university that I learned of the phenomenon of hunger. It appears spontaneously to me.... In the miserable neighbourhoods of Recife ... This was my Sorbonne: the mud of the Recife mangroves.'[2]

De Castro was a good student and after high school he went to Rio to study Medicine at the University of Brazil, where he graduated in 1929 as a physician. In 1932, when he was only 24, he returned to Recife to take up a position as Professor of Physiology at the City's Medical School.

The Problem of Hunger in Brazil

Soon, however, he became interested in more interdisciplinary approaches to understanding the problems of poverty and hunger, and in the following years he went on to become a Professor of Anthropology at the Federal District University and then a Professor of Human Geography at the University of Brazil, where he created the Nutrition Institute and served as its first Director.

During the 1930s and early 1940s his academic work focused on the issues of hunger and poverty in northeast Brazil. He spent time talking to people living in poor communities and sought to understand both the profound impacts of hunger and the social and political factors that enabled and created it. Going against the deterministic approaches that were dominant at the time, such as Malthus's idea that hunger was simply a result of over-population, he developed a much more nuanced and contextualised analysis of the causes of hunger in Brazil, and showed how hunger was a direct result of political decisions and social policies.

Alongside his academic studies, which quickly made him one of Brazil's leading experts on food and food policy, de Castro sought also to engage in practical political activism to reduce the appalling hunger that he saw all around him. In 1933 he chaired a Municipal Committee in Recife which carried out the first major survey of poor people to be conducted in Brazil. In 1935 he became involved in the Campaign for a Minimum Wage, and later he co-founded and directed major associations that studied and campaigned for food security. In these years he was also invited by the governments of several other countries to study their own problems of food and nutrition, including Argentina, the United States, the Dominican Republic, Mexico and France.

In 1946 he published his book, *The Geography of Hunger*. This was a ground-breaking work which brought together his research about the political aspect of hunger in Brazil. He argued that the terrible poverty and the lack of access to clean drinking water and adequate food that affected most of the Brazilian population, was not inevitable, but the result of a particular economic model that perpetuated shocking poverty and inequality.[3]

His book had a huge impact in Brazil and triggered a nation-wide debate on the problem of hunger and poverty as a social and political issue. Based on his diagnosis of the hunger problem, the first collective food services were created, the School Meals Program was established, and programs through which employers paid subsidies for workers' meals were created.

The book also led to the growth of his international reputation as a world-leading expert on hunger, food and nutrition, and to the beginning of his involvement with the newly established United Nations Food and Agriculture Organisation, the FAO. In 1947 he became a member of the FAO's Standing Advisory Committee on Nutrition, and began to take part in high-level international discussions about world food policy and how to eliminate hunger.

The Problem of World Hunger

His experiences at the FAO led him to turn his attention to the situation of world hunger, and in 1951, at the age of 43, he published his next book, *The Geopolitics of Hunger*. This book was a wide-ranging scholarly tour-de-force, looking at the causes and consequences of hunger across the world as a whole, and suggesting radical new paths towards a world with no hunger. The book was soon translated into some twenty five languages and became widely read around the world, setting de Castro as an international expert on the issues of food and nutrition.

The first section of the book set out a detailed description of what hunger is. He looked at not just total hunger, which is a lack of sufficient food in general, but also specific types of 'silent hungers', where there are deficiencies in specific nutrients or vitamins in the food that people do have. In each case he explained how the particular hunger influenced human physiology and had profound impacts on human functioning, physically, cognitively and socially. He described how hunger led not only to starvation and death, but on the way also caused physical stunting, learning difficulties and many other miseries which afflicted the hungry. At this time, around two thirds of the world's population, mainly the black and brown people living in the colonies, were suffering from long-term, chronic hunger, and de Castro indignantly argued that there was a 'conspiracy of silence' about this huge world problem.

The second section looked at the causes of world hunger. It consisted of several detailed case studies from different parts of the world, including India, China, Africa, Europe and the South of the USA, in which he traced historically the underlying social, political, ecological and economic forces that led in each situation to collective hunger and starvation. These detailed studies often yielded surprising results that went against the conventional wisdom of the time. For example, he convincingly showed that the African diet used to be far more varied than it had become in the 1940s, and he provided detailed data about African tribes who had shown no signs of malnutrition when they had lived according to their traditional way of life, but, 'as soon as they go work in the factories and take up a diet under European influence, typical deficiency diseases ... begin to destroy large numbers of them'.[4] And in another example he showed that the rising of vitamin B deficiency in Amazonia during the rubber boom, was due to the shift in eating habits from traditional fare to canned European food.

Putting these and many other detailed case studies together, he argued that the high rates of hunger in Africa, Asia and Latin America were not due to general backwardness and over-population, as was commonly thought, but were rather the direct results of European colonialism and imperialism. European colonialism had destroyed many well-integrated and flourishing societies and re-organised the global arrangement of productive agriculture in a way that suited European interests. It had created large landholdings and single crop cultivation, diverted land use from food production for local consumption to the production of cash crops for export, and led to massive exhaustion of the soil and ecological destruction in the search for quick profits. The result was that food was systemically sucked out of the colonies and sent to the colonising powers. While the colonisers enjoyed a rich and diverse food intake for a low price, the majority of the world's population in the colonies suffered hunger, starvation and misery.

In making this argument, he was seeking to refute the idea promoted by Western scholars such as Malthus that hunger was simply the result of over-population. Instead, he put forward a very detailed and convincing analysis that showed that in fact it was the other way around, that over-population was actually the result of hunger. He brought statistical evidence to show that in a wide range of countries there was an inverse correlation between the consumption of proteins and birth rates, i.e., the less protein in the diet, then the higher the birth rate. And he also drew on evidence from laboratory experiments with animals that showed the same thing. He even pointed to a possible biological mechanism to explain the pattern, arguing that protein deficiency leads to a reduction in the liver's ability to inactivate estrogens in the body, and that the subsequent rise in estrogens increased women's fertility, leading to more babies.

But most importantly, this was not just an academic argument. How scientists understood the cause of world hunger would shape the types of solutions that they offered for it. The Malthusian notion that world hunger was caused by over-population implied that the blame for world hunger rests on the poor people themselves, and that therefore the solution was to reduce fertility and child-birth in the colonies or the so-called 'developing' countries. But if, as de Castro argued, world hunger was actually a social and political creation, caused by the unjust pattern of organisation of world food production and distribution, then the solution would be to change that pattern. De Castro brought convincing data to show that the food produced in the world was more than enough to feed everyone. The problem was not a shortage of food, but the extremely unequal distribution of that food.

This led to the third and final section of the book, where he began to develop proposals for solutions to the world's hunger problem.

While he looked to new technologies to improve levels of food production, his central argument was that the most important thing was to change the structure of the world system. Most basically, this would require, in his words, 'a radical transformation in the social structure of the world', and 'full and harmonious integration, ... At the same time economic, technical, social, and human, permitting the enhancement of resources and possibilities.' [5]

He argued that the 'geography of hunger' could be transformed into a 'geography of abundance' if colonialism would end and there would be 'the transition from a colonial economy to a co-operative world economy based on mutual interests'.[6]

In contrast to international development theory, which was emerging at the time and which called for all sorts of state-led projects of industrialisation under the benign oversight of the Western powers, de Castro instead argued that the contemporary poverty, hunger and inequality was a direct result of the 'under-development' of the colonies that was caused *by* the West. Instead of 'development', he called for 'the collective emancipation of humanity' such that all the areas of the world would be integrated into one global system based on cooperation, mutuality and reciprocity.

In this way, global food reserves could be spread more evenly over the planet, with food surpluses from rich areas being transferred to poorer areas, such that everyone would have a healthy and balanced diet and no-one would suffer the misery of hunger. He thus argued against 'agricultural nationalism' and the competition between states for power, wealth and food, and instead he called for a more humane economy, one that would serve to benefit all of humanity rather than amass never-ending wealth for the few.

Finally, he believed that hunger was one of the main causes of war, and thus he also saw that evening out the world's food consumption and eliminating hunger was crucial to reach world peace, which was a major concern at the time in the aftermath of World War Two. But while many peace activists in the West focused on disarmament as the way to world peace, de Castro called for a deeper look at the root causes of war, and argued that creating a more equal world where no-one was hungry would remove many of the key drivers for war, and thus be a far more effective way to bring about peace. As he wrote,

'We will never achieve peace in a world divided into abundance and deprivation, luxury and poverty, waste and hunger. We must put an end to this social inequality.'[7]

This book, on top of his years of academic study and activism, solidified de Castro's reputation as a world-leading expert on food and nutrition and led to his election, in 1952, as the Chair of the Council of the UN's Food and Agriculture Organisation, the FAO.

Trying to End World Hunger through the FAO

As mentioned above, De Castro's involvement with the FAO had already started five years earlier in 1947, when he became a member of the FAO's Standing Advisory Committee on Nutrition, and indeed much from that experience had fed directly into the analysis of his book. In these earlier years, the FAO had been under the leadership of its first Director-General, John Boyd Orr, a Scottish physiologist and international food policy expert who had been working since the 1930s on hunger and nutrition in the United Kingdom and worldwide through the League of Nations. In the 1920s and 30s, in the aftermath of World War One, food supply had been a very serious issue, and there had been a growing sense that the food system needed to be managed globally. Arthur Salter, who had been Head of the Economic Department of the League of Nations at the time, had proposed the creation of an International Food Board, which would prevent price fluctuations on world markets through the purchase and sale of food commodities and would balance regional deficits in distribution via prompt aid shipments.

Boyd Orr had been much influenced by these ideas, and when he took up the leadership of the new FAO in the years after the Second World War, when again hunger and starvation were becoming massive global problems, affecting not only the colonies but also Europe, he drew on these ideas and developed them further as he sought to make the FAO into an organisation that would abolish hunger, for everyone, everywhere.

In 1946 he developed a proposal to establish a World Food Board, which would have the power to stabilize the prices of agricultural commodities on world markets, to establish a world food reserve adequate for any emergency that might arise through crop failure in any part of the world, and to fund the distribution of agricultural surplus from producers to those countries urgently in need. According to Boyd Orr, the World Food Board would dampen social unrest, stabilize world prices, double the food supply, and eliminate world hunger by absorbing the food surpluses of industrialized nations, and would further global cooperation. The activities of the proposed board would mean that food deficient countries would receive low-priced food, relatively high and stable prices for agricultural goods, and the necessary credit to expand food production for both internal and external consumption. The overall result would be a global management of the food supply, and thus the abolition of hunger.[8]

Boyd Orr's proposal had received enthusiastic support from the scientists and experts involved in the FAO, including de Castro, but when it was presented to the member states at the first FAO Conference in Copenhagen in 1946 the reception was much more mixed. While several governments in Europe, Asia and Latin America expressed support, the governments of the United States and Britain were strongly against. Britain did not want to lose its cheap food imports, and the USA preferred to build its political and economic dominance in the world economy through bilateral agreements, conditional aid and power politics.

Boyd Orr spent the next three years trying to rally support for his plan. But Britain and the United States consistently blocked it, until it became clear that it would not pass. Frustrated and deeply disappointed, Boyd Orr resigned in 1948. By this time the FAO's only contribution to alleviating world hunger was providing some technical assistance and publishing some statistics. As Boyd Orr bitterly put it, 'The hungry people of the world wanted bread, and they were to be given statistics'.[9]

From his position on one of the FAO's Advisory Committees, de Castro had seen first-hand the geo-politics of nutrition and hunger being played out. He supported Boyd Orr's World Food Board proposal as a rational and just way to eliminate poverty and hunger and re-balance a deeply unequal world. He too was deeply angered and frustrated when he saw how the rich countries would reject a scientifically rational plan to abolish world hunger in order to maintain their own narrow self-interest. The two men shared a very similar vision for a just and equitable global food policy that would eliminate hunger and thus also war, and in 1952 Boyd Orr wrote an enthusiastic forward to the English edition of de Castro's book, saluting it as an intellectual instrument for 'saving our civilisation from perishing in a third world war'.

Being younger and earlier in his career than Boyd Orr, de Castro was not yet ready to give up on the FAO. In 1949, after Boyd Orr had already left, de Castro supported another FAO initiative to create an International Commodities Clearing House, in order to control the purchase and distribution of food. This would have been a mechanism to regulate the prices of labour and production globally, by countries cooperating together in the common effort to abolish hunger. But again, the governments and especially the rich governments had refused to set up such a body, and instead created the much weaker 'Committee on Commodity Problems', still active today in the FAO, which is strongly dominated by the interests of the US government and multinational corporations.

Both the idea of a World Food Board and the idea of a Commodities Clearing House drew on ideas of Keynesian economics, which were dominant at the time. Indeed, during the same years, governments were discussing Keynes' proposal for an International Trade Organisation and an International Clearing Union, which would regulate and balance out international trade more generally, in a similar way. But these proposals too, had been vetoed by the US, who wanted to fashion the post-war world order as to consolidate its power as the new hegemon.

And so, in 1952, when de Castro took up the role as Chair of the FAO Council, it was already clear to him and everyone else that the FAO had no powers of its own, but was almost completely dependent on the agendas of national governments, particularly that of the US.

Nonetheless, de Castro tried to further the interests of the world's poor in the developing countries and argued for food policies which would reduce if not eliminate hunger. Less radical and all-encompassing than the proposed World Food Board or the proposed International Commodities Clearing House, he suggested the creation of an Emergency Food Reserve, which would be able to provide food to starving people in crisis situations. But like all the previous initiatives, this too was blocked by Britain and the US. And eventually de Castro too left the FAO in frustration.

The Only Way to End World Hunger is through World Federation

Seeing the lack of decision-making power that scientists and scholars had in international politics, in 1955 he moved from academia into politics, becoming a parliamentarian for the Pernambuco State of Northeast Brazil, and sitting in the Brazilian Chamber of Deputies. That same year he attended two major conferences that would have a big influence on his future thinking and activism. In April he attended the Bandung Conference in Indonesia. As European imperialism was beginning to come to an end, at least in its direct form, many of the leaders of the newly independent countries from Africa and Asia were starting to think about how to collaborate as a bloc and how to work together to change the global system into one that was more equal and just. Their first major meeting took place at Bandung, and, as we discussed in chapter 14, this conference later led to the formation of the Non-Aligned Movement. This was the group of countries, de Castro thought, that would be able to lead the movement to transform the world system. And it was here that he personally met several key leaders, including Nehru from India, Nkrumah from Ghana, Sekou Touré from Guinea and others. Later that year, in July, he attended the 7th Congress of the World Movement for World Federal Government, which would later become the World Federalist Movement, or WFM. It was presumably his friend and colleague, John Boyd Orr, who served as President of the organisation from 1948 to 1951, who encouraged de Castro to come to that Congress and get involved in the movement. Boyd Orr's bitter experience in the ineffective and unjust international system had led him to conclude that the only way to truly eliminate world hunger and to bring about world peace and justice, was to create a democratic world federation. Only such a supra-national institution, he reasoned, would be able to make and implement global policy without being subjected to the national interests of powerful states.

In 1949 Boyd Orr had received the Nobel Peace Prize for his life-long activities to promote a more equitable world order, and in his acceptance speech he had said,

'We are now physically, politically, and economically one world, and nations are so interdependent that the absolute national sovereignty of nations is no longer possible. However difficult it may be to bring it about, some form of world government with agreed international law, and means of enforcing the law, is inevitable.'[10]

These ideas resonated strongly with de Castro's own experience in the international system, as well as his own ideas about world integration and world emancipation, and took them to their logical conclusion. And so de Castro began to get involved with the World Movement for World Federal Government, and also with the World Association of Parliamentarians for World Government.

In 1957 he published *The Black Book of Hunger*, a short manifesto setting out again his vision for how the world could free of hunger. In this manifesto he was now clearer that the way to bring about a just and balanced world food system required a system of supra-national governance, a democratic world government that would have powers over and above that of the national governments. Describing the UN and the FAO, he writes:

'Their decisions depend on assemblies of national delegates who place egoistic national interests above the higher interests of humanity. To resolve a problem of such scope, something more is needed than an inter-national organisation. We need a supra-national organisation, freed from those sterilising injunctions of what is called, without much basis, the 'national interest' of each country. We would need to organise a World Government...'[11]

That same year he also founded and became the first Director of the World Association for the Fight against Hunger, an organisation which would promote the creation of supra-national political structures to assure world food supply and world peace, alongside project to support the socio-economic development of areas threatened by hunger.

In 1962 he moved from national politics in Brazil's parliament to international politics, and became Brazil's Ambassador to the UN in Geneva. Now as a government representative, rather than a scientific expert, he occupied a different position within the UN system, with different possibilities and different limitations. In his new role he spoke up for the developing countries and allied Brazil with countries in Africa, Asia and Latin America during policy negotiations.

However, just two years later, in 1964, there was a military coup in Brazil and suddenly he found himself deemed a 'subversive person' and all his political and civil rights revoked. And thus, at the age of 56, he went into exile in France.

World Federalist Activism: The People's Congress

Establishing himself in Paris, he returned to academia and to activism. He taught Human Geography at the University of Paris in Vincennes, a hub for leftist intellectuals, where he worked alongside other radical scholars such as Foucault, Deleuze and Lyotard. Most of his energy, however, was now devoted to more activist endeavours. He founded the International Centre for Development, an independent think-tank focussing on alternative forms of development and geopolitics from a 'third world' perspective, and became increasingly active in movements promoting global democracy and world federation.

He corresponded with several leading world federalist thinkers, including Bertrand Russell, Leopold Senghor, and Jawaharlal Nehru, and became increasingly convinced that world peace and justice could not be brought about through the contemporary 'international' system in which governments compete with each other for their own self-interest, and would only be possible if all states united into one integrated 'global' system, with supra-national government directly and democratically accountable to the world's people. He got more involved with several world federalist activities and movements, most notably the movement for a People's Congress.

In 1963, on the fringes of a World Federalist Movement meeting in Brussels, de Castro, along with other activists such as Jacques Savary and Jeanne Hasle, launched the idea of a People's Congress to draft a World Constitution, as a radical step towards bringing about a democratic world federation. Most of this group were connected with the International Registry of World Citizens, an organisation which worked to create a register of people who declared themselves to be 'world citizens', that, as we discuss in more detail in chapter 22, had been started by Gary Davis in 1949 and had since grown to include almost a million people.[12]

The group were well aware that there had been several previous attempts to organise similar World People's Conventions, building on the ideas of Rosika Schwimmer and Lola Maverick Lloyd in 1937, and including British MP Henry Usborne's attempts in 1950, as we discussed in chapter 12. But despite the difficulties, they felt that it was the only way to bypass the two great barriers to the rise of a democratic world order at that time – the dysfunctional and undemocratic UN system, and the dynamics of the Cold War.

While many people in the wider World Federalist Movement still believed that the best way to create a world federation was by reforming the UN, de Castro, with his years of experience at both the UN and the FAO, felt that this would never happen. Instead of waiting for national governments to act, he – like Rosika Schwimmer and Henry Usborne before him – thought that it was imperative for citizens to take matters into their own hands.

And so in 1966 The People's Congress launched 'The Declaration of Thirteen World Citizens', a short manifesto calling on people to declare themselves world citizens and to participate in the election of delegates to a People's Congress which would draft a World Constitution. The declaration was signed by thirteen eminent people, including Josué de Castro, John Boyd Orr, Bertrand Russell, Shinzo Hamai (the former mayor of Hiroshima), Linus Pauling (Nobel Prize Laureate in Chemistry), Ivan Supek (Yugoslavian scientist and peace activist) and various other Nobel Prize winners.

The full text of the declaration read as follows:

'In the absence of supernational law, nations are obliged to resort to force to defend their interest. The consequence: war, voluntary or accidental; and war, since the splitting of the atom and the development of bacteriological weapons becomes the absurd "final solution", the genocide of the human race.

Without world institutions able to assure the fundamental needs common to all, man is helpless. Two thirds of humanity suffer from hunger, while immense riches are wasted.

At the same time, scientific and technical progress make it possible to organise a world community of peace and abundance where fundamental liberties would be guaranteed to individuals, peoples and nations.

Why this contradiction? Because governments, blinded by their duty to put national interest above everything, far from accepting the necessary changes, sometimes even hinder the work of the international institutions created to defend universal peace and to serve mankind. Only the people of the world, every one of us, can save the situation. The first simple but effective step we ask you to take is to register as a world citizen, as we have done.

If enough of you answer our plea, we will take the second step together. We will organise on a transnational basis the election of delegates whose duty will be to defend the individual, to voice the needs of the people of the world and, finally, to devise the laws for a peaceful and civilized world.'[13]

In the following years many people responded to this call and registered with the group as world citizens, and de Castro and his colleagues set about organising a transnational, world election of delegates to the People's Congress. The idea was that this would take place in phases, with elections selecting two candidates every few years. In 1969 the first elections took place. Some 10,000 people distributed across eighty seven countries sent in their postal votes to choose the first two delegates to the People's Congress. Josué de Castro was chosen as one of the first two.

Since then, the People's congress has organised several more transnational elections and the organisation has expanded and changed its initial approach, adding also a Consultative Assembly to bring together world citizens organisations, and eventually focussing mainly on promoting the idea that the People's Congress should transform into a democratically elected World Parliament which could then make world law and build supra-national world institutions. Whilst it has not succeeded in its original aims, it did succeed at the time in developing a large, transnational network of world citizens organisations, mainly across the French-speaking parts of the world.

Inspiration and Legacy

De Castro died a few years after that first election, in 1973 at the age of 65. Throughout his life he worked tirelessly to bring an end to world hunger, as a scholar, as a politician and as an activist. Building up from detailed local studies of particular situations of hunger to working at the international level in the UN and the FAO, he came to see that hunger was a social problem, created by the political structures of the world and the way that they shaped agricultural production and distribution in the interests of the rich and powerful.

And thus he came to the conclusion that the only way to eliminate chronic, long-term hunger, was to transform the world system into a democratic world federation, so that democratic supra-national bodies could implement policies that would ensure that everyone in the world would have enough to eat.

His ideas are still deeply relevant for the world today, where millions of people sadly still go hungry and malnourished and where the UN and the FAO remain dominated by the interests of the US and other Western countries, now exacerbated even further with the involvement of huge transnational food and seed corporations. Today the West has a problem of obesity, while the developing countries continue to struggle with hunger and malnutrition. To end this scandal we need to return to the ideas of Josué de Castro, and of his colleague John Boyd Orr, and create supra-national institutions which will act according to the will of the world's people, and not just of the corporations and the elite.

Notes

1 Ferretti, Federico. 2021. A Coffin for Malthusianism: Josué De Castro's Subaltern Geopolitics. *Geopolitics*, 26, 2: 589-614; see also www.josuedecastro.com.br/engl/

2 Castro, Josué de. 1970. *Of Men and Crabs*. Vanguard Publishing, p142.

3 Castro, Josué de. 1946. *Geografia da fome*. [*The Geography of Hunger*]. Rio de Janeiro: Editora O Cruzeiro.

4 Castro, Josué de. 1951. *Geopolítica da fome*. [*The Geopolitics of Hunger*]. Rio de Janeiro: Casa do Estudante do Brasil, p37.

5 Ibid, p99.

6 Ibid, p257.

7 Ibid, p261.

8 Achertz, Ruth and Alexander Nuetzenadel. 2011. Coping with Hunger? Visions of a Global Food System, 1930–1960. *Journal of Global History*, 6: 99-119; Grigg, David. 1981. The Historiography of Hunger: Changing Views on the World Food Problem 1945-1980. *Transactions of the Institute of British Geographers*, 6, 3: 279-292.

9 Cited in Vernon, James. 2007. *Hunger: A Modern History*. Cambridge: Harvard University Press, p153.

10 Boyd Orr, John. 1950, "Science and Peace," *Les Prix Nobel en 1949*. Stockholm.

11 Castro, Josué de. 1957. *The Black Book of Hunger*. São Paulo: Editora Brasiliense.

12 Billion, Jean-Francis. 1996. The World Federalist Movements from 1955 to 1968 and European Integration. *The Federalist Political Review*, No. 2, p96. www.thefederalist.eu/site/index.php/en/essays/1929-the-world-federalist-move-ments-from-1955-to-1968-and-the-european-integration

13 recim.org/cdm/cit13an.htm

16. Kwame Nkrumah: World Federalism instead of Neo-Colonialism

Kwame Nkrumah, the first Prime Minister and President of Ghana, was a key world federalist thinker. He fervently believed that federation, both a Pan-African federation and ultimately a world federation, was necessary in order to create a just and equal world in which the former colonies would be able to determine their own future and not be dominated by the former colonial powers.[1]

Kwame Nkrumah, 1961

Early Life

Young Nkrumah was born on 21st September 1909 in Nkroful, a small village in the south west of the Gold Coast, one of Britain's colonies in West Africa. His father was a goldsmith and his mother was a petty trader. His parents lived apart, as his father had several other wives, and his mother bought him up with the help of her extended family. He had a simple and carefree life in the village until his mother sent him to a local elementary school run by the Catholic Mission, where he was later baptised as a Catholic. He was a good student and was soon noticed by the Reverend Alec Fraser, Principal of the Government Training College in the colony's capital, Accra, who then arranged for Nkrumah to come to his college and train as a teacher. Nkrumah went off to Accra and trained to be a teacher.

While he was at the College he first came across the ideas of radical American black intellectuals, such as Marcus Garvey and WEB Du Bois, mainly through his discussions with the Vice Principal, Kwegyir Aggrey, who had spent several years in the US. Their calls for African independence, of both black Americans and Africans living in Africa under colonial rule, made a big impression on Nkrumah, and he was inspired by the idea of a free and independent Africa in which Africans would live in freedom and govern themselves. He started to think more deeply about the reality of British colonial rule and to develop his own ideas about African freedom.

In 1930 he obtained his teachers certificate and he spent the next five years teaching in various local schools. But he was keen to further his own education and to learn more about the powerful ideas to which he had recently been exposed. A few years later he met Nmandi Azikiwe, the future President of Nigeria, and talked with him about African nationalism. Azikiwe had studied at Lincoln University, a predominantly black university in Pennsylvania in the US, and he strongly encouraged Nkrumah to go there. Coming from a poor family, and with only a teacher's salary, this sounded like a tough prospect for Nkrumah. But he was determined, and he asked around his extended family and somehow he managed to piece together the necessary funds.

Black Radical Thought

In 1935, at the age of 26, Nkrumah set off to the United States, for what would turn out to be ten incredibly important years where he would develop the core of his ideas. In 1939 he received his BA in Economics and Sociology from Lincoln University, and then in 1942 he completed Masters degrees in Philosophy and Education from the University of Pennsylvania and a BA in Theology from the Lincoln Seminary. Alongside his studies he got engaged in student politics, founding the African Students Association of America and Canada, and becoming its first President. He also worked in a range of menial jobs, washing dishes and the like, in order to make ends meet and on Sundays he attended Presbytarian churches.

But perhaps the most important times were the summers, when we went to Harlem, a neighbourhood in the northern part of New York that was the centre of American black life, thought and culture. Harlem was bustling with energy at this time, as black American consciousness was flourishing. In the evenings the streets became open forums where young thinkers and activists stood on soap boxes on street corners and gave impassioned speeches to the large crowds to gathered to listen and discuss. Carlos Cooks, founder of the African Pioneer Movement was on the scene at this time, talking about Pan-Africanism and black liberation. So were Arthur Reed and Ira Kemp, founders of the African Patriotic League, talking about how Africans should start their own businesses in order to overcome the racial labour segregation in the US. Nkrumah walked the streets and watched and listened. The ideas and the energy were intoxicating.

Nkrumah also read the works of leading black intellectuals, such as George Padmore and CLR James. These thinkers developed piercing critiques of the international world order and argued that the imperialist world was built on a dual system of slavery and racial hierarchy. In contrast to many analyses of the time which claimed that the people in the colonies were excluded from the international system, these thinkers argued that the colonies were absolutely included in the world system, but in an unequal way. Their resources and their labour were crucial elements of the international capitalist world order, but their voices were not included in the decision-making.

They argued that the world was organised according to a racialised system of unequal integration, in which the imperial powers and other mainly white sovereign states were fully integrated, while the mainly black and brown colonies were only partially integrated.

This system of unequal integration, along racial lines, was the fundamental political structure which enabled the domination and exploitation of the majority of the world's population in the colonies. Liberation, autonomy and sovereignty, they argued, were needed for Africans and other colonial peoples to have self-determination over their own lives and to integrate, equally, into the world system.[2]

Nkrumah's Ideas about African Federation and World Federation

Nkrumah built on these ideas and took them further. He imagined what would happen if all the African colonies gained independence as separate sovereign states. If this were to happen, he argued, it would lead to what he called the 'balkanisation' of Africa – the creation of lots and lots of small and weak states that would be virtually powerless in the competitive international order. For Africans to really achieve self-determination, the world order needed to be changed in a way that would ensure that the powerful countries did not dominate the weaker ones. A global system of world law and order would need to be created, In the form of a democratic world federation. If this was not possible, or perhaps as a first step towards such a world federation, he argued that Africa must federate.

He modelled his African federation on the US federation. He recalled that the American federation was initially created as a unity of former colonial states who realised that they could only be powerful against their former colonisers if they came together as one large political and economic unit. The US had been hugely successful since then. Nkrumah felt sure that if Africa could come together in a similar way, then it too could develop in a positive way.[3]

If African states were all separate and independent, each one would end up economically tethered to its former imperial master and the global markets. Most colonial economies had been designed to produce and supply a limited number of raw materials to the colonial centre. The Gold Coast, for example, had an economy mainly dependent on the production and supply of cocoa beans. If African states stayed small and separate they would inevitably remain dependent on their former colonial masters. The international system would enable a form of what he called 'neo-colonialism', with the former imperial powers being able to retain economic control of their former colonies, even if their direct rule had been ended.

In order to avert this, and to achieve full, diverse and self-reliant economies, he argued that the whole African continent needed to come together in an African federation, and create one huge political and economic unit for themselves. In this way they could trade with each other rather than always selling to the Europeans or Americans. They could pool resources for regional economic development. They could collaborate on economic planning and create continent-wide systems of defence and security. If Africa came together in this way, he argued, it could become big and powerful. It was full of valuable natural resources which Africans could develop for their own use. And if those outside of Africa wanted access to these natural resources, then they would have to negotiate with the powerful African federation, which would only grant them access on terms that would bring benefits to Africans. Thus for Nkrumah, national liberation and self-determination was only the first step. In order to ensure that Africa was not dominated in a future world order, it was necessary to form both an African federation, and also a world federation.

The Pan-African Congress Calls for African and World Federation

In 1945 Nkrumah left the US and went to London, where he met George Padmore, a leading Pan-African thinker and activist, and the two of them started to collaborate. That same year world leaders were meeting in San Francisco to discuss the formation of the United Nations. Nkrumah and Padmore watched on from the outside. Among the 50 nations who had sent delegates to the meeting, there were only representatives from four African countries – Ethiopia, Liberia, Egypt and South Africa – as these were the only African countries that existed at the time. And South Africa, in any case, was ruled by whites. The rest of Africa, still under colonial rule, had no say in the major re-ordering of the world that was taking place. The injustice and the humiliation was horrible.[4]

In response to the lack of African representation at the San Francisco Conference, Padmore and Nkrumah organised the 5th Pan-African Congress in Manchester from 15-21 October 1945, just days before the UN would officially come into being on 24th October, to set out their alternative vision of post-war world order.

In contrast to the continued imperialism contained in the San Francisco outcome, the 5th Pan-African Congress called for the immediate end to colonialism and for autonomy and independence for black Africa. And in contrast to the very limited confederal approach of the UN, they called for the formation of a Pan-African federation, and ultimately a world federation, which they called 'One World'. The final Congress resolution called for,

'Black Africa autonomy and independence, so far and no further than it is possible in this 'One World' for groups and people to rule themselves subject to inevitable world unity and federation.'[5]

The Gold Coast's Struggle for Independence

After the Congress Nkrumah did not stay in London very long. The stirrings of independence were beginning to rumble in The Gold Coast. In 1947 the first real political party was formed in the colonial Gold Coast – the United Gold Coast Convention – with the aim to bring about self-government as soon as possible. The founders of the new party were looking for someone to run it, and chose Nkrumah. Excited at this turn of events, he accepted the invitation and later that year returned to the Gold Coast and took up his new position.

Nkrumah quickly found the party rather staid and conservative, appealing mainly to the urban intelligentsia. So in 1949 he left and formed his own political party – the Convention Peoples Party, the CPP. As the name suggests, this party would reach out to the masses. The CPP went around the country in vans, waving flags and blaring out music and were incredibly successful in rallying public support. Nkrumah quickly became a well-known and popular figure. In January 1950 he organised a huge general strike. In response the British put him in prison.

The British were nonetheless ready to move slowly towards a system of increased local rule, and while Nkrumah was safely incarcerated in prison they organised an election for the new quasi-government. Nkrumah made sure that the CPP would stand in these elections. His assistant and right-hand man, Komla Agbeli Gbedemah, led the campaign, while Nkrumah managed to smuggle out messages to him written on toilet paper.

The election result was a landslide win for the CPP, with them securing 34 out of 38 seats. Nkrumah was released from prison on 12th February 1951, and the next day the British Colonial Governor asked him to form a government. He became The Gold Coast's first Prime Minister, and Gbedemah became the Minister for Health and Labour.

Following another election a few years later, which the CPP won again, the British finally agreed to give the Gold Coast independence. Nkrumah decided that the name of the new state would be Ghana. And on 6th March 1957 Ghana became the first African colony to achieve full independence as a sovereign state.

The celebrations were huge. Ghana's independence was seen not just as a local victory, but as a victory for all Africans, and indeed for all colonial peoples. Nkrumah became hailed as the 'redeemer', or Osagyefu in the local Akan language.

The Quest to Build a Pan-African Federation

Achieving national independence did not distract Nkrumah from his larger goal of building an African federation. In his augural speech he said: 'our independence is meaningless... unless it is linked up with the total liberation of the African continent'. Just over 12 months later, in April 1958, he hosted the first Conference of Independent African States, bringing together Ethiopia, Liberia, Egypt, Tunisia, Libya, Morocco, Sudan and Ghana, to discuss steps towards coming together to collaborate and form a federation. And later that year he organised the All Peoples' African Congress, a wider event bringing together even more leaders and politicians from across Africa.

Not content with just talking, he also started to practically build a federation. In October 1958 Guinea became the next West African state to gain independence. And just a few weeks later, in November, Nkrumah and Ahmed Sekoe Toure, Guinea's first President, signed an agreement to form the Ghana-Guinea Federation, as the nucleus of a future African federation. In 1960 newly independent Mali joined too, and they changed the name to the Union of African States.

As more and more African states gained their independence in the early 1960s, discussions about African unity continued across the continent. There were several different positions: the Casablanca bloc, consisting of Ghana, Egypt, Algeria and Libya, wanted a full pan-African federation, with a federal continental layer of government, common foreign policy, a free-trade area, customs integration, and coordinated development planning; while the Brazzaville bloc, consisting of Ethiopia, Senegal, Liberia and Nigeria, wanted a much looser confederation, an Organisation of African Unity with a charter and a secretariat, but no political union.

In 1963 a Summit Conference was held to decide on the way forward. To Nkrumah's great disappointment the confederal approach was chosen, and the loose grouping of the Organisation of African Unity was formed. Despite this setback Nkrumah never gave up on his idea of an African federation, and continued to put efforts into increasing African collaboration with the hope that a full federation would be possible in the future.[6]

Trying to Reform the United Nations towards a World Federation

While Nkrumah was putting his efforts into building up both Ghana and the potential African federation, his government was also looking at how to change the broader international order in the direction of a world federation and it was the Finance Minister, Gbedemah, who took on the responsibility for this area. Like Nkrumah, he believed that the first priority was ending colonialism and gaining independence for all peoples, and that then it was crucial to re-fashion the world order into a world federation with a democratically elected federal world government.

Already in April 1951, just two months after taking office in the new colonial Gold Coast quasi-government, Gbedemah had travelled to Rome where he attended the 4th Congress of the World Movement for Federal World Government. The discussions there had been exciting: how to bring about de-colonisation, the need to establish a World Development Authority to help the former colonies once they gained independence, the proposal to create a World Alimentation Office (the World Food Program had yet to be formed), and ideas about drafting a World Constitution for the future world federation.

Gbedemah had been pleased to find a group of people that shared many of his ideas, and he had continued to attend the Congresses in the following years. He had also become involved in the World Association of Parliamentarians for World Government, where he met with parliamentarians from other countries to discuss steps toward the formation of a federal world government.

In October 1957, six months after Ghana gained independence, Gbedemah, now the Finance Minister of the first African state to gain independence from a colonial power, travelled to The Hague to attend the 10th Congress of the World Movement for Federal World Government, which had now changed its name to be the World Association of World Federalists.

Congress participants were excited about Ghana's independence and there was much discussion about how to speed up the process of other colonies gaining their independence too. Many believed that the creation of a third bloc of states, not aligned with either the US or with Russia, and which had much to benefit from the creation of a democratic world federation, would be a powerful force to drive change in the UN. Even though the date of the planned Charter Revision conference had been postponed, there was still hope that it would happen in the next year or two, and the World Federalists were busy discussing options and preparing proposals.

At this Congress Gbedemah was elected as President of the World Association of World Federalists, and he served in that role for the next four years until 1961. In his acceptance speech he emphasised the importance of the anti-colonial struggle and the liberation and freedom of the remining people on the African continent. He also called for the World Association of Parliamentarians for World Government and the World Association of World Federalists to work more closely together to increase their influence and impact. And in particular, he emphasised the importance of working together to revise the UN Charter and to form of a global police force.[7]

In the 1960s, as the Cold War deepened and the possibility of UN Charter revision faded into the background, Gbedemah worked with Nkrumah and others to try reform the UN in other ways. Their initial focus was on increasing representation from African and Asian countries in the UN Security Council, and also in ECOSOC, the Economic and Social Council. Ghana's representative at the UN, Alex Quaison-Sackey, argued that each region of the world – the Americas, Europe, Africa, Asia and the Middle East – should have a permanent seat in the Security Council.[8]

After several years of rather fierce discussion and debate, in December 1963 the UN General Assembly agreed to increase the number of non-permanent members of the Security Council from 11 to 15, and members of the Economic and Social Council from 18 to 27, in order to enable the better representation of the newly forming African and Asian states. This was a significant achievement and set things up for African and Asian countries to be able to have an important impact on UN discussions throughout the 1960s and 70s. The following year Quaison-Sackey was elected as President of the General Assembly, becoming the first black African to hold this position.

Ghana also pushed for the reform of other international organisations, again with the aim of increasing representation from what were now called 'developing countries'. Gbedemah in particular pushed for the representation of Africans in the International Monetary Fund (IMF). While he did not manage to secure increased voting rights, his efforts did eventually lead to the formation of a special Africa Department at the IMF, which was administered by Africans. But all of this, while positive steps, fell far short of achieving a world federation.

During the 1960s Nkrumah and his colleagues were being watched closely by the US intelligence authorities. They believed that Nkrumah was doing more to undermine American interests than any other black African. This may have been true. It may also have been the case that he was doing more than any other black African to advance African interests. Had a true African federation been created, and indeed a true world federation, the history of Africa and its development may have looked completely different.

Despite these innovative struggles to reformulate pan-African and international politics, Nkrumah's actions in the sphere of national politics were less positive. His attempts to unite the different ethnic and religious groups in Ghana and to bring about industrialisation and economic development led him to implement a form of 'developmentalist authoritarianism' with a strong, centralised, government. In the context of an extremely violent approach by the main opposition party, which included two assassination attempts on him in 1962 and 1964,[9] and external intervention by Western powers which sought to undermine him[10], Nkrumah turned increasingly to authoritarianism, instigating single-party rule, jailing opposition leaders and undermining the independence of the judiciary.[11] In 1966, when Nkrumah was on a state visit to China, his government was overthrown in a violent coup that many believe had the tacit, or perhaps not so tacit, support of the US. Nkrumah never returned to Ghana, and instead lived his final years in exile in Guinea, before dying in 1972.

Inspiration and Legacy

Nkrumah's visions of an African federation and a world federation were inspired by a desire to create a world order in which all peoples could enjoy self-determination and would not be dominated by others. He understood that in an 'international system,' rich and powerful states would be able to continue to dominate smaller and weaker ones, and that former imperial powers would be able to retain significant control over their former colonies, in a system which he described at length and which he called 'neo-colonialism'.[12]

Much in his thought and in his writings about international political economy has turned out to be true, and neo-colonialism is an apt and widely used term to describe the current state of affairs, in which the so-called 'developing countries' or 'global South' remain until to-day dominated by, and dependent on, the richer countries, or the 'global North'. Nkrumah's remedy for this unequal world system was federation – a regional federation of Africa, and a world federation. His analysis and his ideas are still important and relevant today.

Notes

1 See Getachew, Adom. 2019. *Worldmaking After Empire: The Rise and Fall of Self-Determination*. Princeton: Princeton University Press.

2 For more on Padmore's ideas see, James, Leslie. 2015. George Padmore and Decolonization from Below: Pan-Africanism, the Cold War, and the End of Empire. New York: Palgrave Macmillan; Williams, Theo. 2019. George Padmore and the Soviet Model of the British Commonwealth. *Modern Intellectual History*, 16,2: 531-559.

3 Getachew, op. cit.

4 Sherwood, Marika. 1996. There is No New Deal for the Blackman in San Francisco: African Attempts to Influence the Founding Conference of the United Nations, April – July 1945. *The International Journal of African Historical Studies*, 29, 1: 71-94.

5 Padmore, George. (ed). 1947. History of the Pan-African Congress: Colonial and Coloured Unity; A Program of Action. London: Hammersmith Bookshop, p5.

6 Biney, Ama Barbara. 2007. *Kwame Nkrumah: An Intellectual Biography*. PhD dissertation, SOAS, University of London, p250-259.

7 Haegler, Rolf Paul. 1972. *Histoire et Idéologie du Mondialisme*, Zurich: Europa Verlag. See also *The World Federalist*, November 1957, vol. IV, n° 7.

8 Getachew, op. cit., pp99-100.

9 Biney, Ama. 2008. The Legacy of Kwame Nkrumah in Retrospect. *Journal of Pan African Studies*, 2, 3: 129-159.

10 Mwakikagile, Godfrey. 2015.*Western Involvement in Nkrumah's Downfall*. Dar es Salaam: New Africa Press.

11 See also Drah, F. 1992. Nkrumah and Constitutional Democracy: 1949-1966 Revisited. *Research Review*, 8,1; 1-27; Lundt, Bea and Christopher Marx. (eds.). 2016. *Kwame Nkrumah, 1909-1972: A Controversial Visionary*. Stuttgart: Franz Steiner Verlag.

12 Nkrumah, Kwame. 1965. *Neo-Colonialism: The Last Stage of Imperialism*. London: Thomas Nelson & Sons. See also www.marxists.org/subject/africa/nkrumah/neo-colonialism/index.htm

17. Hideki Yukawa: World Peace through World Federation

This chapter looks at the life and thought of Hideki Yukawa – world leading physicist, Japan's first Nobel Prize winner, and a major supporter of world federalism. Yukawa, like Einstein, thought that the world needed to be organised into one federation in order to bring an end to war in general, and to the threat of nuclear war in particular. And as a citizen of Japan, the country that suffered the devastating destruction of the American atomic bombs in Hiroshima and Nagasaki, his voice had a particular weight and importance in the post-world war peace movements for nuclear disarmament and world federation.[1]

Hideki Yukawa, 1949

Early Life

Yukawa was born in Tokyo in 1907 to a family of scholars. He was the fifth of seven children, most of whom also went on to become scholars. His father was a geologist, studying the nature of the Earth, and soon after Yukawa's birth he took up a position as Professor of Geography at Kyoto Imperial University and the family moved to Kyoto.

His grandparents also lived in the household and had a great influence on Yukawa as he grew up, immersing him in traditional Japanese and Chinese thinking. His mother's father had been a samurai warrior at the Wakayama castle until the Meiji regime abolished the samurai class, and he had a great knowledge of both Chinese and Western thought. His father's father was a retired Confucian scholar and teacher of Chinese classics. Thus the young and super-talented Yukawa learnt to read *kanji*, the Chinese characters, and indeed to read the Chinese classics, even before he entered school. He found the Taoist works of Lao-tse and Chuang-tse particularly interesting, as they focussed on man's relation with the world of nature, and his one-ness with it. Their holistic style of thinking and use of parable and metaphor also enchanted the young Yukawa and deeply influenced his later thinking and approach to both physics and world affairs.

Yukawa was a quiet and bookish child. He found it hard to express himself and was often silent and withdrawn. He was not very sociable and while at High School he took little notice of the normal run of student life around him. He took little interest in student politics or in the momentous social changes that were taking place in Japan at the time, as the country industrialised, workers moved from the countryside to new urban factories, and agitation for both labour rights and democracy started. Instead, Yukawa immersed himself in the world of books and ideas about the fundamental nature of the material world. He even taught himself German, the leading language of science at the time, so that he could read the most updated and advanced theories of physics that were available. He found a copy of Max Planck's *Introduction to Theoretical Physics* in a local bookshop and poured over it for hours, finding it fascinating and inspiring.

In 1926, at the age of 19, he went to Kyoto University to study a degree in Physics, graduating in 1929. Then in 1932 he took up a po-sition as lecturer at the same university and married his wife, Sumi. Even as the political situation in Japan started to change in the 1930s, with the rise of ultra-nationalism, militarism and imperialist moves into Manchuria, Yukawa stayed in his ivory tower and focussed all his attention on the world of particle physics.

Scientific Breakthrough and the Discovery of the Meson

In 1933 he moved to Osaka and joined the modern new university that was being built up there. It was a stimulating place with a strong Physics department, and Yukawa began to focus on the question of how protons and neutrons were actually bound together in the nucl-eus of atoms. In 1932 the leading German physicist, Werner Heisen-berg, had proposed that this binding force was created through the exchange of electrons between the protons and neutrons, But there were many problems with this theory and Yukawa was convinced that there was an alternative explanation.

Yukawa reasoned that a very strong force was required to keep neutrons and protons from flying apart due to electromagnetic repulsion and this force was far stronger than the force that could be supplied by the exchange of electrons. One night he woke up with an insight – there must be a relationship between the intensity of that force and the mass of the binding particle. And thus, drawing on his distinct ability to think outside the box, he suggested the existence of a new sub-atomic particle with a mass some two hundred times that of an electron. He called this particle the meson.

In 1935, at the age of 28, he published his first major academic paper, in which he proposed a new field theory of nuclear forces and predicted the existence of the meson. This paper would eventually go on to earn him the Nobel Prize for Physics and win him fame in the national and international scientific worlds, but at this point in time it was simply ignored. For two years it had absolutely no impact at all. Nicolas Kemmer, one of the first Western physicists to work on meson theory, later wrote, 'Yukawa in 1935 was ahead of his time and found the key to the problem of nuclear forces when no other theoretical physicist in the world was ready to accept it.'

Yukawa was not deterred, because he was completely convinced that his ideas were correct and he believed that what was true must sooner or later be understood and accepted. Then, in 1937, American physicists Carl Anderson and Seth Neddermeyer, who were studying cosmic rays in cloud chamber experiments, found particles that appeared to fit Yukawa's requirements and had the mass he predicted. Suddenly his theory began to receive a lot of attention, but it was still highly debated and controversial because the other properties of the newly discovered particle did not quite match up with Yukawa's predictions.

In 1938 he received his PhD from Osaka University and in 1939, at the age of 32, he took up a position as Professor at Kyoto Imperial University. His reputation was beginning to grow now, and that same year he was invited to attend the Solvay Conference in Brussels, a highly prestigious meeting of a small number of world-leading physicists. This was Yukawa's first trip outside of Japan and he was excited to meet and network with foreign scientists. However, the conference was disrupted by the outbreak of World War Two, and all the Japanese people who were in Central Europe at the time were evacuated to the United States. And so, unexpectedly, Yukawa suddenly found himself in New York. He made good use of the opportunity and spent a month visiting nine universities and meeting many eminent physicists, before returning to Japan.

World War Two and the Atomic Bomb

On 7th December 1941, the Japanese bombed Pearl Harbour in the United States and officially entered the war, allied with Nazi Germany and Fascist Italy. Yukawa, like most Japanese nuclear physicists, continued on with his research work, and also did not refuse to engage in wartime military research for the government. There was a strong team of Japanese theoretical physicists involved in nuclear research and they were well aware of the significance of the discovery of nuclear fission in Germany in 1938. Several of these scientists were asked to look into the possibility of the development of an atomic bomb by the Japanese government. Yukawa himself was involved in a nuclear bomb project organised by the Japanese navy. These scientists tentatively concluded that it was not possible to make a nuclear bomb at the time.

However, in 1945 they were proved wrong. Even as Germany and Italy had surrendered and the leaders of many countries had met in San Francisco to draft the United Nations Charter, and then sign it in June, Japan continued to fight. On 6th August, airplanes of the US army dropped an atomic bomb on the Japanese city of Hiroshima, immediately killing around 80,000 people and causing tens of thousands more to die later of radiation exposure. Three days later, on 9th August, they dropped a second atomic bomb on the city of Nagasaki, killing another 40,000 people. A few days later Japan's Emperor Hirohito announced his country's unconditional surrender.

The Japanese Constitution's Article 9 and the Peace Movement

After the war Japan was occupied by US forces until 1952. During this period a new constitution was written, which included the famous Article 9, which states that:

'Aspiring sincerely to an international peace based on justice and order, the Japanese people forever renounce war as a sovereign right of the nation and the threat or use of force as a means of settling international disputes.'[2]

This path-breaking article received widespread support from the Japanese public, who were by now war-weary and keen to rally around peace and pacifism. It also seemed important and sensible to many nuclear scientists, including Yukawa, who were still reeling from the shock and surprise of the US-created atomic bomb. And as we shall see, it came to play an important part in Yukawa's thinking about the route to world federation.[3]

The post-war years were a time of great reflection and debate in Japan, as intellectuals, scientists and the broader public pondered on the effects of ultra-nationalism, militarism and the devastation caused by the war. The huge suffering and destruction caused by the atomic bombing of Hiroshima and Nagasaki was initially censored by the occupying US forces, but as the terrible and terrifying news became apparent a strong movement not just for peace, but specifically for nuclear disarmament, began to develop. A wide and popular peace movement began to develop, initially springing out of the labour movement, but quickly spreading more generally across the society.[4] A central slogan was 'No more Hiroshimas'.

In these early days, the peace movement was heavily tinged with remorse over the war and the misuse of science, as well as a sense of human conscience and an uncontrollable fury against atomic bombs. Scholars and scientists, particularly nuclear scientists, took a leading role in these discussions. They were still shocked that the results of their research had been used to cause such devastation and suffering, and they felt a new social responsibility to lead the way towards peace. In 1948 over fifty leading Japanese scholars met to discuss the conditions of peace, and in December they issued 'A statement by scientists in Japan on the problem of peace'. They wrote:

'War is originally a method, a most primitive method, resorted to by man in an attempt to solve certain problems.... Today both winners and losers alike ... suffer from almost incurable wounds from war. Furthermore, inasmuch as any future war is bound to be atomic and/or biolog-

ical, humanity faces the danger of extermination once it breaks out...
Therefore, it devolves as an urgent responsibility upon present-day scientists ... that they make vividly clear the tragic consequences of any
future war and carry on the task of enlightening the people and statesmen of every nation upon this matter'. [5]

Following this they created a permanent study group of scientists,
known as The Peace Study Group, to continue discussing these issues.

World Federation for World Peace

Yukawa mainly kept quiet at this time and was not involved in most
of these early initiatives. The one major exception was his support of
the movement for world federation as a route to peace, which was also
coalescing in Japan at this time, as in many other countries around
the world. While there had been earlier discussions about world federation in Japan in the 1930s, particularly with Indian colleagues such
as Mahatma Gandhi and Raja Mahendra Pratap, it is perhaps not surprising that the world federalist movement grew quickly in Japan in
these post-war years. As the first and only target of the new and powerful nuclear weapons, it was in many respects a natural place from
which new and creative proposals for a political re-ordering of the
world that would prevent a final apocalyptic clash between nations
should arise. Many leading Japanese intellectuals at this time supported world federation, including Economics Professor, Masamichi
Rōyama, Sociology Professor Sugimori Kōjirō, and future Supreme
Court judge Yokota Kisaburō.

In the early post-war years a number of world federalist organisations were formed in Japan, including the Association for World
Peace, formed in 1946 by Christian evangelist, labour activist and
social reformer Kagawa Toyohiko, who had been calling for world
peace through world cooperatives since the 1930s, and The Institute
for Permanent Peace, formed in early 1948 by Morikatsu Inagaki, a
leading publisher, friend of Einstein, and translator of Emery Reves'
book about world federalism, *The Anatomy of Peace,* into Japanese.

Perhaps the leading voice for world federalism was that of Yukio
Ozaki, a long serving parliamentarian, former mayor of Tokyo, and
champion of democracy, civil rights and liberty. During the 1930s
he had been a vocal and consistent supporter of parliamentary gov-

ernment and a staunch critic of the autocratic politics of the imperial regime. He had pressed for universal suffrage, for both men and for women, and for liberal freedoms. In the post-war years he worked to promote world federalism, both inside the Diet, the Japanese parliament, and outside in wider society. Already in December 1945 he moved a resolution in the Japanese Parliament, backed by some thirty supporters, proposing the establishment of a world federation in order to keep the peace. And in the following years he published prolifically in a variety of journals calling for world federation.[6]

For Ozaki, world federation was the natural product of an evolution in humankind's capacity to identify and show compassion for an ever-growing community, beginning with the self, then the family, and then expanding to one's village, the nation, and finally the whole world. He looked at Japanese history and recalled the transformation that took place at the beginning of the Meiji period, starting around 1868, when the separate 'han' domains ruled by local lords had united to form the modern state of Japan. For him, uniting the currently separate countries of the world into a world federation was the obvious next step along this path, and the next step of human progress. In many respects, these views drew on ideas in Confucian philosophy, which called on people to climb further up the hierarchy of relationships into a greater and greater whole.

In 1948 several of the nascent world federalist organisations in Japan came together to form the Union for World Federal Government. Ozaki became its first President, and Tagawa became its Vice-President. Along with Morikatsu and several others, Yukawa was also a founding member. Soon afterwards the organisation became a member of the World Movement for World Federal Government, the international umbrella movement that had been formed in Montreux, Switzerland in 1947, and which would later change its name to the World Association for World Federation, and then again to the World Federalist Movement.

In 1949 the world federalists established a multi-party body in the Japanese parliament, or Diet, called the Diet Members' Committee for World Federation, with around one hundred parliamentarians from across the political spectrum.

The movement grew quickly and by 1950 the Union for World Federal Government had over 4,000 members, organised in fifty chapters, and a lively monthly journal called *The World State*. That same year they held a public meeting in Tokyo and some 5,000 people attended. The crowds were so large that the police had to turn people away.

Like many in the wider peace movement, the world federalists sought to use Hiroshima as a symbol for future world peace. In 1950 a group of young people began a protest fast in front of Hiroshima train station, with the slogan: 'The way to realise 'No more Hiroshimas' is to build a world federation!'

In 1952 the Union for World Federal Government organised the first Asian Congress on World Federation and held it in Hiroshima. This Congress was attended by Redhabinod Pal, Justice of the Supreme Court of India; Abdul Rehman, later the Prime Minister of Malaya, and other leaders of several Asian countries. John Boyd-Orr, former Director-General of the UN's Food and Agriculture Organisation and then President of the World Movement for World Federal Government, also attended. The Congress issued the Hiroshima Declaration, a particularly Asian and post-Hiroshima take on world federalism, with an emphasis on nuclear disarmament, ending racial discrimination and building understanding between the world's different religions:

'The Asian Congress for World Federation in the atom-bombed Hiroshima, recognising the historic significance of this Congress, vowing solemnly to work for the abolition of war and in order to strengthen the spirit of brotherhood among men which is basic to world federation, unanimously declares to the entire world its determination to strive for:

1) Prohibition of the production as well as the use of atomic weapons;
2) Drastic reduction of existing armaments leading to their total abolition in each nation;
3) Elimination of racial discrimination and establishment of fundamental human rights;
4) Removal of religious prejudice and promotion of cooperation among all faiths of the world;
5) Release in the immediate future of war criminals as well as prisoners of war detained in various countries;
6) Opening up of natural resources for the solution of population problems.

For implementation of the principles enunciated above and the matters agreed upon, we hereby resolve, basing our efforts on Mahatma Gandhi's Sutya Graha (Power of Truth), to promote with all our strength the movement for the establishment of world federation.'[7]

Yukawa Awarded the Nobel Prize for Physics

Whilst Yukawa had been present in 1948 as a founding member of the Union for World Federal Government, he was only marginally involved in these subsequent activities in the next few years. This was because he spent the years 1948 to 1953 in America.

From 1948 to 1949 he was a Visiting Professor at Princeton University's Institute of Advanced Study. It was here that he met Albert Einstein, and developed a friendship that would last until Einstein's death in 1955. Both men were nuclear physicists who felt a sense of responsibility after the detonation of the atomic bomb, and both had come to the conclusion that nuclear disarmament and world federation were necessary to maintain world peace and stop humankind from obliterating itself. While Einstein had encouraged the Americans to develop an atomic bomb so that they would have one before the Nazis, he was filled with remorse at its use in Japan. When he first met Yukawa, he took his hand, apologised and cried.

In 1947 a group of experimental scientists finally found the meson, the particle that Yukawa had predicted in 1935. His theory was proved correct, and in 1949 he was awarded the Nobel Prize in Physics. He was the first Japanese to receive a Nobel Prize, and he immediately became a national hero, well-known across all of Japan.

He stayed in America a few more years, as a Professor at the University of Columbia, and only returned to Japan in 1953, after the American occupation had come to an end. To honour him the Japanese government established the Research Institute for Fundamental Physics at Kyoto University, and invited him to be its first Director. He stayed there until his retirement in 1970, continuing his research into theoretical physics and making several further advances.

The Lucky Dragon Incident

On his return to Japan he initially continued to stay silent regarding the atomic bomb and was little involved in the ongoing discussions and debates about peace and disarmament. But this was soon to change. In 1949 the Soviet Union had succeeded in developing their own atomic bomb and since then a nuclear arms race had developed between the USA and the USSR, with each country developing and testing bigger and more powerful nuclear bombs. In 1954 the US carried out a test explosion of a hydrogen bomb on the Bikini Atol of the Marshall Islands. The estimated yield of 15 megatons was much larger than predicted, and consequently 23 Japanese fishermen on the Lucky Dragon tuna-fishing boat were exposed to radioactive fallout, and became ill from radioactive poisoning. One of them, Aikichi Kuboyama, died some months later.

The Japanese public were enraged. It was simply intolerable that their countrymen should fall victim to the dangers of nuclear weapons again. Many were also panicked about the radiation that was detected in the contaminated tuna fish and in radioactive rainfall in some parts of Japan. They began to feel that their daily lives were directly threatened by nuclear weapons. And thus numerous groups, including labour unions, women's groups, religious groups, pacifist groups, academic societies, and many local assemblies of cities and prefectures, started to call for a ban on the use, production, and testing of nuclear weapons.

The Lucky Dragon event, and the suffering it caused, also deeply shocked Yukawa. It was the tipping point that started him to break his silence about the atomic bomb and to speak publicly about disarmament, peace, and the social responsibility of scientists.

A few weeks later he published a piece in a leading newspaper, Mainichi Shimbun, called 'Atomic Energy and the Turning Point for Mankind', in which he argued that humanity needed to come together in order to protect itself from the potential destruction of nuclear weapons and that scientists had a particular responsibility to be involved in these efforts.[8]

Later that year, he and Saburo Yamada, President of Japan's Academy of Arts and Sciences, established the Japan Council Against Atomic and Hydrogen Bombs, and they coordinated with many Japanese anti-nuclear groups to organise the first World Conference Against Atomic and Hydrogen Bombs held in Hiroshima in 1955. Also in 1955 Yukawa became one of the founding members of the Committee

of Seven for World Peace. This was, and still is, a group of seven influential Japanese public figures that were brought together by Yasa-
buro Shimonaka, a leading publisher and then Director of the Union
for World Federal Government. The group started to publish appeals
calling for the abolition of nuclear weapons and the peaceful resolution of international conflicts based on the humanism and pacifism
contained in Article 9 of the Japanese Constitution.

The impact of the radioactive poisoning of the Lucky Dragon crew
stretched far beyond Japan and reverberated around the world. It led
to the formation of many anti-nuclear groups and campaigns, including the international Campaign for Nuclear Disarmament, the
CND.

The Russell-Einstein Manifesto and the Pugwash Conferences

In 1955 the renowned British philosopher Bertrand Russell wrote to
Albert Einstein, suggesting that scientists should take a leading role
in campaigning for the elimination of nuclear weapons. He proposed
that a group of eminent scientists should issue a Manifesto on the
matter and then set up regular conferences in order to get into the
details about how this should be achieved. Einstein of course agreed
and some months later they issued the Russell-Einstein Manifesto.
Yukawa was one of the eleven scientists, almost all Nobel Laureates,
who signed the manifesto.[9]

This Manifesto led to the establishment of a series of high-level
conferences on Sciences and World Affairs, in which a small group of
elite scientists would meet to discuss what humanity should do about
nuclear weapons. The first conference was held in the town of Pugwash, in Canada, and the conferences have since then been known as
the Pugwash conferences.

Yukawa was one of the twenty two scientists that attended the first
conference in 1957. Shimonaka, his wealthy world federalist colleague, covered his travel costs and together they drafted an appeal
from the Committee of Seven calling for a ban on nuclear testing. But
in Pugwash the scientists had a wide array of opinions on how to deal
with nuclear weapons, with many Americans arguing that each side
in the Cold War should maintain their weapons as a deterrent. While
Yukawa, and several of his Japanese colleagues, argued strongly ag-

ainst the policy of nuclear deterrence, this eventually became the dominant view of the Pugwash scientists.

For Yukawa, the notion that peace could be brought about by two enemies arming themselves to the teeth seemed just ridiculous. In contrast to the more supposedly 'pragmatic' scientists, Yukawa was a man of vision. For him world peace was not just about the balance of power, but about creating the right kind of world structure which would make war impossible. This, he believed, was a world federation, in which each country would give up some of its sovereignty to a higher body, disarm itself, and renounce its right to wage war. And he strove to promote this idea among both Japanese scientists and among the broader population.

A Vision of World Federation Built on Article 9

In 1962 Yukawa and two of his colleagues initiated a similar series of conferences for Japanese scientists in Japan, which informally became known as the Japanese Pugwash. The final statement of the 1962 conference argued against the principle of nuclear deterrence and instead emphasized the significance of the Japanese constitution's Article 9, which stipulates the renunciation of war. It said,

'As the country which has experienced the disastrous effects of nuclear weapons, and which has openly renounced war in its constitution, Japan is in a position to make a special contribution to world peace [...]

Today, when the danger of the destruction of the human race by nuclear warfare is growing ever more serious, Article 9 of the Japanese Constitution has a new significance, even greater than when the Constitution was first adopted.'

The statement also criticized traditional thinking and practices of international politics based on the concept of national sovereignty. Instead, it claimed,

'Confronted as we are by many pressing problems, our thinking must advance to a new dimension, transcending the current habit of looking upon national sovereignty as the highest of all values.'[10]

Yukawa brought his particular views about world federalism and world peace also to the World Movement for World Federal Government, which by now had changed its name to the World Association for World Federation. In 1961 he was elected as President of the Association and held this role until 1965, with Senegalese President, Leopold Senghor[11], as his Vice-President. In 1963 he presided over the 11th Congress of the World Association for World Federation, which was held in Tokyo and was a huge Congress, with around 1,800 delegates from Japan, along with well over a hundred delegates from some twenty other countries.

In his Presidential speech, Yukawa again set forth his idea that the best way to realise a world federation would be for each country to renounce its right to wage war. Japan had already done this, in its Article 9, and he suggested that it was eminently possible for other countries to follow suit. This, accompanied by a massive global reduction in armaments, could pave the way for the United Nations to transform into a true world federation.

Yukawa retired in 1970, but he continued his involvement with the world federalist movement and his writing and speaking about peace, nuclear disarmament and world federation through the renunciation of war. In 1980, just months before his death, he gave a powerful speech at the 30th Pugwash Conference. In it, he asked why, after all these years, there was still an arms race? What had gone wrong? His eloquent answer is worth quoting:

'One of the fundamental causes of the present awful situation of the arms race, I think, is that we have rejected as unrealistic the original idea of Bertrand Russell that nuclear weapons are an absolute evil and must be eliminated....

Another fatal cause may be that we have been so indolent, if not rather timid, in pursuit of a new world order where one can live without armaments... Designing such a new world order is indeed a difficult task because it will be associated with some change of the present political status...

A future scenario is not explicitly depicted in the Manifesto. Insofar as I know however, Russell and Einstein were considering this problem. In fact in order to control the sovereignty of states both were thinking of a world federation, an idea with which I am also sympathetic...'[12]

Yukawa died in September 1981 in Kyoto. His wife, Sumi, long his ally and supporter in the cause of world federalism, continued his activities in the peace movement and in the World Federalist Movement for many years more.

Inspiration and Legacy

There is much that we can learn from Yukawa's approach to world federalism. For him, world federation was necessary to bring about an end to war, and particularly to the potential total destruction of a nuclear war, a shadow which still hangs over our heads today.

Yukawa was not interested in ideological issues and ideological divides, he was perhaps somewhat unaware of important social and economic issues, and he spoke little about colonialism, equality or justice. But he was motivated by a deep love of humanity and a desire for humanity to continue, and to not blow itself up in a huge explosion derived from the results of his scientific research.

He drew on both Eastern and Western forms of thought, combining scientific rationalism with the more holistic and intuitive approaches of Taoism. He saw the world as a whole and believed that the most sensible, balanced and peaceful way to organise it was as a world federation. For many people, across all cultures and political flavours, his vision can remain an inspiration.

Notes

1 Kemmer, Nicholas. 1983. Hideki Yukawa, 23 January 1907 – 8 September 1981. *Biographical Memoirs of Fellows of the Royal Society*. royalsocietypublishing.org/doi/abs/10.1098/rsbm.1983.0023

2 japan.kantei.go.jp/constitution_and_government_of_japan/constitution_e.html

3 Schlichtmann, Klaus. 2021. Shidehara Kijuro and the Japanese Constitution's war-abolishing Article 9. *Japan Forum*, 1.1: 1-25; Schlichtmann, Klaus. 2009. *Japan in the World: Shidehara Kijuro, Pacifism, and the Abolition of War*. Lanham: Lexington Books.

4 Gibson, Ian. 2012. Japan's Peace Actors and their Socio-Political Origins. *Peace and Conflict Review*, 11,1: 1-21/ www.review.upeace.org/pdf.cfm?articulo=126

5 Cited in Toyoda, Toshiyuki. 1984. Scientists Look at Peace and Security. *Bulletin of the Atomic Scientists*, 40, 2: 15-31. (p17).

6 Lawson, Konrad. 2020. Reimagining the Post-War International Order: The World Federalism of Ozaki Yukio and Kagawa Toyohiko. In *The Institution of International Order*, edited by Simon Jackson and Alanna O'Malley. London: Routledge.

7 Sekai Renpo Kensetsu Domei. 1953. Sekai Renpo Ajia Kaigi Hiroshima Ketsugi. *Sekai Kokka* 7: 1: 50-51.

8 Cited in Toyoda, Toshiyuki. 1984. Scientists Look at Peace and Security. *Bulletin of the Atomic Scientists*, 40, 2: 15-31. (p17).

9 www.atomicheritage.org/key-documents/russell-einstein-manifesto

10 Kurosaki, Akira. 2018. Japanese Scientists' Critique of Nuclear Deterrence Theory and Its Influence on Pugwash, 1954–1964. *Journal of Cold War Studies*, 20,1: 101-139.

11 For more on Senghor's views about federation see Wilder, Gary. 2015. *Freedom Time: Negritude, Decolonization and the Future of the World*. Durham: Duke University Press.

12 Yukawa, Hideki. 1981. The Absolute Evil. *Bulletin of the Atomic Scientists*, 37, 1: 37. www.tandfonline.com/doi/abs/10.1080/00963402.1981.11458807?journalCode=rbul20

18. The History of the World Federalist Movement

This chapter looks at the history of the World Federalist Movement, or WFM. Today WFM is a network of dozens of organisations in many countries of the world, all working to promote the idea of global democracy and world federation. Understanding the evolution of this movement and its ideas, and the challenges that is has faced, can help us think about how best to drive it forward in the 21st century, when our world is in need of political unification more than ever. [1]

The 19th Century Peace Movements and the Quest for World Law

The idea of uniting the world into a world federation existed long before the creation of WFM. As far back as the mid-19th century, peace movements started to develop the idea that the best way to stop war was to create a legal structure, above states, though which they could solve their differences through non-violent means. Instead of going to war, they could go to court.

In 1840 William Ladd had written an essay called 'A Congress of Nations', in which he had suggested the formation of a Congress of Nations that would make world law, and the creation of a world court that would adjudicate it. This became the guiding aspiration of the peace movement and led to the creation, in 1899, of the Permanent Court of Arbitration in The Hague.

Many in the peace movement realised that if world law was going to become a reality, then it would require a world parliament to make this law and a world government to enforce it. And thus, in the early part of the 20th century many of these peace movements started to also call for world government and world federation. [2] However, peace was not to be, and the First World War broke out. Afterwards, states formed the League of Nations and the International Court of Justice, hoping that this would be sufficient to keep the peace.

Many in the peace movement were convinced that this weak confederation of nations, with no ability to make world law and no real
enforcement power, would not keep the peace for long. And so,
throughout the 1920s and 1930s, a growing number of activists and
thinkers began to publish books calling for a world federation. There
was a wide variety in the proposals – many wanted to federate only
certain countries, and left out Germany or Russia or Japan; others
wanted to have different tiers of membership for different types of
country, and most of them assumed that colonies would remain colonies. Intellectuals from the colonies developed their own ideas of
world federation, in which they were included as equals with everyone else. There was a huge diversity of world federation models: some
thinkers proposed a liberal model, others proposed a socialist model.
These inter-war years were a time when many, many people were
thinking how best to organise the world.

The First World Federalist Organisations

In the late 1930s, as the winds of war were beginning to rumble again
in Europe, a number of organisations dedicated to promoting an inclusive world federation with a democratic federal world government began to form. One of the first, as we discuss in more detail in
chapter 12, was the Campaign for World Government, founded in
the US in 1937 by feminist peace activists Rosika Schwimmer and
Lola Maverick Lloyd. The following year Federal Union was formed
in the UK[3], and separate organisations with the same name were also
founded in the US and in New Zealand. World federalist groups were
also formed in several Scandinavian countries and in the late 1930s
they organised the first Inter-Nordic Meeting on World federation,
in Sweden.

As the Second World War started and progressed, more and
more organisations were formed calling for world federation. In
1940 the Mouvement Populaire Suisse en Faveur d'une Fédération
des Peuples was formed in Switzerland, and the World Federalist
were established in the US. In 1942, fifteen year-old Harris Wofford
set up the Student Federalists, again in the US. In 1946 Een Verden
(meaning 'One World') was formed in Denmark and several other
world federalist groups were set up in Canada, Ireland, France, Aus-

tralia, Southern Africa, India and Argentina. When the war came to an end there was a huge surge of interest in the idea of a world federation. The shock of the scale of death and destruction in the war, and the creation of the atomic bomb and its deadly use against Japan, made many people think that another world war simply could not take place. And thus, the question of how to organise the world so that countries could sort out their differences in a non-violent manner was very high on the agenda, both among politicians and among the ordinary public.

In 1945, shortly after the bombing of Hiroshima, the University of Chicago had set up the Committee to Frame a World Constitution, including leading professors from across the social sciences, including Robert Hutchins, Chancellor of the University, Wilber Katz, Dean of the Chicago Law School; Richard McKeon, Dean of Humanities, Giuseppe Antonio Borgese, Professor of Literature, Robert Redfield, Professor of Anthropology; Rexford Guy Tugwell, Professor of Political Science, and several others. They felt that it was imperative to act quickly to make sure that war could never happen again. They were very much against the newly-formed UN, which they saw as just another powerless league, like the League of Nations. They thought that it was impossible to reform the UN into a real federation because the basic structure was all wrong. Instead, they thought that a totally new form of world order was needed. And they thought that, between them, they had the intellectual strength and leadership to lead the way. And thus, they sat down and started work on drafting a World Constitution for a future federal world government.[4]

In 1946, a survey of candidates for the US Congress revealed that fifty three out of the sixty five who responded to the survey approved of changing the United Nations into a world federation with majority rule legislation. And in 1947, on the other side of the Atlantic, British Labour MP, Henry Usborne, set up the All-Party Parliamentary Group on World Government, which at its peak had around two hundred members from the House of Commons and the House of Lords. At this time there was a very real fear that a third world war might erupt at any moment, and many statesmen felt the need to create a higher power, above the states, that would settle disagreements between them by non-violent methods.

The Montreux Congress and the Formation of the WFM

In 1947 several world federation activists decided to hold a congress to try and bring together all the various world federation organisations so that they could work together in a concerted effort to bring about a world federation and a world government in the next few years. The British Federal Union took the lead in organising the conference, which they decided should take place in Montreux, Switzerland. They sent out invitations to the hundred or so world federalist organisations that they knew, mainly in Europe and America, inviting them to come to Montreux and join forces.

In August that year, 51 organisations, and many independent delegates, came together at the Montreux Congress. All in all, there were about 300 people from fourteen countries. Approximately half of them were students. Messages of support were sent from a variety of important people, including Britain's Foreign Minister, Ernest Bevin; Italian Foreign Minister Carlo Sforza, and of course, Albert Einstein.

This was the Congress that founded the World Movement for World Federal Government, that would later change its name to the World Association of World Federalists, and then again, to the World Federalist Movement, or WFM. It also founded a student movement, the World Student Federalists.

The discussions at the Montreux Congress were energetic and intense. The two key questions which dominated the discussions were what should the future world government look like? And how do we make it happen?

Broadly speaking, there were two major views about what the future world government should look like. Most of the American delegates favoured a 'minimalist' approach, in which the powers of the federal level of world government would be limited only to security issues so as to stop war; while most of the European delegates preferred a 'maximalist' approach, in which the federal level of government would also deal with socio-economic issues. Or in other words, the Americans mainly wanted to focus on security, while the Europeans also wanted to deal with justice.

There was also a divide in views regarding how best to get there. Most of the Americans favoured a gradual and incremental approach, focussed on reforming the UN. The UN was still very young then and there was a Charter Reform Conference that was expected to take place in 1955, and the Americans favoured drawing up proposals and lobbying politicians in order to achieve change which would lead the UN in the direction of becoming a world government.

Most of the Europeans, on the other hand, thought that the UN was fundamentally the wrong organisation, and that instead a new world government had to be created from scratch. Building on the ideas first put forward by Rosika Schwimmer and Lola Maverick Lloyd, they suggested holding a World Constitutional Convention to draft a World Constitution. They believed this this could be drafted, amended and ratified within a few years so that the new world government would be in place by 1955.

Another group believed that the best route to a world federation was through the formation of regional federations. They thus felt that it was important to devote energies to the fledgling unification process that was beginning to start in Europe and to push for the creation of a European Federation. They set up a third organisation, the Union of European Federalists.[5]

The speeches on each side were long and detailed, and when they got too theoretical the student delegates would urge them to a conclusion by chanting, 'action, action, we want action!' That was the energy of the meeting – a desire for action and a belief that world federation was a possible achievement in the next few years.

By the end of the Congress, it was agreed that the movement would pursue both strategies, UN Charter Reform and a World Constitutional Convention. Edith Wynner, who was now running the Campaign for World Government that had been set up by Rosika Schwimmer and Lola Maverick Lloyd, and young Harris Wofford of the Student Federalists, himself then a student at the University of Chicago, sat down with all the suggestions and resolutions raised by delegates and drafted the text of what would become the Montreux Declaration, the founding charter of the WFM. It is worth quoting it in full:

'We world federalists meeting in Montreux at the first international Congress of the "World Movement for World Federal Government", call upon the peoples of the world to join us in our work. We are convinced that mankind cannot survive another world conflict. Two years have passed since the fighting ended, but Europe and Asia are still strewn with the wreckage of war. The work of rehabilitation is paralysed; the peoples suffer from lack of shelter, food and clothing, while the nations waste their substance in preparing to destroy each other. The second attempt to preserve peace by means of a world organisation, the United Nations, is powerless, as at present constituted, to stop the drift of war.

We world federalists are convinced that the establishment of a world federal government is the crucial problem of our time. Until it is solved, all other issues, whether national or international, will remain unsettled. It is not between free enterprise and planned economy, nor between capitalism and communism that the choice lies, but between federalism and power politics. Federalism alone can assure the survival of man.

We world federalists affirm that mankind can free itself forever from war only through the establishment of a world federal government. Such a federation must be based on the following principles:

1) Universal membership: The world federal government must be open to all peoples and nations.

2) Limitation of national sovereignty, and the transfer to the world federal government of such legislative, executive and judicial powers as relate to the world affairs.

3) Enforcement of world law directly on the individual whoever or wherever he may be, within the jurisdiction of the world federal government: guarantee of the rights of man and suppression of all attempts against the security of the federation.

4) Creation of supranational armed forces capable of guaranteeing the security of the world federal government and of its member states. Disarmament of member nations to the level of their internal policing requirements

5) Ownership and control by the world federal government of atomic development and of other scientific discoveries capable of mass destruction.

6) Power to raise adequate revenues directly and independently of state taxes.

We propose to make use of any reasonable methods which can contribute to the early achievement of world federal government to prevent another world war.

We consider that integration of activities at regional and functional levels is consistent with the true federal approach. The formation of regional federations – insofar as they do not become an end in themselves or run the risk of crystallising into blocs – can and should contribute to the effective functioning of federal government. In the same way, the solution of technical, scientific and cultural problems which concern all the peoples of the world, will be made easier by the establishment of specialist functional bodies.

Taking into account these principles, we recommend the following lines of action:

1) The mobilisation of the peoples of the world to bring pressure on their governments and legislative assemblies to transform the United Nations Organisation into world federal government by increasing its authority and resources, and by amending its Charter.

2) Unofficial and concerted action: in particular the preparation of a world constituent assembly, the plan of campaign for which shall be laid down by the Council of the Movement in close cooperation with the parliamentary groups and federalist movements in the different countries. This assembly, set up in collaboration with organised international groups, shall meet not later than 1950 for the purpose of drawing up a constitution for the world federal government. This plan shall be submitted for ratification, not only by the governments and parliaments, but also to the peoples themselves, and every possible effort shall be made to get the world federal government finally established in the shortest possible time.

Without prejudging the results of these two methods of approach, we must expand our action as quickly as possible, so that we may take advantage of any new opportunities which present themselves to the federalist cause. One thing is certain we shall never realise world federal government unless all the peoples of the world join in the crusade.

More than ever time presses. And this time we must not fail.'[6]

A People's Convention to Draft a World Constitution.

In the following years many world federalist activists rallied around the idea of a World People's Convention to draft a World Constitution. The UN just seemed like another version of the League of Nations, doomed to failure, and instead something else seemed both possible and necessary. British MP Henry Usborne led the way. In 1948 he set up the Crusade for World Government and turned his Westminster office into its unofficial headquarters. His parliamentary group met there once a week, and young people from the Student Movement for World Government often came by to volunteer and help out.[7]

Usborne drew up a detailed plan for the People's Convention, which he proposed to hold in Geneva in 1950. His plan included a methodology for how delegates would be elected from each country according to the population of that country, with one delegate per million people. Since the UK had a population of 38 million at the time, he proposed they would elect thirty eight delegates, and he made plans for an unofficial election to be held, modelled on the Peace Ballot of 1934, when activists had organised an unofficial vote to gauge if there was support for the UK to remain in the League of Nations as Hitler started to create waves in Europe. Usborne thought that if he could get a quarter of the British population to vote for world government then he would have sufficient popular support to make ratifying the World Constitution an issue in the next parliamentary elections.

He and his colleagues travelled around the country, explaining the vision and winning considerable support from peace societies, churches, industry groups, trade unions, and political parties. He also went on a tour of the US to try to build up support there. While the United World Federalists, the largest world federalist group in the US, favoured UN reform over the World People's Convention approach, other more radical groups supported him, including the Campaign for World Government, World Republic, the Chicago Committee, and several of the student groups. He organised a conference in Pennsylvania where participants discussed the pros and cons of his idea and tried to work out the method by which the US would elect delegates to the People's Convention.

One of the lead activists in America who supported a People's Convention was historian and classics professor, Stringfellow Barr. He suggested that it was important to include people from a wide range of countries in the Peoples Convention, not just people from western countries. In particular he thought that Nehru, how Prime Minister of independent India, should be involved.

Nehru had spoken publicly about his support for the idea of a world federation, which he called 'One World', and he had recently

met with American World Federalist, Edward Clark, and spoken en-
thusiastically about world federation on the University of Chicago ra-
dio. Barr thought that Nehru could lead a group of newly emerging
post-colonial countries to support world federation and send delegates to the People's Convention. Usborne, who had been born in
India and was well-aware of Nehru's views on world federation,
heartily agreed, and he wrote to Nehru about the People's Convention idea.

Nehru was cautiously supportive of the idea. He had read many of
the western proposals for world government and knew that some of
them did not include the people of the colonies. He saw that Usborne
and the World Movement for Federal World Government *did* include
everyone, and so he replied positively, although taking the opportunity to stress again the importance of including all people from all
countries in the future world federation and ensuring equality and
justice. Or, as he wrote in his letter to Usborne in 1948:

> 'I have little doubt that the great majority of our own people would wel-
> come the idea of international cooperation or some kind of a world gov-
> ernment. But it is important that they must not think of this as a rever-
> sion to European or any other domination'.[8]

In 1948 the World Movement held its second congress, this time
in Luxembourg.[9] Again, some 300 people attended, including several
heavy-weight figures, such as Lord William Beveridge, former Director of the London School of Economics and designer of Britain's new
welfare state, and Sir John Boyd Orr, the first Director-General of the
Food and Agriculture Authority. The Congress discussed the People's
Convention and set up an international steering committee to coor-
dinate the preparatory work.

Just a few months earlier, American peace activist Gary Davis,
had publicly renounced his American citizenship while in Paris and
declared himself a world citizen. As we discuss more in chapter 22,
he was drawing huge support across Europe with his message of
world peace through world government and world citizenship, and
starting a mass movement with thousands of people coming out on
rallies, and literally hundreds of thousands of people registering with
his World Citizens Registry. Davis also supported the idea of a People's

Convention and his voice amplified the calls for it far and wide, across Europe and beyond.

However, by late 1948, tensions were beginning to flare up again between the Soviet Union and the European countries, and people began to fear that a Third World War may be about to erupt. Discussions in political circles moved away from the idea of a world federation, at least in the immediate future, and instead turned to various kind of western alliances. British politicians debated the various options. Foreign Minister, Ernest Bevin, previously cautiously supportive of the idea of a world federation, now turned to the idea of a so-called 'Western Union', what would later become NATO. In opposition, Winston Churchill favoured unifying Europe, what would later become the European Union. Parliamentary support for Usborne's idea of world federation began to diminish.

Nonetheless Usborne and his colleagues continued preparing for the People's Congress. But by 1950 it was already too late. The Korean War had started and the world was splitting into communist and capitalist blocs. People began to rally around nationalist causes, and even popular support for the idea of world federation lost its fervour. While some 500 people from forty two countries attended the People's Convention in December 1950, and John Boyd-Orr and Albert Einstein sent messages of support, the Convention was not a success.

Usborne's system of electing delegates to the Convention never found its way into practice, with the one exception of the American state of Tennessee, which did indeed hold formal elections for delegates to the People's Convention and elected three representatives, who duly arrived in Geneva ready to vote on a World Constitution. Eyo Ita, a professor and politician from colonial Nigeria, also turned up and declared that he had been elected by the various tribes and people of his region[10]. However, these were the only elected delegates.

The elected delegates looked over the draft World Constitution prepared by the Chicago Committee, and also another draft constitution that had been prepared by advocate Sanjib Chaudhuri of Calcutta, India, who presented his text at the Convention. But there was little that they could really do. And so instead, the six-day convention turned into a general talking shop about how a real People's Convention could be organised, what should be in a future World Constitution, and so on.

The world had now changed and the plausibility of states ratifying a World Constitution in the coming years now seemed remote. While some groups decided to keep on with the People's Convention plan nevertheless, including the Campaign for World Government and then the World Constitution and Parliament Association, most people now turned away from the idea. Usborne himself decided to change tactics, and the following year he set up the World Association of Parliamentarians for World Government, to bring together parliamentarians from many different countries to discuss how to reform the UN in the direction of world government.[11]

Reforming the United Nations

But most of the world federalist organisations that continued to operate after 1950 changed direction and started to focus on working to reform the UN. The promised Charter Revision conference was still tentatively scheduled for 1955 and most of the energies of the World Movement and its member organisations shifted now to thinking just how the Charter should be changed.

In 1951 Usborne organised a conference of the World Association of Parliamentarians for World Government to discuss UN reform. 250 parliamentarians from twenty four countries attended and together they came up with a detailed proposal of how to improve the UN. First, they proposed replacing the General Assembly with a two-house legislature – a Council of States to represent states and a Council of Peoples to represent the world's people. Secondly, they proposed replacing the Security Council with a World Executive Council consisting of representatives elected from both the Council of States and the Council of People. Thirdly, they proposed that the International Court of Justice would be given compulsory universal jurisdiction, which would turn it into a real, world court. And fourthly and finally, they proposed that a UN police force should be formed, and that all states should go through a process of complete and simultaneous disarmament. This was essentially a minimalist approach that would create a very thin layer of federal world government that would deal solely with security issues.[12]

These ideas were very much in line with those of American lawyer Grenville Clark, who in 1950 had published his book, *Plan for Peace,* which was built on the idea of UN Charter revision.[13] He later developed his ideas further with Harvard professor Louis Sohn, and together they published *Peace through Disarmament and Charter Revision* in 1953[14], and then later in 1958, their magnus opus, *World Peace through World Law*.[15] All these ideas flowed into the movement.

In 1953 the World Association of Parliamentarians for World Government and the World Movement for Federal World Government held a joint Congress in Copenhagen and together they decided to focus on the UN reform plan. They adopted the plan of the parliamentarians and agreed to work together to lobby their governments to support the plan when the Charter Review conference would finally take place. The movement was again energised because they had a clear plan of action.

In 1955 the tenth General Assembly of the UN agreed that there was indeed a need to review the UN Charter and they nominated a Commission which was charged with presenting a report to the General Assembly in 1957. The world federalists stepped up their efforts to win support for their plan. However, 1957 came and went, and still no UN Charter Review conference was scheduled. The movement carried on in hope, because surely it would happen any year now.[16]

Their discussions also began to broaden out. The world was changing, European empires were disintegrating and colonies in Africa and Asia were becoming independent states. The World Movement started to discuss decolonisation and also issues of poverty and development. The proposed the establishment of a World Development Authority and a Fund for Economic Development.

At the Hague Congress in 1957 Komla Agbeli Gbedemah, the Finance Minister of newly independent Ghana, was elected as the movement's President. As we discuss in more detail in chapter 16, Gbedemah had been involved with the movement, and also with the World Association of Parliamentarians for World Government, since the early 1950s, and strongly supported the idea of UN reform.

This marked the beginning of a short period in which the World Movement began to diversify beyond its predominantly European and American membership and begin to reach out to peoples in the newly emerging countries in Africa and Asia. As they began to think more broadly about world justice issues, and particularly about the colonial and post-colonial world order, many world federalists at this time thought that they would find allies and supporters in the newly emerging states in Africa and Asia, as these poorer and weaker states would have much to gain from a world order in which power politics would be subordinated to international law, and in which greed would be subordinated to justice. And as these new countries joined the UN, they reasoned, they could form a third bloc, separate from the American and Soviet blocs, and they could have a real impact in shifting the UN in the direction of a democratic world government.

A few months later a regional Congress was held in Kyoto. As we discuss in chapter 17, the Union for World Federal Government had been created in Japan in 1948, on the 3rd anniversary of the bombing of Hiroshima, and several of its members had been attending the World Movement's Congresses since then. This regional Congress focussed mainly on the issues of ending colonialism, cooperation among the peoples of Africa and Asia, and economic development. Plans were laid to create new world federalist organisations in a range of countries, including Ghana, Senegal, Nigeria and Sierra Leone.

Over the next few years more and more delegates from African and Asian countries started to attend the World Movement's Congresses and the discussions focused increasingly on de-colonisation and economic development, and the changes needed in the UN to bring this about. The 1961 Congress, held in Cologne, included delegates from Pakistan, Japan, India, Vietnam, Cameroon, Congo, Ivory Coast, Tunisia, Senegal, Nigeria, Sierra Leone and Egypt, as well as several countries in Latin America. Leopold Senghor, President of the newly independent Senegal, attended and was elected as Vice-President. Japanese Nobel Prize-winning physicist, Hideki Yukawa, was elected President. The Movement was changing.

While the UN Charter Review conference never in fact took place, in 1963 a small number of Charter reforms were in fact agreed by the UN General Assembly. In order to accommodate the growing number of newly independent African and Asian states that were taking up their seats at the UN, the Security Council was expanded from 11 to 15 members, and the Economic and Social Council, ECOSOC, was expanded from 18 to 27 members. Whilst important, these changes were so small that to many it finally became clear that changing the UN Charter in any significant way was, by now, extremely unlikely.

And thus, the energy for UN reform began to run out. Many of the African and Asian delegates who had been attending the World Movement Congresses began to drop out. They saw more potential to affect change in the UN through direct political channels, such as the G77 or the Non-Aligned Movement, which united the developing countries to vote together as a bloc in the UN. In the late 1960s and early 1970s these movements developed an outline for a New International Economic Order, which sought to offer more opportunities to the developing countries and even out the unfair existing international order. Forming a majority in the General Assembly, they managed to vote through their Declaration. But then the real weaknesses of the UN system became clear, as the rich countries simply ignored it.[17]

Most of the European and American world federalists also came to the realisation that UN Charter Reform was now unlikely. The Youth and Student Division called for a shift in strategy. It was time to move away from the legalist approach of UN reform, they argued, and time to focus on more immediate world problems, such as securing human rights, improving East-West relations, working for international arms control, reshaping the world's economy and preserving the environment. And so, starting from the early 1970s the movement started to focus its efforts on such issue-specific goals. They called their new policy 'dynamics for peace'.

The Wilderness Years

In certain respects this new approach was broader than the UN reform approach – it was more of a maximalist approach, focussing on justice and not only on security. But it lacked a clear vision of how world federalism would deal with these issues. And thus, they fell into just trying to tinker with the existing international order to try to achieve some small improvements here and there.

While this approach might have seemed more practical and realistic, it meant that the movement had basically lost its fundamental *raison d'etre*. Instead of talking about structural change to the world order, it instead got bogged down in a whole variety of discussions about small improvements to specific issues here and there. There were many other NGOs talking about how to make these types of small improvements and the world federalists basically lost their identity and their core message.

Numbers dwindled as members left the movement to pursue other avenues. A small group continued on. Some were waiting for the political situation to change so they could start calling again for world federation, others were content to engage in countless discussions about world improvement projects. There were, of course, many activities, but in all honesty, this was a low-point for the movement.[18]

World Federalism in the Era of Globalisation

However, by the 1990s, the political situation did indeed change. In 1989 the Berlin Wall came down and the Cold War finally came to an end. The world was no longer divided into two separate blocs, with two competing ideologies. Instead, all countries were now taking part in the capitalist world economy and the global market. US political scientist, Frances Fukuyama called it 'the end of history'. In the coming years it came to be known as 'globalisation'. Suddenly, it was indeed possible to imagine a unified world. Energy and enthusiasm began to return to the world movement. In 1990, the popular and famous actor Sir Peter Ustinov assumed the Presidency of the WFM.

Furthermore, the 1980s had witnessed a major transformation in civil society. Many largely voluntary social movements had professionalised and transformed into 'Non-Governmental Organisations', or NGOs, with paid staff and offices and large grants from philanthropic or government donors. WFM decided to follow this pattern. In 1994 William R. Pace was hired as the Executive Director, a new office was established in New York, close to the UN, grants were sought, and a new strategic approach was agreed. WFM would now work with networks of other NGOs on specific campaigns, with the aim of getting new institutions created at the global level which would improve the governance of global issues.

Pace had attended the Earth Summit in 1992 and he thought that global environmental governance would be the area where there would be most support for new institutions, in particular, turning the small and powerless UN Environmental Program into a proper UN Environmental Organisation which would be able to make and enforce international environmental laws. But the leading environmental NGOs of the time were sceptical that international law could actually work, and so there was not a lot of interest or support in this idea.

Instead, developments were starting in a different area altogether, that of international human rights law. In 1989 Trinidad and Tobago had proposed that the UN General Assembly should discuss the creation of an International Criminal Court to hold individuals accountable for the worst kinds of war crimes. The General Assembly had referred the issue to the Sixth Committee (the Legal Committee) and by 1994 a draft Statute for a future International Criminal Court, or ICC, had been prepared and presented to the General Assembly.

WFM and the Coalition for the International Criminal Court

Even though there was strong opposition from larger states, such as the US and Russia, the creation of an International Criminal Court looked like a process that was moving and that actually stood a chance. Pace, who had previously worked at Amnesty International, started talking to other NGOs in the human rights and disarmament sectors and found that many of them were also excited about these events. Amnesty International, in particular, were keen to rally support for the process. And so, in February 1995, a meeting of around 25 interested NGOs was organised and the Coalition for the ICC was formed. Pace became the Convenor and WFM hosted the small secretariat to organise the work.

Over the next few years there were several discussions at the UN General Assembly about the proposed ICC. There were states that supported, states that opposed, many arguments about how it should be composed, what powers it would have, and so on. The Coalition attended these meetings and provided input and analysis. They also brought NGOs from the developing countries to participate so that they too could have a say. And they formed a partnership with the 70 or so states that supported the creation of the ICC. As these activities started to bring results, more and more NGOs joined the Coalition, and the pressure on the states to create the ICC increased.

In 1996 the UN General Assembly formally decided to hold a special treaty-establishing conference in Rome in 1998. This is where the ICC would either finally be agreed, or fall by the wayside. The Coalition stepped up its activities, lobbying governments, providing analysis, proposing solutions to technical problems, and keeping the pressure on. In 1998 the Rome Conference took place. The fate of the ICC was still very much in the balance. The US, Russia and others were very much against it and doing everything they could to find a way to block it. But a large group of smaller countries were determinedly pushing ahead. The Coalition, now consisting of some 800 NGOs, attended the Rome Conference in force. While most states sent one or two delegates, and even the larger states sent 10 or 15, the Coalition sent over 500 delegates. Their presence was huge. They set up a website and wrote daily updates so that people all round the world could know what was going on. If they saw a state beginning to back off from supporting the ICC, they would speak with their coalition members back in the capital city of that state, and get them to talk to the ministers there. All this work massively increased the transparency of the process and put pressure on the wavering states to stand by their previous positions.

Eventually the Treaty was passed and the Rome Statute to create the ICC was adopted. According to Bill Pace, who of course was there, there was a thunderous applause that went on for about 25 minutes. A partnership between a group of states and a group of NGOs had succeeded in creating a new international institution, an international court that would be able to investigate and prosecute individuals for four international crimes – genocide, crimes against humanity, war crimes, and the crime of aggression. This would be the first international court able to prosecute individuals, rather than states, and thus it represented a huge breakthrough in international law.

In 2002, after the required state ratifications were achieved, the Statute entered into effect and the ICC was created. The Coalition decided to continue working together to support the fledgling ICC and to try to improve it. Over the next 20 or so years Bill Pace and the WFM led the coalition, which during that time consisted of between 2,000 and 4,000 NGOs, to work towards improving the ICC and keeping ordinary people aware of and involved in its activities, as well as achieve further state ratifications from across the world.

This formed the bulk of WFM's work during the past 20 or so years. The staff in the offices in New York and The Hague focussed most of their energies on the Coalition for the ICC. They also carried out some other smaller projects, such as leading the NGO Working Group on the Security Council, which sought to improve the UN Security Council and make it more transparent, and contributing to the Responsibility to Protect initiative that was developing at the time.

The 'Movement' Part of WFM

While WFM became a well-known and well-respected NGO in New York, a disconnect began to develop between the NGO part of the WFM, and the movement part of it. While the member organisations continued to meet and discuss their ideas in the WFM Congresses, and continued to work in their own countries to promote world federation, they were only marginally involved in the activities of the NGO in New York.

And since the early 2000s there has been a great influx of new energy and a significant growth in these organisations. In 2003, for example, the Committee for a Democratic UN was formed in Germany and joined the WFM. In 2007 they set up the Campaign for a United Nations Parliamentary Assembly and set about lobbying politicians and diplomats in order to win support. After several years, the Campaign had gained considerable traction. Its proposal has been supported by the European Parliament and was discussed in various other international fora, and over 1,500 parliamentarians have given it their endorsement.

In 2017 the Committee for a Democratic UN transformed into Democracy Without Borders and began a process of worldwide expansion, setting up branches in India, Kenya, Greece, Spain, Sweden and Switzerland, and others on the way. They have also worked together with other democracy-promoting NGOs and in 2019 launched a campaign for a World Citizens Initiative, a proposal similar to the European Citizens Initiative, in which ordinary people could join together to get particular issues discussed in the UN General Assembly.

In 2005 a new world federalist organisation was formed in Argentina, called Democracia Global, and they too joined the WFM. They worked with leading academics to issue a Global Democracy Manifesto and have also created the Campaign for a Latin American and Caribbean Criminal Court against Transnational Organized Crime– or COPLA, the acronym of the campaign's Spanish name – as a step towards building up more supra-national institutions at the regional level.

In 2013 One World was formed in Israel-Palestine, bringing together young Jews and Arabs to call for global democracy, and producing educational materials about global democracy and world federation. In 2014 Professor Joseph Schwartzberg, Emeritus professor at the University of Minnesota, set up the Workable World Trust, to support activities focusing on UN reform and on global democracy more generally. And in 2019 the Young World Federalists burst onto the scene, bringing new youthful energy to the movement, engaging on internet platforms and social media, and rallying millennials and Generation Z to the cause of world federation.

WFM in the 21st Century

So now is probably another inflexion point for the movement. Bill Pace has retired and the task of convening the Coalition for the ICC has been passed onto another NGO. The WFM has new leadership, new energy and a desire for new directions. The NGO part and the Movement part need to be brought back together so that they can support each other in the complex task of bringing about real political change.

In today's highly globalised world it is now very much possible to imagine a unified world, a world federation, with global democracy and global citizenship. The problems with the international world order are becoming increasingly visible to everyone. A retreat to nationalism does not seem likely, or desirable. So now, finally, it may be the right time for WFM to start again the push for world federation and global democracy.

Notes

1 Billion, Jean-Francis. 1991. The World Federalist Movements from 1945 to 1954 and European Integration. *The Federalist Political Review*, No. 1, p28. www.thefederalist.eu/site/index.php/en/essays/1892-the-world-federalist-movements-from-1945-to-1954-and-european-integration; Billion, Jean-Francis. 1996. The World Federalist Movements from 1955 to 1968 and European Integration. *The Federalist Political Review*, No. 2, p96. www.thefederalist.eu/site/index.php-/en/essays/1929-the-world-federalist-movements-from-1955-to-1968-and-the-european-integration; Laursen, Finn. 2010. Strategies for World Federal Government: The Early Debate Revisited. Paper prepared for delivery at Workshop, 'Present Futures and Future Presents – World State Scenarios for the 21st Century' at Klitgaarden, Skagen, Denmark, 23–25 June. finnlaursen.com/downloads/papers-ByFinn/Skagen%20paper%202010.pdf

2 For more on the peace movement and the early moves towards the idea of world federalism see Tryon, James. 1911. The Rise of the Peace Movement. *Yale*

Law Journal, 20,5: 358-371; Mazower, Mark. 2012. *Governing the World: The History of an Idea, 1815 to the Present.* New York: Penguin; Yoder, Jon. 1972. The United World Federalists: Liberals for Law and Order. *American Studies*, 13, 1: 109-129.

3 For more on Federal Union, see the Federal Union archives, London School of Economics and Political Science, UK. federalunion.org.uk/federalism/archives/

4 Baratta, Joseph. 2004. *The Politics of World Federation: United Nations, UN Reform, Atomic Control.* Westport: Praeger. Chapter 15: Robert M. Hutchins: Framing a World Constitution, pp315-330.

5 See also Flessenkemper, Tobias. 2013. A Short History of the Young European Federalists. www.thenewfederalist.eu/a-short-history-of-the-young-european-federalists?lang=fr

6 www.wfm-igp.org/about-us/montreux-declaration/

7 Baratta, op. cit., Ch. 16: The Crusade and the World Movement, pp331-347.

8 Letter from Nehru to Usborne, 6th April 1948, Schwimmer-Lloyd Archives T63, cited in Baratta, Joseph. 2004. *The Politics of World Federation: United Nations, UN Reform, Atomic Control.* Westport: Praeger, p385.

9 For more on the congresses of the World Federalist Movement see Carter, Richard. 2001. *Survival Meetings: Highlights of the World Government Movement, 1947 to 1952: A Personal Journey.* New York: Writers Club Press.

10 In the early 1950s Eyo Ita wrote a letter to Tracy Dickinson Mygatt, of the Campaign for World Government, in which he said: 'It was my impression of the failings of the League of Nations in 1931… that first led me to the conclusion that the peoples of the world would have to elect their representatives directly to a world parliament to seek the broad vital human interests of equal justice, peace, health and communication , in order to create order out of chaos in the new world community…. When in 1947 and 1948 I started receiving papers from the American and British federalists on World Government Movement I was happy to discover such serious-minded leaders as Dr A Einstein, Lord Boyd Orr and Beveridge were thinking the same way I did…' Cited in Mygatt, Tracy Dickinson. 1952. Torchbearer of Nigeria. *The Crisis*, 59, 6: 361-366.

11 For more on this see World Association of Parliamentarians for World Government Archives, Sussex University, UK. archiveshub.jisc.ac.uk/search/archives/5a8a9470-7b74-3446-8c0f-bcee204610ff

12 Laursen, Finn. 2010. Strategies for World Federal Government: The Early Debate Revisited. Paper prepared for delivery at Workshop, 'Present Futures and Future Presents – World State Scenarios for the 21st Century' at Klitgaarden, Skagen, Denmark, 23–25 June. pp14-16. finnlaursen.com/downloads/papersByFinn/-Skagen%20paper%202010.pdf; McAllister, Gilbert. (ed).1952. *Report of the London Parliamentary Conference on World Government. September 24-29, 1951.* London: The Parliamentary Group for World Government.

13 Clark, Grenville. 1950. A *Plan for Peace.* New York: Harper and Bros.

14 Clark, Grenville and Louis Sohn. 1953. Peace through Disarmament and Charter Revision: Detailed Proposal for Revision of the UN Charter. Dublin, NH.

15 Clark, Grenville and Louis Sohn. 1958. *World Peace through World Law.* Cambridge: Harvard University Press.

16 Scott, Shirley. 2005. The Failure of the UN to Hold a Charter Review Conference in the 1950s: The Future in the Past? *Australia and New Zealand Law and History E-Journal,* 70-79. www.anzlhsejournal.auckland.ac.nz/pdfs_2005/Scott-.pdf. For a discussion of the potential or UN Charter reform see Sharei, Mahmoud (Shahryar). 2016. *Reconstructing Article 109(3) of the UN Charter: Towards Constitutionalisation of the United Nations and International Law.* PhD dissertation, Kent Law School, University of Kent. kar.kent.ac.uk/57034/1/212Sharei-PhD-Thesis-Rev%20II-R2-%2020%20July%202016%20%28uploaded%29%20-Electronic%20Submission.p.pdf

17 Renninger, John. 1976. After the Seventh Special General Assembly Session: Africa and the New Emerging World Order. *African Studies Review,* 19,2: 35-48.

18 For more about the United World Federalists during this period see Baratta, op. cit., Chapter 25: World Federalists in the Cold War, pp505-526.

Section IV
Ways Forward

19. Debunking the Objections to Global Democracy

As humanity is increasingly facing global problems that, by definition, are beyond the scale of any nation state – problems such as global warming, inequality, pandemics and so on, as we have discussed in the previous chapters – an increasing number of people are daring to ask the question: 'Wouldn't it be so much better if instead of having 200 legally separate governments, all in competition with each other and looking out only for their own interests, we also had a federal level of democratic state above all of them, that would have the right size to address those global problems?'

But when they share that thought with others, they often get a cold shower of objections that tell them, 'Oh no! That's just a naïve utopia. It goes against human nature, and could even end up in a dystopia of a global tyranny. So forget that idea and focus on realistic solutions'. This type of objection can come even from rather educated people, and yet it reflects a profound ignorance about what's really going on in the world, and a complete failure of imagination of how different it could be.

In this chapter we will take a look at these objections, and we will answer them, one by one.[1] As it turns out, it is actually quite easy to refute them all. In fact, when we look at them closely, many of them seem much more like excuses than real objections, poor arguments that are actually just trying to serve the interests of a certain group of people against the greater interests of humanity. As we go through them, pay attention to a pattern that will repeat over and over again, of A, B & C:

A. At first glance, each objection to the idea of global democracy seems to stand on solid rational logic.
B. But upon a closer look, we quickly begin to see that the logic is not solid at all. Which then gets us to the tricky part of,
C. That as soon as you just begin exposing the weakness of the first objection, another objection will quickly pop its head out from another direction, saying 'but what about me?'

It's as if all of the objections are connected in some underground mental system of mutual support. Now, that new objection will also be standing only on seemingly solid logic, but if you are not careful and you get distracted to start exposing its own weakness, without first making sure that you have properly destroyed the first objection, then later down the line that first one might rise up again to help the other objections. So it's really important to take the time to properly dismantle the foundation of each objection in its entirely, so that it cannot rise again.

Objection (1): Global Identity is Impossible

Let's begin with the classic objection number one, which goes like this:

> People will never agree to live in a federation of the world because their nature is egoistic and tribal. They can't affiliate emotionally with something so remote and as big as the whole world, just as they can't identify with a group so large and so diverse as the whole of humanity.

Sounds familiar? How do you answer that? At first glance it looks like it's standing on the solid logic that naturally, every one of us cares more about our close circles of family and friends than about more remote circles of acquaintances and people that we don't even know. So surely, the argument goes, we couldn't care about the whole of humanity.

Well, while indeed human nature has plenty of egoism and tribalism in it, it's important to notice the tension between those two things. For example, going to the army and perhaps even to battle to protect one's own tribe or country is in tension with one's egoistic tendency to protect oneself as an individual. Humans are complex, and by our nature we can hold multiple allegiances to different social circles and levels of social circles, even when they are all in some tension with one another. Think of the different levels of family and friends, or the commitment to going to work versus pursuing one's own hobbies. It's surely not easy to find the perfect balance between all the social circles and communities of which we are members. But we, humans, have the basic ability to do just that.

And so, having some measure of affiliation to the very largest circle, to the world as a whole, alongside all the other circles or layers, and naturally, with some tension between them, is certainly not beyond our human nature. This is why it's easy for us to imagine, for example, that if only we had some serious external threat, like aliens from space, or an asteroid coming our way, then we would quickly put aside all our differences and disagreements and come together to protect our shared homeland, our planet.[2]

Think of it, just as many people today indeed care for their respective national or religious communities, who can be groups of millions or hundreds of millions of people, they can also have some level of care for a group as large as humanity. The very fact that we have some affiliation with any group, doesn't mean that we personally know, or love, or agree with everyone in that group. Of course not! So the same can go for humanity. And democracy is really helpful here, because it creates a framework in which we can passionately disagree with each other, but in a non-violent manner. Are you aware of any rule of human nature that determines that we can't have that also at the global level?

Some people argue that in order to have a global democracy we need first to have some shared identity and interests. Well, guess what? We are all one species, and we are all vulnerable to the same diseases. We live on the very same planet and thus have many shared interests, because if someone is wrecking the climate by pumping greenhouse gasses into the atmosphere on the other side of the planet, it's very much our problem, too. So we have a very tangible basis of common identity and shared interests to build on. These things are far more real and far more important than many national differences or cultural symbols that people rally around today.[3]

And just before another objection pops its head up from anywhere else, and to make sure that this one will not rise again later, let's quickly look at another variant of it. This version of the argument is built on the simple and unrefusable observation that the vast majority of the borders that today divide the nation states of the world have been relatively stable for many decades, and haven't changed since roughly World War Two. Many people point to this as the success of the current division of humanity into nation-states. They argue that it's thanks to the strong national sentiments that people have for their nation-states, that nation-states came into being and continue to exist. Hence, the fact that we don't yet have a federal state of the Earth reflects, they argue, the fact that humans just don't care enough for the world and for humanity as a whole.

But what's missing in this picture is that it also goes the other way around. Just as national sentiments do create and strengthen nation-states, the existence and action of nation-states creates and strengthens national sentiments. And that makes a very big difference with regard to the proposed idea of a world federation.

Today, the simple fact is that it's only within nation-states that we can see examples of somewhat functional systems of large-scale social justice and solidarity, such as democratic decision-making, taxation of the rich and redistribution to all, and the rule of law that protects civil rights and liberties. So naturally, people who care for all these extremely important things, care strongly for the political framework that enables them, which today is only the nation-state.

From this perspective it is quite amazing that so many people already today profess a great care for the Earth as a whole and for our shared identity as humans, even *before* we have any of those state-systems of justice and solidarity and democracy at the global level. Just imagine how many more people would have these sentiments of care and solidarity, and how much more strongly they would feel them, if we had those state mechanisms up and running globally.

Global democracy, in which people would have a framework to disagree with each other in a non-violent and politically constructive way, has a huge potential as a possible alternative to the existing international system, in which we can only 'solve' our disagreements through war.

Objection (2): Not Everyone Wants Democracy

So now we can move on to the next objection, number two. It's also a very common one, and it goes like this:

> Global Democracy is impossible because a very significant portion of the world's population does not want democracy. Democracy is a western and liberal idea that is alien to the traditions of many other cultures, who prefer a clear system of social hierarchy. One may hope that maybe, one day, they will also develop a liking for democracy, but surely it's not up to us to intervene in any way in their decisions about that.

Right. It's possible to see a certain logic here, but we have just one small question. How do we know? How can we be so sure that the reason that so many countries around the world are not democratic, and we leave it up to you to say which ones those are, is because the people there just don't want democracy? Is it because it's clearly shown in the results of the free and fair elections that are held there? or surveys? or something? Are the people there really given a free and fair chance to make up their minds about it?[4]

While we warmly embrace the liberal principle of tolerance, which says that we should keep out of other peoples' lives, and mind our own business, the problem is that whenever we do business with those who themselves are intolerant and exploit and harm others, we end up going against our own noble principle. How? Well let's take an example to show what we mean.

Let's imagine a stereotypical liberal guy from Germany, who would proudly tell anyone, including himself, that he strongly believes in democracy and the values of democracy. But to warm up his home in winter, he uses gas that arrives in pipes all the way from Russia. That gas is really good, but what about the democracy in Russia? Well, a little less so. And while he might like to tell himself that these things are not connected, the simple fact is that a portion of the price that he pays for the gas every month covers the taxes or fees or bribes or other payments that the gas company has to pay to the Russian government for the right to pump this gas. So while in principle our German guy just minds his own business, and surely doesn't support any form of oligarchy, in practice he does. And not with mere words, but with his cold, hard cash. And it is this very money that allows the Russian government to pay for the guns and the prisons with which they oppress the Russian people, to pay salaries to their collaborators, to fund the media that tells the Russian citizens that they live in the best country, and so on.

So the fact is, the decision about what kind of government there should be in Russia, is in practice not just a matter between the Russian people and their leaders, but also includes the actions of many other people. There are millions of people outside of Russia who effectively put their money on the side of the Russian oligarchy, and against the Russian people and against democracy. And Russia is just one example, it's true in many other cases around the world.

Don't let anyone take you down the rhetorical road of 'Oh, this German guy, he's just a small consumer, what can he do? Life is so complicated and you expect him to investigate each product that he buys? How can he know how it was produced, who did what to whom in the process, who is benefitting from the profits? He's just an innocent consumer, it's not his fault.'

But of course we don't mean to put all the responsibility on the individual consumer. When we say that market players, like consumers or shareholders, have some undemocratic power over people in other countries, it doesn't mean that it is up to them to investigate every product and only buy things that pass the test. No. The 'ethical buying' movement may have ideas like this, but we think that this is completely unfeasible on a large scale, and that there are better and more effective solutions. The whole idea of democracy is that there is a system in which those who have any power to govern others should be restrained by those who are governed. A full circle. So the system, the political and judicial system, should function to stop this kind of behaviour.

To carry on with our example, let's imagine that our guy in Germany is a truck driver, transporting, let's say, apples that are grown in the countryside to the big city markets. Why is he doing this job? Mainly because consumers who are interested in those apples incentivise him, financially, to get up in the morning and hit the road. But at the same time, they create also a similar or even greater financial incentive for another guy, who doesn't have a truck but has a gun, to stop the truck on a small side road, get the driver out, and then himself drive the stolen goods to the market, where he can sell the apples, and the truck, to the oblivious local vendors for a cheap price.

In such a case, do we expect the consumers in the market to start investigating where the apples came from and whether they are fine or stolen? Of course not! Do we expect the truck driver to somehow find the robber, fight with him, and try to take back his truck? Maybe in the movies, but not in real life in somewhere like Germany. All the driver needs to do is pick up a phone and call the police and tell them what happened. And they then have the means and the authority to investigate the case, find the robber, charge him in court, and bring him to justice.

And notice, the German police and the German courts work on behalf of the German public. Not only that their salaries are paid by the German public taxes, but the rules that they enforce are written by representatives of the German public in the German parliament. This is extremely important, because it creates within Germany a nice democratic circle on the national level: the government and the police and the courts that have power to govern, are themselves governed by the public.

But when it comes to the global market, when those who buy and those who sell are located in separate countries, under completely different and independent systems of law and justice and politics, then that circle is broken.

If it's not a truck, but a whole country that is somehow taken over by a group of what are essentially armed robbers, who dispose of democracy and establish an oligarchy, then those robbers should not be allowed to sell stolen goods without recourse to justice. They should not be able to export the oil or gas or other natural resources of that country and keep the money for themselves in private overseas bank accounts. And they should not be allowed to use this money to buy guns from overseas suppliers which they can use to continue to oppress the local population.

And of course, it cannot and should not be the role of the consumers anywhere to make sure that this is not happening and to do that enforcement work. That should be precisely the role of democratic government agencies that work on the same scale as the market, which in this case, stretches beyond national borders. So there should be, on the global level, a democratic justice system with a federal police force and federal courts, that work on behalf of the global public, with salaries funded by global taxes, that enforce the rules written by the representatives of global citizens in the federal world parliament. A full circle of global democracy.

But as long as we don't have such a global democratic system, while we do have a global market system, we actively create the financial incentivise for the oppression of people in other countries. Even if we are lucky enough to live in a country that is democratic on the national level, we still participate in this system of global oppression, as consumers of global goods and as shareholders in global companies, mainly through our pension or saving funds. So right now, by just living our lives and minding our own business, we are participating in what should be understood as a sophisticated system of global oligarchy.

Then there's the argument that goes: 'Oh, but if we don't buy all that stuff from these countries, they will lose their only source of income and livelihood, the poor people there will suffer, and their children will go hungry. So we better rush to the nearby shopping mall in order to help them'.

Really? What nonsense. In Germany, if the management of a factory exploits its workers, pays salaries below the minimum wage, doesn't allow them to form a union, or employs children, you don't hear German people saying 'Oh how awful! Let's buy the products of that factory in order to support its workers.' No! What happens is that the state authorities come to supervise. They investigate and prosecute on behalf of the German citizens.

Saying that people in undemocratic countries don't want democracy, while you pay those who oppress them, is not just illogical, it's also inhumane.

It's time to realise that what we have right now is a system of global injustice. And we need to change it! But in order to change it, we first need to clearly understand what's the problem with it. And we also need to realise that there is an alternative. Global democracy, a government of humanity, by humanity and for humanity, is the alternative to the existing system of global injustice.

Objection (3): Democracy Can't Work on a Large Scale

Now we can move on to the third objection, or maybe it's more accurate to call them 'excuses', for why that alternative supposedly cannot work. This one argues that:

Democracy can work well only on a small scale, where you personally know all the members of the community, or where at least you can easily access and speak with your representatives in the parliament when you need to. But on the global level, where the scale of the Earth and the size of humanity supposedly make both of these things impossible, some people like to claim that the voice of the individual citizen will get lost and each person will remain unheard and neglected.

At first glance this sounds logical, but let's take a closer look. First of all, let's not idealize small communities too much as places of peace and harmony and good relations. Sadly, it is all too often precisely in small-scale tight communities, in which everyone knows each other and has the same culture – indeed, even in families – that you find the greatest hatred and the most bitter conflicts. If you know anything about the statistics of violence and abuse, you will know that it's often the larger circle of community, such as the state, that protects individuals from violence or abuse in the smaller social units. So smaller is not necessarily better.

Secondly, while it's true that you can find examples of small countries that are internally more democratic than larger ones, it is also true that if you make a proper study of all countries, you will find that there are many small countries that are far less democratic than many larger ones. Contrary to what many might think, there is absolutely no empirical correlation between the size of a country and the quality of its democracy.

And why is that? Here are three reasons. The first is that the federal model that you find in many large countries, in the right conditions and if done correctly, as we outlined in chapter one, can enable a good balance between the benefits of centralisation and de-centralisation, and between uniformity and diversity, even on a very large scale. While some people fear that a world federation would mean imposing some grey homogeneity on the whole world, this is not true at all. Alongside a very limited degree of centralization and uniformity, there would be plenty of room for diversity, between communities and regions and individuals. Only things that concern everyone, like global warming or global taxes, would be decided together at the global level.

The second reason that democracy can be successful on a very large scale has to do with the fact that larger societies are, indeed, inevitably more diverse. And while diversity can be a challenge for democracy in some respects, it can also be a major advantage, as it incentivises the creation of a more tolerant political space, in which people are more open towards each other's differences. In a relatively homogenous society, such as a nation-state with a clear majority of just one ethnic or religious group, a politician can easily gain cheap popularity simply by enflaming hatred towards the minority. But in a very diverse society, made up of multiple groups with none of them being a majority, politicians are incentivised to appeal to a much broader and more diverse crowd, and to form coalitions of diverse communities. And that is a very big advantage in creating an open and tolerant political culture.

In today's world, where we are all divided into 'nation-states', many people are obsessed with preserving the demographic superiority of their respective majority groups against the 'threat' of minority groups and immigrants. But in a federation of the whole world, you'll be happy to find that no single ethnic or religious group comes even close to being a majority. And that fact, in a world federal system, would necessarily incentivise politicians to appeal to diverse crowds, to form coalitions, to emphasize what is common in our human identity, and to work for our shared interests on this planet. Now that would be so, so much better than today's politics!

The third reason that democracy can work well even on a very large scale has to do with the fact that the democratic mechanism of elections, if done properly, creates a powerful incentive for politicians and parties to find out what voters care about, even without having to hold private conversations with every single voter. Because the type of problems that we want the government to do something about are rarely things that bother only one individual voter. For example, if there is a big crack in the street where you live, it bothers not only yourself, but also your neighbours and everyone who passes in the street. Therefore, a local politician who wants to be elected in your neighbourhood had better say and do something about it. In just the same way, global elections would create an incentive and a mechanism for politicians at all levels to listen and find out what world citizens care about when it comes to shared issues, such as climate change or how do deal with global pandemics.

Why do we think that it would be so hard to have a federal level of global government, when we know that it is quite possible to have a global level of management for huge transnational corporations? Why is scale not an impediment there? Why is cultural diversity not an insurmountable challenge? While there are of course many differences between democratic states and commercial corporations, it is certainly interesting to note how effectively corporations have managed to scale up to the global level and overcome many potential management and governance challenges. In fact, they have done it so well that local states now find it very difficult to restrain and regulate them –

to tax them, and to stop them from mistreating workers, lying to consumers, or harming the environment.

If global management works so well in the corporate sphere, why should it not work in the political sphere? Why is it that the one system that has the formal ability to tax and regulate the market powers, namely the state, allegedly cannot work at the global level? To us it's clear that it could indeed work at that global level, but it's extremely useful for the corporations that so many people believe that it cannot.

Objection (4): A World Government will turn into a Global Tyranny

This brings us to the fourth and final objection, which is the most powerful, and the most stupid, of them all. It goes like this:

> In a world federation the government will quickly centralise all the power in its hands, and it would turn into a tyrannical dystopia, in which everyone would be enslaved and have nowhere to hide, forever. And if there is even just one chance in a billion that this nightmare would happen, then we should just reject this whole idea right away.

Seems logical, right? Let's look at this bogeyman up close and see if it's real or just a scarecrow, and what it might be protecting.

The first thing we need to ask in order to deflate this scary ghost is, 'why?' Why in a democratic federation of the world would the government become tyrannical? Is it because our tribal human nature cannot affiliate with a social circle that includes the whole of humanity, and therefore only a tyrannical government would be able to maintain power above the different factions? Well, we answered that one already: we can care for many different social levels at the same time. We don't have to love or agree with everyone in all those circles all the time, we just have to engage in constructive discussion with them through institutions such as parliaments and the media.

So is it because some people and some communities don't want democracy? Well, we've answered that one as well. How do we know what they want at present? And how can they make up their minds about it in a free and fair way when the oligarchies that educate and oppress them are funded from the huge global market?

If you look at the world from a global perspective, the democracy that you find today in some countries of the world, is similar, in a sense, to the Athenian democracy of ancient Greece. That ancient democracy was a very nice democracy for the citizens of Athens, but these citizens were only a relatively small sub-set of all the people governed by the Athenian government. Citizens, then, were only men, who had land, and lived inside Athens itself. All the women of Athens, and the landless peasants, and the slaves, and all the people who lived in the lands that were outside of Athens but occupied by the Athenian Empire, they were not counted as citizens. Thus, they did not have a vote in the Athenian 'democracy'. From their perspective it was one big oligarchy, the rule of the few. And, as we discuss in more detail in chapter 23, this is very much how the world is set up today: democracy and freedom and riches for the few, oligarchy and oppression and poverty for the many. It's not right, and it doesn't have to be this way. Instead, we need a real, inclusive global democracy for everyone.

What other reasons are there that a global democracy would turn into a global tyranny? Is it because democracy just can't work on a large scale? We've answered that too. And when we see how corporations flourish when organised at the global level, across borders and cultures, we realise again that there is no reason that the one institution that could restrain these corporations – the state – should remain divided into two hundred separate and competing units, where it falls prey to the 'divide and rule' strategy of those corporations.

The corporations are indeed afraid that in a world federation there would no longer be anywhere for them to hide away their profits. If there were a global federal tax system, then the global rich and powerful would finally have to pay their fair share of tax, just like everyone else. This would raise trillions of dollars and enable all the rest of us, the 99%, to live with dignity.

Today, it's only powerful corporations and rich individuals who can freely cross borders, and set up their factories in countries whose governments are too weak to stand up to them and protect their citizens. The poor citizens don't have a place to hide from the harsh hand that their governments use against them in the service of the corporations. They cannot hide from the pollution, from the exploitation, from the poverty. And they cannot simply cross the border when they want to, and get a visa, or citizenship, in another country. For them, in today's world, there is nowhere to hide.

So what else is there? What other reason is there for the government of a world federation to become tyrannical? Is it because they would want to centralize more power in their hands? Of course they will. This is what governments always want to do. And this is why we divide them in democratic constitutions so that *we* can rule *them*. We divide them into different branches of government that can check and balance the power of each other: we divide them horizontally between the executive, legislative, and judicial branches, and we divide them vertically between the central, regional and local levels. We do this because we fundamentally don't trust anyone in power. This is why we, the people, keep the final sovereignty to decide who will be in government. That's how democracy works. Nothing new. But the division of state power between 200 separate states - this is the one type of division that is not helpful for us. It's helpful for the corporations, and it's helpful for the 1%. But it is dividing us, and it's time we stopped this silly madness.

People look at the successes of local, national, governments and say: 'This is because they are local, but it couldn't possibly work on the global scale', while other people look at their failures and say: 'If it can't work at the local level, then even more so it won't work on the global level'. But it's exactly the other way around. People should see the successes of local, national, governments and say: 'Wow! If governments can do all that despite their unfavourable condition vis-à-vis the global corporations, imagine how much more they could achieve if the government system was global?' Likewise, people should see the many failures of local, national, governments and realise: 'These failures are because they are just local. How could we have ever seriously expected them to be successful when they stand against the power of the global market?' That's a much more accurate way to think about these things.

How to respond to the argument that if there is even one chance in a billion that a world federation would fail, then we shouldn't go for it? Well, we need to realise that there are no risk-free futures on offer. Are we safe in a warming world that has no one in charge of dealing with this problem? Are we safe in the face of global pandemics? Are there no risks in the current situation of rising inequality, injustice and wars, that no one is responsible for addressing? Are the islands of democracy safe against the impact of the global 1% and autocratic forces? Of course not! There are risks all around, and forming a democratic world federation is actually the best chance we have of managing most of those other risks. Because with a world federation we would finally have a global body responsible for maintaining the well-being of everybody on the planet, and indeed of the planet itself.

It's time for people to realise that another world *is* possible. A democratic world federation is the alternative that we need. We need to take this idea and push it forward. We need to stand up to the objections, expose and debunk the myths on which they are built, and spread the vision of global democracy. Once a critical mass gathers behind it, it will suddenly seem easy and obvious to everyone. And then, it will happen.

Notes

1 See also Dooley, Joseph. 1961. *The Social Nature of Man as the Ontological Basis for a World State*. PhD dissertation, Department of Political Science, University of Ottawa; Erman, Eva and Jonathan W. Kuyper. 2020. Global Democracy and Feasibility. *Critical Review of International Social and Political Philosophy*, 23, 3: 311-331; Marchetti, Raffaele. 2008. *Global Democracy: For and Against*. London: Routledge.

2 See also Montani, Guido. 2012. Human Nature, Nationalism and Cosmopolitism. *Il Politico*, 3: 68-90.

3 See for example Koenig-Archibugi, Mathias. 2011. Is Global Democracy Possible? *European Journal of International Relations*, 17,3: 519-542. eprints.lse.ac.uk-/28941/1/__libfile_repository_Content_Koenig-Archibugi%2C%20M_Is%20-global%20democracy%20possible_Is%20global%20democracy%20possible%20-%28LSE%20RO%29.pdf

4 See also Sen, Amartya. 2003. Democracy and its Global Roots: Why Democratization is not the Same as Westernization. *New Republic*, 229, 14: 28-35.

20. Localism or Globalism?

A lot of good people who care about social and environmental issues and about social justice often feel rather scared about ideas of world federation or world government. These ideas somehow seem too big, to out-of-our-control, too bureaucratic. They tend to prefer small-scale solutions, like living in small communities or eco-villages, where they can basically cut themselves off from the world and all its problems and injustices. In their small communities they can create a microcosm of social and environmental justice, discussing issues in small assemblies, living simply and growing their own food. In short, they prefer localism over globalism. But is this really a solution? It might lead to a nice life for these individuals in their eco-villages, but does it really help the cause of global justice? Is it really a remedy for the world's problems?

Can Localist Solutions Solve Global Problems?

If you think about it, then it's obvious that localism cannot solve global problems. It's just a way to try to cut off from the world and essentially put your head in the sand. 'But at least we don't contribute to any of the world's problems or injustices', many of these localists say, 'we just lead a good life and don't harm any others or cause any pollution'. But is this true?

If you still use a computer, or a mobile phone, then you're certainly contributing to pollution and injustice because in order to produce the cobalt that is necessary to make these phones and computers child workers work for long hours in dangerous conditions in mines in Africa and elsewhere. And of course, these mines produce a huge amount of environmental pollution. And if you are wearing clothes, then most likely they were made in sweatshops in Africa or Asia, again by poorly treated workers, working long hours in poor conditions for extremely low pay. And if you are using electricity, it was probably generated from oil or coal, contributing to environmental pollution and to climate change. And so on, and so on, and so on.

If you really wanted to be sure that you weren't contributing to the world's problems and injustices, then you would have to say goodbye to your computer, goodbye to your mobile phone, and goodbye to pretty much all modern tech and gadgets – from ovens to fridges to televisions and air conditioning. If you wanted to use electricity, then you'd have to generate it yourself, through solar panels or wind turbines, that you'd also have to make yourself, from locally-available materials. You'd have to make your own clothes, and also grow your own cotton to make them with.

In essence, you would have to live a life rather similar to the traditional communities of Africa, Asia and Latin America, living in some kind of mud or wooden hut and spending all your days working the land to produce enough food to eat. Now we're not saying that there is anything wrong with such a life. One of us, Dena, is an anthropologist and has spent several years living in a mud hut in a village in rural Africa. In many respects it's a very good life. But we don't think that it is the life that most localists imagine for themselves. We think most of them imagine an idyllic small-scale utopia where they live with other like-minded souls, perhaps grow their own food, but nonetheless live with all modern comforts and gadgets, use computers, mobile phones, wear clothes, use electricity, and so on. Yet they imagine that somehow by living in this way they are doing good for the world and, at the very least, not contributing to its problems and injustices. But this is just not the case.

So, if you want all of these things, and there's nothing wrong with that, then you have to accept that you are still part of the world system, even if you live in a small-scale eco-community. And therefore, what you're actually doing there is creating a nice life for yourself, and simply ignoring the suffering and injustice that is caused around the world to make your nice life possible.

Global Problems Require Globalist Solutions

If you actually care about other people in the world, about poverty and injustice, about human rights, about environmental pollution and climate change, then you have to realise that the only way to do something about those problems is to work to change the world system. These problems simply cannot be solved at the local level. They can only be solved at the global level. And that's why we argue that if you care about social and environmental justice, you need to be a globalist.

Working for global change is not as much fun as living in a small-scale experimental community. It's a bit abstract. It doesn't give you the immediate kick of satisfaction of helping someone face-to-face, or of achieving a goal straight away. It will probably take quite a long time. But changing the global system is the only way that we are ever going to rid the world of poverty and injustice. And it's probably the only way that we have a chance of saving the world from massive climate change and environmental destruction.

If you truly want to solve these issues, then you need to work towards a democratic and just world system, in which all the world's people have a say in how the world system is governed. You need to work towards things like a world parliament and global courts. These things may seem a bit technical, and not much fun, but these are the crucial things that we need in order to make our world a better place. A democratic world federation may seem far off, but if we all work together then it can be much closer than we ever imagined.

21. Domesticating the International System

When we try to understand global politics, the politics of humanity as a whole, and the different relations that occur on different levels, one of the most useful concepts that can help us is what scholars refer to as the 'Great Divide' that can be observed between domestic politics, which happens *within* states, and international relations, which takes place *between* different states.[1] While on the domestic level, politics revolves around things like elections and political parties and parliaments, in international relations you find a very different set of tools and concepts, such as diplomacy, realism, power politics and war. In this chapter we will explore six key differences between the two sides of this great divide. This will help us get a better understanding of the problems that currently plague the international system, and also shed some more light about what it would mean to take domestic politics to the global level.

Difference (1): National Governments Work Differently on the Domestic and International Levels

The first key difference is how national governments work differently in the domestic sphere and in the international sphere. On the domestic level, as we know, all governments appoint issue-specific ministries (or departments or agencies) to deal with different issues, such as health, education, environment and so on. But they only deal with these matters within the borders of the state. Any health-, or education-, or environment-related issues that stretch *beyond* the state border suddenly get re-defined as 'international issues', and responsibility for dealing with them is given to the Ministry of Foreign Affairs.

The name of that Ministry, 'Foreign Affairs', reveals something fundamentally problematic about the whole international system, because it reflects the perception that the entire Earth that is beyond national borders is a 'foreign land', and that the entire rest of humanity that is 'out there' are 'foreigners' – you know, people that are not like you and me, people whom we cannot understand and certainly cannot trust. This is actually a very dangerous mindset, because in reality we live together with all those people on the very same small planet, that is so precious and so fragile. We are all vulnerable to the failures of the global economy, to pandemics and to other global threats. And so a system that defines most of humanity as 'foreign' and 'alien' to us is just the wrong system on so many levels.

And sure, it's nice that despite this, many people still feel a strong connection to the entire Earth as our shared home, and to the whole of humanity as our larger group, just like that ancient sage who said: 'I am a human, and therefore nothing human is foreign to me'. That's great, but we also need a political system that reflects this basic unity. Today, we don't have that.

Difference (2): The Ability to Aggregate Political Power

Which brings us to the second key difference, which has to do with the important issues of identity and citizenship. On the domestic level, in any country you can find a multitude of individuals and groups with a huge variety of opinions, customs, hobbies, preferences, values and interests. People in any one country are certainly not identical. But one fundamental thing that they all share in common is that because they are all legally recognized as citizens of the same country, they can do that thing that is at the heart of the democratic system, they can aggregate their political power by voting on the issues or for the parties that they like, together.

But on the international level they cannot do that. Let's say that you are worried by the fact that some big country that you do not live in is doing nothing to reduce its huge carbon emissions, and you know that these emissions will eventually harm you, and millions of other people, because you all live in the same climate that is getting heated up because of these emissions. But because you, and those millions of other people, are not citizens of that big country, you are not allowed to vote there for a party or a politician that would take serious actions to curb those emissions. So you are included ecologically in the damage caused but excluded from the political process that makes the decisions about what is or is not allowed.

Even if you could find the millions of like-minded people in other countries, who all care about the same thing that you care about, there is no way for you to aggregate your political power together with them. The structure of the international system imposes a permanent and impenetrable legal separation between you all, and defines you as 'foreigners' to each other. You cannot come together to form global political parties and you cannot vote together in global elections. While so many of the things that affect your life are caused by actions that take place outside of your particular country, you have absolutely no say in those actions.

Difference (3): How Conflicts are Solved

Another feature of the international system is that we are all minorities in the world. In any one country its own citizens – its 'us' groups – are always outnumbered by the greater 'them' group of foreigners that are out there in the world. For example, even though the USA has the third largest population in the world, on a global count they are just a small minority. For every US citizen in the world there are 23 people that are non-US citizens. Even for every Chinese citizen, there are globally 6 non-Chinese others, and nearly the same number for every Indian citizen.

Because every nation feels like such a minority in the world, they are all constantly worried and feeling vulnerable and insecure, living in fear, because who knows what those foreigners might have in mind. Each country may say: 'We are not looking to fight with anyone, but we have to be ready to defend ourselves in case others attack. We can't really rely on others to defend us. And if we did, what will they want in return?'

This brings us to the third difference between politics on the domestic and international levels – the matter of what tools exist to solve conflicts and provide security on each level. On the domestic level, if individuals or groups have a dispute that they cannot settle, they are not allowed to use violence, but are invited to turn to the appropriate court, whose rulings can then be backed up by the police. But on the international level, countries don't have the phone number of some world police force that will come to protect them in case they are attacked. And so they pour huge budgets into maintaining national armies that will be ready to defend them in case of attack. And when we say huge, we mean the equivalent of $2 trillion every year. That is the equivalent of $500 million every single day.

Now, you might have heard people speak about 'international treaties', such as the Geneva Conventions that set the norms for how to wage wars in a less barbaric way. And you might have heard about the International Court of Justice (ICJ), now more than a hundred years old, or the much more recent International Criminal Court (ICC), only twenty years old, that are supposed to help solve conflicts and prosecute the worst crimes on the basis of 'international law'. But when push comes to shove, the fact that countries spend $500 million per day on their armies shows you how much these so-called 'international justice' mechanisms are worth. They are far too weak to be counted on. Their toothlessness is not a mistake, it is a basic feature of international system.

Notice also that on the domestic level, all the processes of solving conflicts and ensuring security are, fairly transparent and open to public scrutiny: from the writing of laws in the parliament, through to their adjudication in open courts and their legal enforcement by the police.

But on the international level, the tools for solving conflicts and ensuring security are shrouded in thick fog. Our army forces are a state secret; our diplomatic missions and all their dealings are also secret; and our intelligence agencies – spying on other countries, and trying to weed out foreign spies amongst us – are all completely secret. In fact, even seemingly benign things like trade and investment treaties are kept secret while being negotiated, so secret that even parliamentarians are not allowed to see what's in the drafts.

Why is there all this secrecy at the international level? As US federal judge Louis Brandeis said some ninety years ago, 'Sunlight is the best disinfectant, and electric light is the most efficient policeman.' Today the domestic sphere is the 'realm of light', while the international sphere is the 'kingdom of darkness'. Shedding some light there would surely be a good thing.

Difference (4): Tools to Prevent the Concentration of Power

This brings us to the fourth key difference between the two spheres, and the most important one, and that is about the tools available in each sphere to prevent the concentration of power in the hands of the few. On the domestic level, national democracies have developed some really good principles for how to do that, both with regard to the people, and with regard to the government.

The power of the government is divided in horizontal and vertical ways. The horizontal division is between the three branches of government: the legislative, the judicial and the executive, which roughly correspond to the parliament or congress which write and adopt laws, the courts that rule according to these laws, and the government ministries or departments which execute these laws and enforce them. The vertical division means that in all three branches, state power is divided between several levels: the central level at the top, dealing with national or state-wide issues, the regional in the middle, dealing with simpler or more local affairs, and the local or municipal levels at the grassroots level, managing local affairs.

The underlying assumption behind all these divisions was nicely explained by the writers of the US Constitution, in the Federalist Papers. They said that each branch of government, at each level, can be expected to be greedy and will try to accumulate more power for itself, at the expense of the others. But because all the different branches and levels will be trying to do this, they will each stand guard and make sure that they do not lose their own respective powers. In this way, they will prevent the concentration of too much power in any one place. When the power of the whole government is kept divided and balanced in this way, it is also much easier for the people to check the power of the government, and to make sure it stays a government of the people, by the people and for the people.

With regard to the people, domestic politics also has effective tools to prevent the concentration of too much power in the hands of individuals citizens or their groups or companies. Laws and regulations seek to ensure that everyone plays fair, and taxation and redistribution from the rich to the rest of society ensures that inequality is kept at a reasonable level, balancing the incentive for social mobility, while maximizing the options for it.

However, today many people complain, and rightly so, that this domestic system is failing, and that it does not prevent the concentration of power in the hands of either governments or the economic elite.

This is true. But the reason for this failure, as we have discussed in several other chapters, is the fact that these good domestic mechanisms are today restricted only to the national level, while the frameworks for accumulation of power and wealth have expanded to the global scale, where they are largely beyond the reach and the oversight of the national domestic systems.

This fundamental problem has two possible solutions – we can either down-scale the economy and limit it only to level of the nation-state, or upscale the domestic system of checks and balances to the global level, so that it can function on the same scale as the economy. The first option is very hard to justify from a humanistic or cosmopolitan perspective. It is rather the second option that makes much more sense. Just as our moral sentiments can cross borders and we can care about exploitation and environmental problems that occur beyond state borders, so we should have a shared system for restraining the powerful, everywhere. Just as within our states we don't leave the protection of the weak to the voluntary 'morality' of the strong, but rather we have systems of regulation, law enforcement and redistribution, so too we should have such systems at the global level. All of these domestic measures for preventing the concentration of power can, and should, be applied at the global level.

Furthermore, while it's clear that helping the economy to be as local as possible has many advantages, both ecological and social, the best way to do it is actually by globalising the domestic mechanisms of politics and justice. This might sound counter-intuitive, but if you think about it carefully then it makes sense. You see, one of the main drivers for globalising the economy and doing so much business 'over there', in other countries, is because in those countries the regulation is much weaker: people can be made to work for long hours and be paid less for their work, it is OK to pollute the environment there because no-one bothers to enforce environmental laws, and so on.

But if human rights and the environment were protected globally, through a global justice system, then the economic incentive for this outsourcing of harmful activities would suddenly disappear. And then it wouldn't be worth paying all the additional transport costs to move things round the world during their production, and so we would see a great revitalizing and strengthening of local economies.

By globalizing domestic politics, or domesticating global politics, we can expect to see the economy not only flourishing, but also becoming more local (because of more uniform regulation), more equal (because of redistribution), more just (because of real protection of human rights) and more sustainable (because of real enforcement of environmental laws). Sounds good, doesn't it?

Difference (5): How the Economy is Managed

This brings us to the fifth difference between domestic and international politics – the management of the economy. In domestic political systems, you can find different versions of 'mixed economy', that combine the market system with the economic checks and balances of the state. These can be regulation, taxation and redistribution, and also some public ownership of land, or natural resources or companies, to be used for the benefit of the wider public.

In each democratic country, the exact balance of state and market is the topic of hot arguments between the domestic left and the domestic right. And indeed, in every such country this ratio is dynamic and changes this way and that way over the years. But what we sometime forget is that there is a great agreement among those on the left and those on the right that some mixture of state and market is necessary. Virtually everyone agrees that having just a market economy with no state, or just a state economy with no market, would be a bad thing.

Yet, when it comes to the international level, these same people seem to just take it for granted that the market system has gone global, while the state system has not. And thus, at the global level, we basically have a market system with no state. While this would be clearly bad at the national level, no-one seems to worry about it at the global level. Of course, it is super convenient for the transnational corporations and the economic elites who are the major global market players. The regulatory tools that are supposed to restrain their power are divided between some two hundred separate and competing governments. So it becomes very easy for them to escape regulation and avoid paying any taxes.[2]

Difference (6): The Rights of the Individual

There are many other profound differences between domestic politics and international relations, but we will end here with just a final one, and that is the different rights and powers of the individual in each system. On the domestic level, the individual person is considered the most basic unit of society. In democratic systems each individual has one vote. In this way the demos is supposed to have a portion of power and sovereignty over the government. Thus, the political relationship is not only top-down, where governments rule subjects, but also bottom-up, with citizens also selecting and ruling their governments.

But on the international level individuals have no say. It is as if they don't exist. Instead, as it is conceived now, the basic unit of international society is the state. International relations is a game for governments, and governments only. And as such it is fundamentally top-down. Individuals are effectively governed through this system, but they have no voice and no vote.

We Need to Domesticate the International System

The vision of a world federation, in its most basic manifestation, is to create a domestic-style democratic political system on the global scale. In a world federation we would globalise domestic politics, or domesticate global politics. We would create one political system to bring together everyone on planet Earth.

In such a world we would no-longer share our planet with 'foreigners', but with fellow citizens. We would no longer have to spend trillions of dollars on armies to defend ourselves, but would have a much cheaper and much more effective federal justice system, with federal courts and federal police. We would write the laws together, in a global parliament or congress, in which no nation or religion would have a majority. We would be free to aggregate our political power with other people who share our values, wherever they may be in the world. And finally, we would be able to start dealing seriously with our global problems.

It's a big vision, and it takes a while to get your head around it. But once you grasp it, it really does seem so obvious.

Notes

1 Clark, Ian. 1999. Globalization and International Relations Theory. Oxford: Oxford University Press; Kaldor, Mary. 2007. Human Security: Reflections of Globalization and Intervention. Cambridge: Polity Press.

2 See also Cabrera, Luis. 2005. The Cosmopolitan Imperative: Global Justice Through Accountable Integration. *Journal of Ethics*, 9, 1-2: 171-199.

22. Global Citizenship

There is a lot of talk these days about global citizenship, but the term is often used in a very vague and unclear way. Most of the time it's not really about 'citizenship' at all, with all the rights and responsibilities that come with it, but rather people speak about global citizenship as a general sense of being interested in, and caring about, other peoples and cultures. Or following world events and knowing what is going on beyond your own country. Or perhaps giving to international charities and working in international development. Or even just living a cosmopolitan lifestyle and travelling a lot. In this chapter we're going to have a look at the concept of global citizenship or world citizenship in more detail, and imagine what the world would look like if the individual became the basic unit of global society and we all became world citizens, in the real sense of the term.

Feeling Like a Member of a Global Society

Oxfam defines a global citizen as 'someone who is aware of and understands the wider world and their place in it, who takes an active role in their community and work with others to make the planet more peaceful, sustainable and fairer'.[1] That's all very nice, but a bit wishy-washy, and certainly doesn't have anything to do with real citizenship. In a similar vein, many organisations these days talk about 'global citizenship education'. Again, this is generally understood to mean educating children and adults to take a holistic world perspective, to look at social issues, to value understanding and tolerance across cultures, and so on.

Used in this vague and general way, many people do indeed feel that they are global citizens. A surprisingly large number of people, in fact. In the World Values Survey, a massive survey carried out with large numbers of respondents across many countries every few years, the 2014 results show that 70.5% of respondents either agreed or strongly agreed with the statement, 'I see myself as a world citizen.'[2] And this was no once-off rogue survey. In 2016 in another huge survey was carried out across 18 countries by Globescan and the BBC World Service, it was found that 51% of respondents agreed or strongly agreed with the statement, 'I see myself more as a global citizen than a citizen of my country'.[3] This indicates that a global majority identify as being part of one global society, and that this identification is even more important to them than their national identification. That's amazing. It means that despite what the politicians try to tell us, many, many people are not taken in by nationalism and racism and xenophobia, and instead feel like the world is their home.

Former British Prime Minister Theresa May might have tried to appeal to nationalist sentiments when she spoke to the Conservative party conference in 2016, saying, 'If you believe you are a citizen of the world, you are a citizen of nowhere.'[4] But it seems that many people, even in Britain, actually *do* feel like they are citizens of the world. As our social and economic interactions increasingly spread across the globe, as we travel more, meet more people through social media, and learn about the world through the internet, many of us feel as if we belong to one, increasingly global, society.

Of course, that doesn't mean that we don't also identify as British, or Chinese, or Nigerian, or whatever. Just as it doesn't mean that we don't also identify as men, or women, or left-wing or right-wing, or a whole range of other identities that we manage very easily to hold at the same time. May, and other nationalists, try to imply that if you feel a profound connection to the whole of humanity then you can't possibly also feel a profound connection with your native country. That's as stupid as saying that feeling loyalty to your friends must mean that you feel less loyalty to your family. Of course not! We can feel loyalty and connection to many people, all at the same time.

What Does World Citizenship Actually Mean?

But there are also some truths in Theresa May's words. What she said in full was actually this: 'If you believe you are a citizen of the world, you are a citizen of nowhere. You don't understand what citizenship means.'

It is this last bit which is true. All this vague and general talk of being a citizen of the world has nothing to do with what 'citizenship' actually means. Citizenship is a relationship between a person and a state in which the state gives that person particular civil, political, and social rights. Social contract theory defines citizenship as 'a bundle of rights – primarily, political participation in the life of the community, the right to vote, and the right to receive certain protection from the community, as well as certain obligations.' So real world citizenship would require some kind of world state which could grant people certain rights, and indeed guarantee them.

This was the vision of Rosika Schwimmer and Lola Maverick Lloyd, who, as we discussed in detail in chapter 12, wanted all refugees and stateless people to be able to claim world citizenship. It was also the vision of Gary Davis, a peace activist who in 1948 renounced his US citizenship and declared himself World Citizen Number One. These activists, and many others like them, talked about world citizenship in the very real sense of the term. They wanted a federal layer of global government which could grant real rights to everyone. Let's consider what this might look like.

A World Passport and a World Without Borders

First of all, pretty much all states grant their citizens the right to move around freely within the state, and to live and work anywhere. So let's imagine that world citizens had this right. This on its own, would be huge. It would mean that everyone, no matter where they were born, would have a world passport and be able to travel anywhere, and to live and work anywhere, just like it is today within the US or within the EU. Borders would become minor details and everyone would be able to cross them freely. There would be no more refugees and no more stateless people. Everyone would be citizen of the world and have rights and freedoms whatever the situation in their home country and wherever they happened to find themselves.

In a world without borders it would be impossible to fence people into countries in which there are no opportunities, or where they cannot earn a decent living, or where their government is persecuting them. No, they would simply be able to leave and go somewhere better. 'But hang on', you say, 'wouldn't that mean that everybody from the poor countries would suddenly rush to the rich countries? Then there will be over-crowding and tensions between people of different religions and ethnic groups, there won't be enough jobs to go around, it will be awful'. Well, let's think about that. If the world continued to be as unequal and as unjust as it currently is, then yes, there probably would be a huge movement of people from poor to rich countries. But if that were possible, and the politicians and everyone knew that, then that would be a huge incentive to balance out the inequalities and injustices in the world, so that all the countries would be more or less similar in terms of wealth and freedoms and opportunities.

Rather than keep the majority of the world's population imprisoned against their will within the borders of their countries, where they have no other choice than to work in poorly paid jobs, in dangerous conditions, in order to produce the food and commodities which rich people in the west consume, we could create a fair and balanced world where everyone, no matter where they were born or the colour of their skin, would be able to make a good life for themselves. Opening all the borders would very quickly lead to a much more balanced and just world, because suddenly it would be in the interests of the rich countries to do so.

Global Democracy and Human Rights

Most states grant their citizens the right to vote in elections to choose the government. So let's assume that world citizens would also be able to vote in elections to choose the federal level of the global government. We would finally have global democracy and a say in global affairs.

Most states also grant their citizens many other social, economic and political rights. So what rights would the world government grant to world citizens? Well, we actually already have a draft of this – the Universal Declaration of Human Rights, and indeed all the other human rights that have been drafted in international law since then. As we showed in chapter 8, in the current system all of these 'rights' are just aspirational, because there is no world government to actually grant and guarantee them. But if we did have a world government, and a world parliament and world courts, then we could make human rights *real*. In such a system, all world citizens would actually have real human rights. If we only went this far, the world would be a hugely more just and more equal place. But we could go even further.

A Global Welfare State

If the world's population chose to do so, through democratic elections at the global level, we could decide to set up the world state on a similar basis to the European model, with a strong welfare state based on a system of taxation and redistribution. If we did this then we could institute some global taxes, as we discussed in chapter 10 – perhaps a wealth tax, or a financial transaction tax, or a carbon tax, or even a tiny income tax – and then the world state could give everyone the right to free education, free healthcare, some form of welfare, and so on. This would even out the economic inequalities, and the inequalities of opportunity, even more. But even if we didn't go this far, even if we just chose a more right-wing, US style model of citizenship, even that would make a huge difference.

Supra-National Citizenship

Now this all might sound fanciful, but there are already several kinds of supra-national citizenship – citizenship that is granted at a level higher than the state. Citizenship in the European Union is the best-known example. People retain citizenship of their home country, of France or Italy or where ever, but also gain citizenship of the European Union, and this grants them rights to travel freely in the area and to live and work where they please.

Just recently, in 2021, the Mercosur bloc of countries in Latin America decided to do something very similar, and launched the Mercosur Citizenship Statute, which grants a supra-national Mercosur citizenship to citizens of Mercosur countries, such as Argentina, Brazil, Paraguay and others. Mercosur citizens can now travel freely in the bloc, and live and work in any Mercosur country.[5]

So setting up supra-national citizenship is not particularly hard to do. In fact, it is eminently possible. There is no legal or technical reason that we could not create a supra-national world citizenship for everyone. It just requires political will, and for enough people to demand it.

It is probably because world citizenship, real world citizenship, is such a radical and powerful idea, that the powers-that-be have found a way to warp and twist the term until it has come to mean something quite different – something that is much less radical and much less challenging to the status quo. But if we want real world citizenship, then we need to start saying so, and using the term in the proper way.

The Movement for World Citizenship

In the 1940s there was a massive movement calling for world citizenship. Rosika Schwimmer and Lola Maverick Lloyd wrote one of the earliest descriptions of what world citizenship could look like and then set about lobbying governments to make it a reality. A few years later Gary Davis took a more novel and direct approach, renouncing his US citizenship and simply declaring himself to be a world citizen. He had a background in show business and knew how to catch the attention of the press and the people, and used creative tactics to get himself and his cause on the front pages of newspapers. On 19th November 1948, for example, he caused a stir by interrupting the United Nations session that was meeting in Paris and shouted out from the observers' balcony, demanding a world government and world citizenship in order to end war and bring about peace.

Another tactic he used was to camp out in international territory – places like the UN, or the borderlands between two countries – where national police forces could not evict him, and then give press conferences about the stupidity of dividing the world into separate countries.[6]

Davis also worked with Lola's daughter, Mary Maverick Lloyd, to establish the International Registry of World Citizens, and they registered over 950,000 people who declared themselves world citizens. Later on, he also set up an organisation that issued world passports, symbolic world passports, and he and other activists tried to use them when they travelled to other countries. Sometimes they succeeded, sometimes they were arrested, but many of the times their antics made it into the newspapers, and made people think about what a passport is, and why it works as it does. Arthur Kanegis, an American filmmaker who made a documentary about Davis recalled,

'He used to say: 'The World Passport is a joke — but so are all the other passports. Theirs are a joke on us and ours is a joke on the system.'[7]

These creative actions helped him build up a following of hundreds of thousands of people. They came out to the streets, thousands or tens of thousands at a time, calling for an end to war and the creation of world citizenship and world government.

But in the 1950s, the Cold War brought an end, or at least a major reduction, to these and other movements for world citizenship. For the next 40 or 50 years the world seemed to be literally split into two opposing camps, communist and capitalist, with completely different political and economic systems. With the Iron Curtain cutting the world in half, many found it impossible to think about world unity.

World Citizenship in an Era of Globalisation

But then, in 1989, the Iron Curtain came down. And since then, economic globalisation has accelerated at a phenomenal rate. Today it is very much possible to imagine a unified world. Indeed, we're partway there. The global economy is to a very great extent unified. Air travel and the internet have enabled our social relations and even large parts of our culture to increasingly unify. It is only our political system that remains resolutely fragmented and disparate.

We are so much closer to a unified world than we were in the 1940s. So much closer. So perhaps it will be possible now, with the aid of internet and social media, and possibly other new technologies still on the horizon, to galvanise an even larger mass movement than the one in the 1940s – with people from the north and the south, the east and the west; social movements, NGOs and ordinary citizens; farmers, students, factory workers, indigenous peoples, environmentalists, refugees; everyone who cares about justice and human rights – to make that final push to make global political unification a reality. Because only then can we get a say in the democratic running of our world, only then can there really be human rights, and only then can we really become world citizens.

Notes

1 www.oxfam.org.uk/education/who-we-are/what-is-global-citizenship/

2 Inglehart, R., Haerpfer, C., Moreno, A., Welzel, C., Kizilova, K., Diez-Medrano, J., Lagos, M., Norris, P., Ponarin, E., Puranen, B., et al. 2014. World values survey: Round Six: Country-Pooled Datafile Version. www.worldvaluessurvey.org/-WVSDocumentationWV5.jsp.

3 www.weforum.org/agenda/2016/04/bbc-poll-suggests-more-people-identify-as-global/

4 www.bbc.com/news/uk-politics-37788717

5 www.mercosur.int/estatuto-ciudadania-mercosur/

6 Baratta, Joseph. 2004. The Politics of World Federation: United Nations, UN Reform, Atomic Control. Westport: Praeger. Chapter 19: Garry Davis: World Citizen in France, pp399-419; Davis, Garry. 1961. My Country is the World: The Adventure of a World Citizen. London: Macdonald & Co.

7 www.latimes.com/local/obituaries/la-xpm-2013-aug-01-la-me-garry-davis-20130801-story.html

23. From Global Oligarchy to Global Democracy

Our world, at present, is organised as a global oligarchy. This may be obvious to people in the global South, but to those who live in the global North it can sound like a strange claim. We are often told that all the bad things in the world come from the 'less developed' places – things like poverty, war, corruption, and so on. While apparently, the 'developed', western world is a paragon of law and order, democracy and clean values. Well, we need to challenge this rosy story and think again. We are all part of one global system, and when you zoom out and look at things this way then you see that the actions of the west are not so sparkling clean after all. This chapter helps us to understand our respective places in today's global oligarchy, and sketches the outlines of a much brighter alternative, world federation and global democracy.

The Growth of Local Democracy within a Global Oligarchy

Let's start with looking at the evolution of democracy, but from a global perspective. One of most famous historical landmarks with regard to the development of democracy is the medieval Magna Carta, the 'Great Charter', in which the King of England was forced to share power and authority with the English Barons. Initially, it was with a Council of only 25 barons, and of course it didn't include any of the peasants who did all the hard work, but later, over the centuries, that Council was broadened into a parliament, and representation in that parliament was gradually increased until eventually all the men of England were included, and then a little later, also all the women too. So over time, the very limited British 'democracy of the elites' gradually expanded and became a 'democracy of everyone', manifesting the democratic principle that those who are governed should have power over those who govern them.[1] However, what often gets ignored in this tale is that most of that evolution of democracy within England, as in several other European countries, happened at the same time as they were busy conquering the rest of the world. Imperialism was surely not a European invention, but when the European empires rose, they possessed the technology and the mindset to go global. And so we can see a tension between two contradicting trends. On the domestic scale, within England or France, we see the evolution and growth of an inclusive democracy – a government of the people, by the people and for all people – while on the global level, at the same time, those people become members of what can only be understood as a global ruling class, which profits from the exploitation of their new subjects in the colonies, otherwise known as 'the rest of the world'.

From the perspective of the masses of people in those colonies, of course, this was not a democracy but an oligarchy, a rule by the few over the many. And so that system, that global order that emerged, had a huge internal contradiction built into it: on the one hand there was the rise of democracy on the local level, in the west; while on the other hand, and at the same time, there was the formation of an oligarchy on the global level.

The tension between the justice of the first and the injustice of the second, could have been resolved in three ways. Two have already been tried in history, and failed, and there is just one way that remains for us to try now. Let's take a look at all three.

(1) The Philosophy of Racism

The first way that Europeans tried to resolve the awkward tension between local democracy for themselves alongside a global oligarchy for everyone else was for the Europeans to tell themselves that the people that they were ruling over were not really 'people,' but some inferior beings that were incapable of taking part in democracy. We know this philosophy now as 'racism', and it was at its strongest during the 19th century. But as scientific enlightenment and simple human solidarity increasingly exposed the huge falsehood and cruelty of this belief, racism was then largely abandoned for the sake of an updated, repackaged version of it, that said that it was the culture, rather than the biology of the people in the colonies, that made them unfit to be included in a shared democracy of 'civilized people'. The people in the colonies themselves, of course, did not find these arguments convincing in the slightest. And eventually even the Europeans came to accept that culture, like race, could not justify the profound injustice of their oligarchic rule over the non-Europeans. This realisation, which occurred mainly during the 20th century, then led to the second great attempt to resolve the tension between the democratic standards that the Europeans applied to themselves, and their oligarchic rule over the rest of the world.

(2) De-Colonisation and the Formation of Nation States

In this second attempt, the European empires were formally dismantled, supposedly to allow the people of the colonies to govern themselves freely. And so, soon after the middle of the 20th century the whole of humanity and the whole of the Earth were divided into some two hundred separate political units, which we call states, with borders that almost everywhere were identical to those that were drawn by the colonial powers. This new arrangement, that we still have today, was supposed to finally resolve the contradiction between local democracy for Europeans alongside a global oligarchy for everyone else. Now that the Europeans no longer directly governed the world, it would appear, at least at first sight, that the system of global oligarchy had been taken apart, and that the people of the world were finally free to shape their own futures as they like.

But surprise, surprise! After more than seventy years of the formal independence of most of the colonies, what do we find? We find that the basic unjust pattern of global exploitation didn't really change. Before the so-called 'independence', many people in the colonies had to work long hours in the plantations, the mines and the sweatshops, to produce things that were shipped to the happy markets of Europe. And now? Their grandchildren and grand-grandchildren are still working in the plantations, the mines and the sweatshops to produce things that are still shipped mainly to the happy markets of the European countries.

It's not a coincidence, of course. The only thing that really changed in the new arrangement is that the Europeans, who used to directly govern the colonies, have now out-sourced that hard and dirty work of undemocratic rule to local governments made up of non-Europeans. And these new local rulers were allowed to enjoy a part of the loot in return for their good services. So the European system of global oligarchy didn't really end with the official end of colonialism and empire, it just got a little bit more sophisticated. The newly created 'international order' didn't really resolve the tension between local democracy and global oligarchy, it just made it a little less obvious.

(3) Global Democracy

This brings us to the third possible solution, the one that hasn't been tried yet, even though it's the most obvious one. And that is the idea to expand the boundaries of democracy until it includes the whole of humanity. Then we could have one integrated political system that will exist on the same scale as our society, our economy and our ecology. This is what democracy should have evolved into already a long time ago, but some powerful interests diverted it in another direction. It's time to rectify that now.

As humanity is increasingly facing more and more global problems, and as nation states and the so-called 'international system' are finding that they cannot solve them, the imperative to take democracy to the global level is becoming ever more pressing, and ever clearer to more and more people.

How Would a Global Democracy Function?

So what would it be like? What does it mean to apply democracy at the global level? Well, the basic principles are pristinely simple and obvious. The two basic components of democracy, the demos and the kratos, the people and the system of government, should be recognized globally.

With regard to the demos, this would mean that every person would be recognized as a world citizen, with the right to vote not only at the local, city or state levels, but also at the federal global level. There would be democratic global elections to elect the government and parliament at the federal global level, as well as, of course, national and local elections for state and municipal officials. There would probably be global political parties, which set out their different ideas about how to solve global problems, such as climate change or economic inequality, or how to institute global laws protecting human rights. And people all around the world would consider these various ideas and vote for the party that they thought offered the best solutions. In this way, as we discussed in chapter 21, people from around the world would be able to aggregate their political power and act together, *politically*, to create the type of global society that they want.

With regard to the kratos, it would mean that the classic division of power between the legislative, the executive and the judicial branches of government, would also be applied at the global level. There would be a world parliament, a world government and world courts. The definition of the respective capacities, responsibilities and limitations of these three branches of government would be clearly outlined in the federal World Constitution. Besides this horizontal division of power, there would also be a vertical division of power within each branch, so that authority would be devolved and dispersed over several different levels. In this way the central authority, such as the federal court or the federal government, would have only a subsidiary function, performing only those tasks which cannot be performed at lower, or more local, levels. There would be no all-powerful, centralised world government.

Thus, the basic institutional outlines of global democracy are incredibly simple and straightforward. We know them well from the national context. The only task would be to implement them globally. The problem is not that we don't know how to do it, but rather that the powers-that-be, the global oligarchs, have brainwashed us into believing that it is neither possible nor desirable.

Ending Global Oligarchy Once and for All

It is high time that we, people who care for justice and for humanity, rise and speak truth to power. We need to re-think, and help others to re-think, the stories that we have all been told about our history and our present, and about what is possible or impossible in the future. We must no longer accept the poor substitutes of global democracy that we have, but demand the full package: a world parliament, a world government, world courts, a world constitution and world citizenship. The whole thing! A truly democratic and inclusive system that will do away with the injustice of global oligarchy. Nothing less.

Note

1 See also Kiser, Edgar and Yoram Barzel. 1991. The Origins of Democracy in England. *Rationality and Society*, 3: 396-422.

24. A World Parliament

One of the central institutions in a future global democracy would be a world parliament, an institution where representatives of all of humanity can sit together, discuss and debate, and make decisions about common global issues that affect us all.[1]

The idea of a world parliament has a long history. During the French Revolution at the end of the 18th century, cosmopolitan revolutionaries called for the creation of a world republic with a world parliament. And in 1842, the British poet Alfred Tennyson, mentioned the idea of a parliament of mankind as a solution to the world's problems in the poem 'Locksley Hall', where he writes,

> 'Till the war-drum throbb'd no longer, and the battle-flags were furl'd
> In the Parliament of man, the Federation of the world.
> There the common sense of most shall hold a fretful realm in awe,
> And the kindly earth shall slumber, lapt in universal law.'[2]

In recent years the idea of a world parliament has moved from being just a vague and poetic aspiration, to being the centre of scholarly and activist calls to democratise the world system. There are now lively discussions about what a world parliament should look like and how it could realistically be established, and several campaigns and initiatives aiming at making a world parliament a reality. This chapter considers in more detail why we need a world parliament and looks at the major present-day campaigns to make it a reality.

Why We Need a World Parliament

The need for a world parliament is obvious. It would give people a say in politics and decision-making at the global level. At the moment we are excluded from expressing our wishes and opinions at this level, and can only express them at the national level, if we happen to live in a country with a national democracy. But since the 1980s and 1990s more and more important decisions have started to be taken at the global level, where we, the people, have no say. This is really important, because decisions taken at the global level can and do affect our lives in many ways. And the basic principle of democracy is that people should have a say in decisions which affect their lives. Let's look at a few examples. Decisions taken at the World Trade Organisation (WTO) impact on many people around the world in all sorts of ways. They can lead to workers losing their jobs, or to consumers finding that their food is now grown from genetically-modified seeds, or is full of chemical additives, or to patients finding that the drugs that they require are now very expensive because of WTO patent rules. Decisions taken at the global level about how to deal with climate change, or not to deal with it, affect us all, as our lives and livelihoods are disrupted on a warming planet. Decisions about global finance and sovereign debt impinge directly on our savings and on our country's ability to provide public services. And there are many other examples that affect all areas of our lives. Since these decisions affect us, we should have a say in them. But at the moment we don't, and this is a serious problem.

A world parliament would provide a place for citizens' representatives to have their say in these kinds of global decisions. It would provide a mechanism to connect the decision-makers with the people affected by their decisions. And it would provide a mechanism of accountability, so that if we don't like the decisions, then we have a way to vote these people out. As in national democracies, this would help incentivise politicians to act according to the wishes of the people.

A world parliament would bring into being a very different kind of voice within global politics. Whereas the UN General Assembly is composed of representatives of the executive branches of governments who ultimately represent institutional interests within the nation-state system, a world parliament would be made up of elected individuals who would speak for citizens, and be accountable to them. While the General Assembly is similar to the US Senate, representing states, a World Parliament would be like the US House of Representatives, representing individuals.

A world parliament would also help to develop a global or planetary consciousness. It would be a place where discussions centre on what is best for the world as a whole, and not what is best for my particular country. In a world parliament, rather like in the European Parliament, there would be representatives from both government parties and opposition parties. These representatives would not sit or vote in country blocs. Instead, they would sit and vote in ideological blocs. So left-wing politicians from many different countries would sit together and vote together on left-wing ideas, while right-wing, or green, or liberal politicians would similarly vote together in their blocs. This could lead to the formation of global political parties and to parliamentary debates about how best to organise the world system from different ideological perspectives. Then there could be open discussion and debate about different approaches to globalisation. Now that would be refreshing.

There would be discussions about how to solve the major global problems that are facing us all – climate change, COVID, inequality, biodiversity loss. Rather than states negotiating according to their national interests, which as we have seen gets us nowhere, we would have citizens' representatives discussing collectively how to solve these problems.

Ultimately, a fully developed and fully democratic world parliament would be able to legislate world law. This would be completely different from so-called 'international law', which, is largely voluntary and unenforceable, and which applies only to states, and not to citizens or corporations. World law would be democratically-created, enforceable law, that would apply to everyone, everywhere. It would apply to the rich as well as the poor, to the trans-national corporations as well as to states, and to those in powerful countries as well as those in weaker countries. World law would be law created by the representatives of the people of the world, and it would be a kind of supranational law that would be able to constrain states. With world law, human rights could be enforced, global taxes could be legislated, and world-wide maximum levels of carbon emissions could be set.

A world parliament would probably not start out with all those powers, and in itself it would not fully democratise the whole global system. But it would be a very important first step, even without having legislative competences initially. It would be the first institution to provide a direct link between global politics and the grassroots, between global governance and global citizens. And it would be the first institution to take a global, rather than international, approach to world problems. Once up and running, a world parliament could lead the effort to further transform and democratise the world system. So, the reasons that we need a world parliament are clear. But how do we get there? How do we make a world parliament a reality?

The Movement for a World Parliament

Activists have been pushing for a world parliament for quite a long time.[3] In the years before and after the First World War activists in the Peace Movement called for the creation of a world parliament and world law, because they saw these as necessary for the establishment of a rules-based world system in which countries could solve their disputes through legal means, rather than resorting to war. Their efforts contributed to the creation of the Permanent Court of Arbitration, the Permanent Court of International Justice, and the League of Nations, but they did not lead to the creation of a real world parliament or world law.

There was another push for a world parliament in the years immediately after the Second World War, when the notions of world federation and world government were extremely popular. But at this time we got instead the United Nations, and again, no supra-national world parliament.

In the late 1970s and early 1980s discussions started up again about creating a world parliament. In 1978, a 'Peoples Assembly for the UN' took place over five weeks, in parallel with the first UN Special Session on Disarmament. And in the following years the Swedish Peace Council and the Swedish UN Association organised a 'Swedish Peoples Parliament on Disarmament'. Building on these ideas the People's Assembly Movement began to grow, holding World Citizen Assemblies in several cities around the world.

Then, in 1982, during the second UN Special Session on Disarmament, the Medical Association for Prevention of War, an organisation based in the UK and led by Jeffrey Segall,[4] presented a proposal for a study on 'a UN Second Assembly' or 'UN Peoples Assembly'. This proposal suggested that such an assembly could be established at the UN in a relatively straightforward manner, under Article 22 of the UN Charter, which allows the General Assembly to establish any subsidiary bodies that it deems necessary to support its functions.

In 1983 Segall brought a number of like-minded organisations together to form the International Network for A UN Second Assembly, or INFUSA. In the following years they worked to promote this idea in the NGO community and they also submitted a request to the UN, calling for it to study proposals for the establishment of a second chamber. Whilst they did not receive a response from the UN, their ideas *did* get support from a number of NGOs, particularly those dedicated to world federation and world citizenship, including the World Federalist Movement, The People's Congress and the Bertrand Russell Peace Foundation.[5]

But whilst all these organisations wanted to create a second chamber at the UN which would represent individual citizens, there were very many different ideas about what this chamber should look like. Should it consist of parliamentarians chosen by national governments? Or parliamentarians directly elected by the people? Or maybe it should consist of NGOs and civil society representatives? Should it be subsidiary to the UN General Assembly, or equal to it? Should it have legislative powers to make world law or should it only make recommendations? And so on.

So, in 1989 INFUSA, in collaboration with the New York-based World Citizens Assembly, created CAMDUN, Conferences for a More Democratic United Nations, a series of conferences where activists could come together to explore and discuss the various options and issues.[6] Building on these discussions, in 1992 the World Federalist Movement (WFM) published a small booklet, written by Dieter Heinrich, setting out their vision for a United Nations Parliamentary Assembly, or UNPA. It was the first publicly available thorough analysis and it set out a pragmatic and realistic proposal for developing a world parliament in a staged, evolutionary process, modelled on the progressive development of the European Parliament.[7]

During the 1990s the idea of a UN Parliamentary Assembly began to gain ground beyond activist circles. In 1993 the Standing Committee on External Affairs and International Trade of the Canadian House of Commons recommended that Canada should support the development of a United Nations Parliamentary Assembly and offer to host the preparatory meeting in the Canadian parliament buildings as the centrepiece of its celebrations for the UN's 50th anniversary in

1995. UN policy experts Erskine Childers and Brian Urquhart recommended the establishment of a UNPA in their 1994 report, 'Renewing the United Nations System'.[8] That same year both the European Parliament and the InterAction Council, an association of former heads of state and government, suggested that the possibility of establishing a UNPA should be studied. And in 2000 the president of the Czech Republic, Vaclav Havel, called for an elected world parliament in his speech at the UN's Millennium Summit.[9]

Throughout the 1990s various groups circulated more detailed UNPA proposals and began publishing analyses of how to proceed in the current political situation. Academics also began to get interested in the idea of a world parliament, and in the late 1990s and early 2000s international law professors Richard Falk and Andrew Strauss published a series of academic articles exploring the need for a world parliament and considering possibilities for establishing such a body.[10]

Policy Discussion: How Should a World Parliament Function?

As more activists, academics and policy experts began to think about a world parliament, a variety of ideas began to emerge. In particular there was a divide between those who thought that a world parliament should consist of elected parliamentary representatives and sit *within* the UN system, and those who thought that a world parliament should consist of directly elected individuals and sit *outside* of the UN system and indeed, outside of the formal state system altogether. The latter view was mainly voiced by the Global People's Assembly Movement, who in 2000 held the First Global Peoples Assembly. Despite the advantage of being able to move forward without having to wait for states' agreement, they soon found that their assembly had little legitimacy amongst the broader public and could simply be ignored.

Nonetheless, there have been several other attempts to try to organise a world parliament outside of the UN system. In the early 2000s British journalist George Monbiot suggested that the World Social Forum, the annual meeting of thousands of social movements and activists from around the world (which we discussed in chapter 4), could form the nucleus of a future world parliament if it were properly expanded and democratised.[11] His ideas were discussed at the World Social Forum in 2004, but at that time many activists favoured localist approaches and were nervous about globalist approaches (see chapter 20), and thus the participants could not agree on a way forward.

There is also the idea that a democratic world parliament could effectively exist on the internet. Blockchain technologies could be developed to build a transparent and incorruptible system, and then individuals from all round the world could simply log-in and vote directly on all manner of key issues. This would lead to a form of decentralised world parliament, based not on representative democracy, but on direct democracy. There are many challenges with this approach, not least getting the technology right, but there are several groups working on it at the moment, including academics such as Liav Orgad[12] and Ehud Shapiro[13], and activists such as Rasmus Tenbergen with his United Humans[14] approach, and Santiago Siri with his organisation Democracy Earth.[15]

Other activists thought that the world parliament should sit *within* the UN system, so that it would be properly recognised and have widely-accepted legitimacy. While the flaws of the UN system are obvious, it is still the central organisation that brings together all the countries of the world and which sits at the centre of the contemporary global governance system. Rather than trying to create a parallel system outside of the UN, they argued, it would be much better to create a world parliament inside the UN. And these activists suggested three different ways that it could be established.

One idea was that it could be created through a stand-alone treaty, signed initially by around 30 states. This would be enough to get the body established, but then obviously more states would need to join in order to give it democratic legitimacy. The promoters of this approach argue that it would be much easier to get states to join a body that already exists, than to vote to create it in the first place. And thus, starting with a small 'coalition of the willing' would be a good way to get things moving. Once a larger number of states had joined, its powers could be redefined and its place within the UN system agreed.

At the other end of the spectrum, another idea was to establish a world parliament in the UN by amending the UN Charter under article 109. If done this way, then a much stronger and more robust parliament could be created right at the outset, with considerable legislative powers. However, amending the UN Charter requires the support of a two thirds majority of all UN member states, plus the agreement of all the permanent members of the Security Council, and is thus extremely difficult to achieve.

In the middle was a third idea, to establish a Parliamentary Assembly at the UN, as an advisory body to the General Assembly. This could be done under article 22 of the UN Charter, which, as mentioned before, allows the General Assembly to establish any subsidiary bodies that it deems necessary to support its functions. This approach would not need any reform of the charter, and would only require a decision of the General Assembly. Crucially, it would not require the support of the Security Council. Once established, this Parliamentary Assembly could itself become a force for change within the UN. Over time it could evolve into a stronger body, in a similar way to how the European Parliament had started out as a purely consultative body in the 1950s and then over time gradually transformed and taken on more powers. In much the same way, the nascent UN Parliamentary Assembly could be expected to evolve into a stronger body, and ultimately become a real world parliament with legislative powers.

It was this third option that quickly began to emerge as the most popular, as activists, parliamentarians and scholars recognised its potential to bring about a change that was both achievable and sufficiently inclusive.

The Campaign for a United Nations Parliamentary Assembly (UNPA)

In 2003 the Congress of the Socialist International, meeting in Sao Paulo, endorsed the goal of a UN Parliamentary Assembly, or UNPA, followed in 2005 by the Congress of the Liberal International, and in 2008 by the Green World Congress. And in 2005 a majority of Swiss parliamentarians published an open letter to UN Secretary-General Kofi Annan, asking him to look into the proposal of a UNPA.

Seeing the momentum beginning to build, in 2007 the Committee for a Democratic UN, which had been formed in Germany on 2003, and which would later become Democracy Without Borders, initiated the launch of the International Campaign for a UNPA, in collaboration with the World Federalist Movement, the Society for Threatened

Peoples, and several other partners. The idea was to bring together the various different organisations promoting a UN Parliamentary Assembly so that they could work together in a concerted effort to bring a UNPA into reality.

Former UN Secretary-General Boutros Boutros-Ghali was a patron and as such sent a supportive message to the participants of the new campaign, saying,

> 'Democracy within the state will diminish in importance if the process of democratization does not move forward at the international level. Therefore, we need to promote the democratization of globalisation, before globalisation destroys the foundations of national and international democracy'.[16]

And in 2008 he presided over the first international meeting of the campaign at the UN in Geneva.

The UNPA Campaign suggests a three-stage approach to creating a world parliament in the UN. The first stage would be the creation of a UN Parliamentary Assembly as a consultative body of the General Assembly. In this initial stage, the functions of the UN Parliamentary Assembly would be limited to providing support for the work of the General Assembly's committees, improving communication between the UN, the national parliaments and the world public, and to playing an oversight role. Delegates would be initially chosen by their parliaments, from the members of their respective national parliaments.

In the second stage the UN Parliamentary Assembly would consolidate into a more democratic institution, with its representatives directly elected by the world's citizens. Its powers would also increase. For example, it might have co-decision powers with the General Assembly with regard to the UN budget and the appointment of the UN Secretary-General, and it could have the right to submit draft resolutions to the General Assembly and to ECOSOC for consideration. As a democratically elected parliamentary body, it would have tremendous moral authority and would be able to hold other powers to account. It could review the decisions taken by governments, by international bodies such as the UN General Assembly, the World Bank and the World Trade Organisation, and if appropriate, publish critical reports and bring matters to light. And people affected by the negative actions of governments, international bodies or transnational corporations would be able to petition the world parliament to look into the matter. While not yet a full legal and judicial system, a critical report from the world parliament would be able to bring to bear a significant moral authority on the body in question.

Finally, in the third stage, the UN Parliamentary Assembly would evolve into a true World Parliament, directly elected by the world's people and with substantial parliamentary powers. It would be a primary organ of the UN, like the General Assembly or the Security Council, and would be able to legislate universally binding regulations and world law.[17]

For the time being, the campaign is pushing to reach stage one, with the creation of a UN Parliamentary Assembly as a simple, consultative body with very limited powers. For some, this approach is too slow and gradual, while for others it is far too radical. For many, it offers a sensible and balanced way to try to bring about incremental institutional change.

Since the creation of the Campaign, support for a UNPA has continued to grow. In 2007 the Foreign Affairs Committee of the Canadian House of Commons announced that it supported the establishment of a UNPA. This was soon followed by the Pan-African Parliament, and then also the Latin American Parliament, the Mercosur Parliament and the European Parliament. The campaign's call has so far been endorsed by over 1,700 current and former members of parliament from 135 countries, and this number continues to rise. It also has the support of a long list of current and former heads of state, foreign ministers, Nobel laureates, professors, and numerous eminent people from a variety of sectors, ranging from Tibetan spiritual leader, the Dalai Lama, to British actress Emma Thompson, and from former NASA astronaut Edgar Mitchell to the popular Senegalese musician Youssou N'Dour.[18]

The Campaign's Coordinator and Director of Democracy Without Borders, Andreas Bummel, regularly meets with parliamentarians, ambassadors and UN officials to advocate for the creation of a UNPA and to move it up the policy agenda. In 2021, on the initiative of Democracy Without Borders, CIVICUS and Democracy International, a large group of now over 200 NGOs, including Greenpeace, ActionAid, Open Society Foundations and Global Justice Now, came together to issue a call for more inclusive global governance, including a UN Parliamentary Assembly[19], and many of them took part in the Global Peoples Assembly, which took place in September in parallel to the 76th meeting of the UN General Assembly.[20] Under the name of 'We The Peoples', the initiative has coalesced into a new ongoing campaign that embraces a UNPA.

Momentum for a United Nations Parliamentary Assembly is building. As more organisations and more individuals get involved in the campaign, carry out academic studies and publicly call for the creation of this body, it begins to become part of public consciousness. The creation of a UNPA would be a huge step in the direction of a world parliament, and ultimately, a world federation.

Notes

1 For an extremely thorough discussion of a world parliament see Leinen, Jo and Andreas Bummel. 2018. *A World Parliament: Governance and Democracy in the 21stt Century*. Berlin: Democracy Without Borders.

2 www.poetryfoundation.org/poems/45362/locksley-hall

3 For a detailled history see Part I in: Leinen and Bummel, op. cit.

4 See also Poteliakhoff, Alex. 2008. The Rise and Fall of Professions for World Disarmament and Development. *Medicine, Conflict and Survival*, 24, 3: 188-200; Segall, Jeffrey. 1990. Building World Democracy Through the UN. *Medicine and War*, 6,4: 275-285. Segall, Jeffrey. 1990. Come to the UN. *Medicine and War*, 6,2: 81-83.

5 Lerner, Harry. 1991. INFUSA and the Dynamics of Democracy. In *Building a More Democratic United Nations*. London: Routledge.

6 See also Barnaby, Frank. 1991. Building a More Democratic United Nations: Proceedings of CAMDUN-1. London: F Cass.

7 Heinrich, Dieter. 1992. *The Case for a United Nations Parliamentary Assembly*. New York: World Federalist Movement. Available at www.unpacampaign-.org/files/2010heinrich_en.pdf.

8 Available at www.daghammarskjold.se/wp-content/uploads/1994/08/94_1.pdf

9 www.unpacampaign.org/proposal/history/

10 Falk, Richard and Andrew Strauss. 2000. On the Creation of a Global Peoples Assembly: Legitimacy and the Power of Popular Sovereignty. *Stanford Journal of International Law*, 36: 191-219; Falk, Richard and Andrew Strauss. 2001. Toward Global Parliament. *Foreign Affairs*, 80: 212-220; Strauss, Andrew and Richard Falk. 2012. *A Global Parliament: Essays and Articles*. Berlin: Committee for a Democratic UN.

11 Monbiot, George. 2004. The Age of Consent: A Manifesto for a New World Order. London; Flamingo.

12 See for example Orgad, Liav. 2018. Cloud Communities: The Dawn of Global Citizenship?. In *Debating Transformations of National Citizenship*, edited by R Bauböck. Springer: IMISCOE Research Series.

13 See for example Shapiro, Ehud. 2018. Foundations of E-Democracy. Communications of the ACM, 61, 8: 31-34. arxiv.org/ftp/arxiv/papers/1710/1710.-02873.pdf

14 See Tenbergen, Rasmus. 2018. United Humans: Internet Voting for a World Parliament, A Global Cyberspace ('World Parliament Experiment') and a New World Organization of the Third Generation. A Discussion Paper. Berlin: Democracy Without Borders. cdn.democracywithoutborders.org/files/DWBDPRT-2018.pdf

15 democracy.earth

16 www.unpacampaign.org/about/message-from-dr-boutros-boutros-ghali/

17 See Brauer, Maja and Andreas Bummel. 2020. *A United Nations Parliamentary Assembly: A Policy Review by Democracy Without Borders*. Berlin: Democracy Without Borders. www.democracywithoutborders.org/files/DWB_UNPA_Policy_Review.pdf

18 www.unpacampaign.org/supporters/

19 www.wethepeoples.org/

20 www.democracywithoutborders.org/events/global-peoples-assembly-2021/

25. Pathways to World Federation

We have argued that in order to bring about global justice and environmental sustainability we need to have global democracy. We have pointed out many of the problems with the current 'international system' and shown how it makes it virtually impossible to solve any of our pressing shared challenges, mainly because it separates and divides us so that we are trapped, politically, in the boxes of our nation-states and unable to join together, *politically*, with other people around the world who share our vision of justice and sustainability. We have also discussed the history of movements calling for global democracy, world citizenship and world federation, and sketched the outlines of what a future possible democratic world federation might look like. All this leaves one burning question: how do we make this vision a reality, now, in our lifetimes?

This final chapter will address this question head-on and will have a look at some of the different possible pathways towards reaching a democratic world federation, and the things that you can do to help make it happen.[1]

Sudden or Gradual Change?

In the heydays of the World Federalist Movement, soon after World War Two, many believed that we could jump from the present world order to a democratic world federation in one leap. And thus, as we discussed in chapter 18, the two main pathways pursued at that time were either to radically reform the UN Charter to transform the organisation into the global layer of a world federal government, or, alternatively, to organise some kind of a World Constitutional Assembly in which representatives of the world's population – either states, or parliamentarians, or otherwise elected people – would draft a World Constitution, which would then get ratified by states and create a world federation.

While both of these pathways still have those who work for their realisation, most groups, scholars and activists at this time agree that the transition towards a world federation seems much more likely to be staged and incremental, moving forward in small steps which hopefully get us closer and closer to the goal over time.

Reforming and Democratising the United Nations

One of the current ideas is to try to reform the United Nations but using a more gentle and gradual approach than that envisioned in the 1950s. The idea is not to turn it into the centrepiece of a world federation in one jump, but rather to make many small changes which will incrementally make it more transparent and more democratic. There are many campaigns that work in this direction, and some have had notable success.

For example, in 2014 the World Federalist Movement, together with Avaaz, the Friedrich-Ebert-Stiftung New York, and the United Nations Association of the UK, formed the 'One for 7 Billion Campaign'. The campaign's aim was to make the election of the UN Secretary General more democratic. It quickly gained a lot of momentum and was supported by over 750 NGOs from all around the world.[2]

Prior to that campaign the five permanent members of the Security Council used to discuss potential candidates in secret and choose the next Secretary General themselves, bringing their agreed nominee as a single candidate to be 'elected' by the General Assembly. But this, of course, was just a technicality and the General Assembly always accepted the candidate dictated by the Security Council. This process was highly problematic, as it meant that only the governments of these five countries – the USA, Russia, China, the UK and France – got to choose who they would like in the top job, while the governments of all the other countries, not to mention anyone else, did not have any real say. Since the UN Secretary General is a position of considerable power and influence within the organisation, it is important to have someone who is both well-qualified and also neutral. The non-democratic selection procedure that existed until recently did not guarantee either.

So the One for 7 Billion Campaign proposed ten very specific reforms to the process which would make it much more open and inclusive. They proposed that the UN would issue an open call for nominations to member states, parliaments and civil society, with a clear list of selection criteria and a clear timetable. They suggested what should have been obvious, that the list of candidates, with their CVs, should then be published for all to see, and that candidates should publicly present their leadership vision and goals if they were to get the position, and participate in question-and-answer sessions with member state governments, the public and the media. They further argued that the whole process should be transparent and that there should be no secret, backroom deals in the Security Council. And finally, they proposed that the Security Council would not make the final choice, but that they would present at least two candidates to the members of the General Assembly and that it would be this wider, more inclusive grouping of states, that would make the final choice.

After considerable pressure from the Campaign, as well as from several supporting governments, in 2015 the United Nations adopted a resolution which accepted many of these changes. They initiated a totally new process, which included a call for candidate nominations, a list of basic criteria, the circulation of candidates' names and CVs, and the holding of informal dialogues with candidates.

This was a big win for the One for 7 Billion Campaign and has led to the election of the current UN Secretary General, which was held in 2017, becoming more open and inclusive than it has ever been. The process is of course still far from perfect, and the Campaign continues to work to improve it further. But it shows that it *is* possible to make some incremental improvements to the UN system. And if enough small changes are made, one could hope that they would eventually add up to a significant transformation.

Recently, the World Federalist Movement has been central in launching another such 'reformist' Campaign, the 'Coalition for the UN We Need', which includes many NGOs, working towards making the UN stronger, more inclusive and more democratic.[3] And indeed, there are several other campaigns and initiatives that are working to slowly, bit by bit, push the UN in the direction of becoming a democratic layer of federal world government which would be at the centre of a future world federation.[4]

Building New Global Institutions

Another pathway towards a democratic world federation is to start building new global institutions, which will eventually become the institutional building blocks of a future world state. This could include global courts, like an Environment Court or a Human Rights Court, or important global institutions, such as a Global Tax Body or a more effective Global Health Organisation. Whilst these organisations would first have to be created within the current 'international' system, and thus would be far from perfect at the outset, they could hopefully become seeds for the institutional infrastructure of a future world federation. National states often evolved like this, only coming fully into being after the basic structures were already in place. So there is good reason to suggest that this is a necessary step in preparing for a future world federation.

As we discussed in some detail in chapter 18, this approach was successfully pursued by the World Federalist Movement in the second half of the 1990s, when it led the NGO Coalition for the International Criminal Court. The members of the coalition put pressure on governments to create a global court to hold individuals, including state officials, accountable if they caused the worst kind of human rights abuses, such as genocide. Even though several major states were against the initiative, the huge pressure put by the Coalition, consisting of thousands of NGOs, eventually tipped the balance and led to the International Criminal Court being established in 2002.

And at present the Campaign for a United Nations Parliamentary Assembly, or UNPA, is, as we detail in chapter 24, pushing hard for the creation of a new assembly within the United Nations. Unlike the General Assembly, which is made up only of representatives of governments, this new assembly would be made up of parliamentarians, as the first step towards hopefully creating a real-world parliament. The special importance of the UNPA would be that it would allow parliamentarians from all political parties, including opposition parties, to get involved in the UN and increase the connection between the UN and the people of the world.[5]

There are many more global institutions that need to be created if we want to make global democracy and world federation a reality. If the time is right, and the pressure is big enough, it *is* possible to get new institutions created. So forming more NGO coalitions and pushing for the creation of more global institutions is another important pathway towards world federation.

Democratising Existing International Institutions

Another pathway is to democratize the existing intergovernmental institutions. This could increase the democratic accountability of their decision-making and could push them in the direction of becoming truly democratic, global institutions.[6]

For example, the International Monetary Fund, or IMF, is extremely undemocratic because, as we discussed in chapter six, the voting rights of the member governments are dependent on how much money they put in. So instead of 'one state, one vote', it's more like 'one dollar, one vote'. This is obviously very problematic as it means that the rich and powerful countries dominate the decision-making process while poorer countries have hardly any say at all. The USA, in particular, with just above 15% of the votes, effectively has a veto on the most important votes which require an 85% majority. So campaigning to change this voting system would be a very important way to make this key inter-governmental institution more democratic.

Another major feature of contemporary intergovernmental organisations that makes them undemocratic is that they do not reach down to the world's people. There is no way for individual citizens to have their say or to influence discussions in these bodies, or even to know much about what is being discussed there. So another way to democratise these bodies would be to form parliamentary assemblies within them. In this way delegates who are chosen by citizens, and are accountable to them, would be involved in these organisations. Just as the Campaign for UNPA is pushing for a Parliamentary Assembly at the UN, there could also be campaigns calling for the creation of parliamentary assemblies at the IMF, and the World Bank, and the World Trade Organisation, and so on.[7]

Democratising these powerful intergovernmental organisations, both in terms of balancing the voting powers of different governments and of including citizens voices, would begin to change the way that these organisations function and the types of decisions that they make. Over time it could lead to important shifts in the world system and push us closer to global democracy.

Building and Democratising Regional Federations

Another major pathway is to start by building up regional federations. The idea here is that either one successful federation would continue to expand and accept more countries until the whole world would be united, or that several different regional federations would form and then later unite into one big world federation. So, activists on this pathway push to deepen existing projects of regional integration and to strengthen the democratic structures in these blocs.[8]

The European Union is the obvious example here, as countries in the EU are slowly and gradually integrating closer and closer together. There are several organisations, including the Union of European Federalists, the Young European Federalists, and DIEM25 (Democracy in Europe Movement 2025) who are campaigning and advocating for a democratic European Federation. As we discussed in chapter one, over time the EU has transformed from a simple confederation into a kind of hybrid structure that is part confederation and part federation, and it is becoming increasingly democratic with new structures such as a parliament and a constitution. Over time it can hopefully continue transforming until it becomes a truly democratic federation.

Other projects of regional integration are much further behind, but they are slowly moving in a similar direction. As we discussed in chapter 22, Mercosur, the South American common market, recently created a system of supra-national citizenship, allowing citizens of its member states live and work where they please in the union. The African Union, as we discussed in chapter 16, may one day transform into a Pan-African Federation, as Nkrumah and others had wanted right from the beginning. And ASEAN, the Association of South-East Asian Nations, may one day become more deeply integrated and democratic. One way to work towards world federation is to work to strengthen these nascent regional unions and push them in the direction of democratic federation, by encouraging them to form new policies and new institutions.

For example, Democracia Global, a WFM member organisation in Argentina, is leading a campaign to establish a Latin American and Caribbean Criminal Court that will be dedicated to combat the problem of Transnational Organised Crime. Known as COPLA, the acronym from its name in Spanish, this campaign seeks to establish a new regional court which would be able to deal with major transnational crimes, such as drug trafficking, human trafficking, and money laundering, which take a huge toll on communities across the whole region and that have escaped the control of national governments. As well as solving a pressing issue in the region, the proposed new court would be an important institutional steppingstone towards building a future Latin American Federation.[9]

A Mass Movement for Global Democracy

It is very likely that the way towards a democratic world federation includes all these different pathways. So it's not about choosing one over the other, but about pushing from many directions at the same time. And the absolutely crucial thing is to build mass support. We need a mass movement of people, all around the world, demanding global democracy and world federation.[10]

The issues of global democracy and global justice need to become matters that are publicly discussed in newspapers, on TV, on social media. There need to be discussions and debates, education, and awareness raising. At present, as long as people don't have a democratic say beyond their national borders, most of them, if they think about politics at all, are focussed only on their own countries and their own political systems and incorrectly believe that local problems can be solved by local politicians. But those days are over. In our highly globalised world, most problems can only be partially resolved at the local level, if at all. Most local problems require global solutions.

So the more that people write about this, and talk about this, then slowly – or quickly – this awareness will grow. And as awareness grows, then action will soon follow. The results of public opinion surveys, the spectacle of mass demonstrations and protests and social media hashtags, will send an important message to our national politicians that the people want global democracy. This will encourage them to put global democracy on their platforms, so that they will win votes and support. And the rise of world federalism on the political agenda of some countries will greatly help the issue to also rise in other countries, and once this starts to happen new transnational political movements can develop in order to work together, for example, to promote initiatives to democratize international institutions.

Transnational Political Parties

Existing political parties could put global democracy on their agendas, or we may see the rise of new political parties which will promise specifically that if elected they will lead the move to democratise the international system, from within, in their role as ambassadors and state representatives to the UN or the World Bank and so on. If the state officials of a few powerful countries started to push for actions to democratise these organisations, then there is a good chance this change would happen, especially if there were also a large civil society coalition pushing in the same direction.

One approach would be to set up transnational political parties, pushing for global democracy. Imagine say, that we had a Global Democracy Party standing in national elections in the UK, France, Germany, India, Japan, Ecuador, and other countries, with a shared platform of specific ways that they would further global democracy if elected. If the national branches of the party won the elections and came to power in their respective countries, their Ministers and officials could then work together at the UN and other international organisations to bring about change.[11]

This is a very exciting possibility, and something very similar has already started within the European Union, where a transnational political party, the European Spring, stood in the 2019 elections in several European countries with a shared platform of turning the EU into a democratic federation. While they were not successful in those elections, their path-breaking initiative has started to pave the way for new, transnational politics.

A Great Convergence of NGOs and Social Movements

As well as getting the issue of global democracy into mainstream politics, it is also hugely important to build support among NGOs and social movements. At present, most NGOs and social movements focus their energies on trying to improve one particular thing, such as human rights, inequality, refugees, or climate change. But what this means is that all that positive energy is being dispersed in lots of different directions, trying to make a small change here and a small change there, instead of a *structural* change. However, underlying all of these other problems is the basic problem of the lack of global democracy. If we, the people, had a say in global decisions then we could decide to institute a global system that would truly protect human rights, make and implement policies that would reduce inequality, make life around the world so good that people would not be forced to dream of leaving their countries as migrants or fleeing as refugees, to finally take serious steps to address climate change, and so on.

Instead of standing on the side-lines and begging government representatives to consider our views, we should change the system so that we become the decision-makers. Then we will be able to solve all of these problems much more effectively. If all the social justice NGOs and movements would realise this, and then come together to push for global democracy, we would truly be a force to reckon with!

'Impossible' Things Do Happen

So the pathways to global democracy and world federation are many and complex. And it might seem that it is too difficult or that it will take too long. Or that it is simply impossible. But it is important to remember that things that at first seem to be impossible, do happen.

At the beginning of the 19th century, the idea of democracy at the national level seemed to be an impossible, utopian dream. But around a hundred years later, after years of struggle and demonstrations and protests, as we discussed in chapter three, it finally became not just a reality in many countries, but one that is taken so much for granted that it's hard for people to believe that it was ever any different. Similarly, in the 1980s people were so used to the Cold War that they couldn't imagine that it would ever end, but then suddenly it did. And there are many other examples. Change *does* happen, sometimes slowly and sometimes in an unexpected bang. But it is actually far more unusual that things just stay the same.

Our current system, with nation states and a very weak international confederation, may seem normal and natural, the only way that things can be. But that is simply not true. 150 years ago the world was organised in a completely different way. There were huge empires, most states had different borders than the ones they have today, and very few people had the right to vote. In a relatively short time empires have disappeared, nation-states have become dominant, democracy has become widespread, and a whole range of international organisations have been established. That's a lot of change! So the next hundred years, or the next fifty or twenty years in our fast-changing world, will more than likely see a lot of change too. The key issue is not *if* there will be change, but *what* that change will look like?

And probably the most important question within that is whether we will move towards deepening global oligarchy or towards global democracy. Do we want a future with rising poverty and inequality, violent conflict, climate change and environmental degradation, constant surveillance through artificial intelligence and big data? Or do we want a future that is peaceful, just, democratic and sustainable?

We are sadly well on the way to deepening the system of global oligarchy, in which a relatively small minority of the world's population make all the decisions and do so in their own interests with little concern for other people or for the planet. If we sit quietly now or put our efforts into initiatives that are simply distractions and that do not bring about real change – like the Sustainable Development Goals or giving some charity here and there – or just zone out and entertain ourselves on Netflix, Facebook and so on, then that's where we will end up. We will sleepwalk into a more intense global oligarchy.

If we want a global democracy, then we need to start acting now! The exact path forward may not be super clear – it never is – but if we all come together and push in the same direction, then that's the best chance we have of getting there.

What You Can Do

If you want to help create a global democracy, there are many concrete things that you can do right now. See if there's a world federalist organisation near you. If there is, then join and get involved. If there isn't one, then set one up. If you contact the World Federalist Movement[12] or any of the member organisations, such as Democracy Without Borders or One World, they'll help you and give you some ideas and starting points.

Or you can get involved with the Young World Federalists.[13] Their activities happen online, so you can take part wherever you are.

Importantly, you can endorse the Campaign for a UN Parliamentary Assembly. Check out their website[14], sign the petition, offer to volunteer with them, write to your member of parliament about the need for a UN Parliamentary Assembly, and take part in the Global Week of Action for a World Parliament.[15]

If you're a good writer, write articles or posts about global democracy for your local or national newspaper, or in online journals, or on your blog. If you're good at creating social media memes, create some about global democracy and spread them around Facebook, Twitter, Instagram and so on. And if you're not so great at creating new content, then like and share good stuff that other people make to boost their visibility. But in any way you can, get a conversation going about global democracy and let your friends and family and colleagues know that you are a supporter.

You can give copies of this book to your friends or share the video lectures on which they are based on social media.[16] You could organise a book club to meet and discuss the book, or a group to watch the video lectures together and then discuss the issues. You could even organise a regular study group, like a course or a workshop, which would meet regularly for a period of time and go through the book, chapter by chapter, or watch the video lectures, one by one. It can be fun and stimulating to discuss these ideas with a group of other people. And it might inspire you and your friends to set up a new world federalist chapter or organisation or to organise other campaigns or activities.

If you're involved with an NGO or social movement, then raise the issue of global democracy at the next board meeting or at a policy meeting. Show people how the lack of global democracy underlies the issue that your NGO or movement is working on, and how bringing about global democracy would enable your particular issue to get more easily resolved. See if you can get your NGO or movement to support some of the world federalist campaigns and join the Great Convergence for global democracy.

If you are involved in a political party, raise the issue there and try and get it included in their manifesto. See if you can get the issue raised in parliamentary discussions. See if you can make links with similar parties in other countries, with a view to establishing a transnational network of members of those political parties in support of global democracy.

If you're an academic, then check out the website of the World Government Research Network and join them.[17] Write books and articles analysing how the existing problems that humanity faces need nothing short of global democracy to be really solved. Organise conferences and seminars on the topic. Build up a vibrant research community which will take forward the thinking about how to democratise global politics.

If you're a student, raise the issue of global democracy in class discussions. Read what the academics are writing about it. You can also choose to write your own thesis on a topic related to global democracy, and then send it to the World Government Research Network so that it can be shared with others.

If you are a policy specialist or work with a think-tank, then get the issue of global democracy on the agenda. Write research and policy briefs with proposals for how to move forward.

If you're a funder or a philanthropist, or even just a reasonably wealthy person with some money to spare for a good cause, then make a donation to a world federalist organisation. Get in touch with the World Federalist Movement[18], or with Democracy Without Borders[19], or with us at One World[20], or with any of the other WFM member organisations, and discuss how you can help. What new initiatives could be carried out to bring us closer to global democracy, if only they had your financial support? You might be surprised at what an impact even a relatively small amount of money can have.

Whoever you are, and whatever you do, get involved! The struggle for global democracy is the major struggle of the 21st century. It is only with global democracy that we will be able to implement real human rights, reduce economic inequality and deal with climate change. We have little chance of solving these problems in an international system of oligarchy. Our voice needs to be heard and our vote needs to count. And that will only be possible if we have real global democracy.

Notes

1 See also Archibugi, Daniele. 2004. Cosmopolitan Democracy and its Critics: A Review. *European Journal of International Relations,* 10(3): 437–473; Archibugi, Daniele and David Held. 2011. Cosmopolitan Democracy: Paths and Agents. *Ethics and International Affairs,* 25, 4: 433-461; Archibugi, Daniele, Urbinati, Nadia , Zürn, Michael , Marchetti, Raffaele , Macdonald, Terry and Didier Jacobs. 2010. Global Democracy: A Symposium on a New Political Hope. *New Political Science,*

32: 1, 83- 121; Little, Adrian and Kate Macdonald. 2013. Pathways to Global Democracy: Escaping the statist imaginary. *Review of International Studies*, 39,4: 789-813.

2 www.1for7billion.org

3 c4unwn.org

4 For other ideas about UN reform see Lopez-Charos, Augusto, Dahl, Arthur and Maja Groff. 2020. Global Governance and the Emergence of Global Institutions for the 21st Century. Cambridge: Cambridge University Press; Schwartzberg, Joseph. 2103. Transforming the United Nations System: Designs for a Workable World. Tokyo: United Nations University Press.

5 www.unpacampaign.org

6 Levi, Lucio, Giovanni Finizio and Nicola Vallinoto. (eds). 2014. *The Democratisation of International Institutions: The First International Democracy Report.* Turin: Centre for Studies on Federalism. www.internationaldemocracywatch.org-/news-books/books-publications/the-international-democracy-report; Patomäki, Heikki and Teivo Teivainen. 2004. *A Possible World: Democratic Transformation of Global Institutions*. London: Zed Books.

7 See for example Cabrera, Luis. 2007. The Inconveniences of Transnational Democracy. *Ethics and International Affairs*, 21, 2: 219-238.

8 Laursen, Finn. (ed). 2010. *Comparative Regional Integration: Europe and Beyond.* Farnham: Ashgate; Mattli, Walter. 1999. *The Logic of Regional Integration: Europe and Beyond.* Cambridge: Cambridge University Press.

9 www.coalicioncopla.org

10 See also Cho. Hee-Yeon. 2000. Civic Action for Global Democracy: A Response to Neo-liberal Globalization. *Inter-Asia Cultural Studies*, 1,1: 163-167.

11 Patomäki, Heikki. 2011. Towards Global Political Parties. *Ethics and Global Politics*, 4:2, 81-102. www.tandfonline.com/doi/pdf/10.3402/egp.v4i2.7334; Sehm-Patomaki, Katarina and Marko Ulvila. (eds). 2007. *Global Political Parties*. London: Zed Books.

12 www.wfm-igp.org

13 www.ywf.world

14 www.unpacampaign.org

15 www.worldparliamentnow.org

16 www.oneworld.network/lectures

17 www.wgresearch.org

18 www.wfm-igp.org

19 www.democracywithoutborders.org

20 www.oneworld.network

Index

Printed in Great Britain
by Amazon

13573976R00149